The Only Sacrament Left to Us

Princeton Theological Monograph Series

K. C. Hanson, Charles M. Collier, D. Christopher Spinks,
and Robin A. Parry, Series Editors

Recent volumes in the series:

Koo Dong Yun
The Holy Spirit and Ch'i (Qi):
A Chiological Approach to Pneumatology

Stanley S. MacLean
Resurrection, Apocalypse, and the Kingdom of Christ:
The Eschatology of Thomas F. Torrance

Brian Neil Peterson
Ezekiel in Context: Ezekiel's Message Understood in Its Historical
Setting of Covenant Curses and Ancient Near
Eastern Mythological Motifs

Amy E. Richter
Enoch and the Gospel of Matthew

Maeve Louise Heaney
Music as Theology: What Music Says about the Word

Eric M. Vail
Creation and Chaos Talk: Charting a Way Forward

David L. Reinhart
Prayer as Memory: Toward the Comparative Study of Prayer
as Apocalyptic Language and Thought

Peter D. Neumann
Pentecostal Experience: An Ecumenical Encounter

Ashish J. Naidu
Transformed in Christ:
Christology and the Christian Life in John Chrysostom

The Only Sacrament Left to Us

The Threefold Word of God in the Theology and Ecclesiology of Karl Barth

THOMAS CHRISTIAN CURRIE

PICKWICK *Publications* · Eugene, Oregon

THE ONLY SACRAMENT LEFT TO US
The Threefold Word of God in the Theology and Ecclesiology of Karl Barth

Princeton Theological Monograph Series 215

Pickwick Publications
An Imprint of Wipf and Stock Publishers
199 W. 8th Ave., Suite 3
Eugene, OR 97401

www.wipfandstock.com

ISBN 13: 978-1-62564-815-0

Cataloguing-in-Publication Data

Currie, Thomas Christian

The only sacrament left to us : the threefold word of god in the theology and ecclesiology of Karl Barth / Thomas Christian Currie.

p. ; cm. —Includes bibliographical references and index.

ISBN 13: 978-1-62564-815-0

Princeton Theological Monograph Series 215

1. Barth, Karl, 1886–1968. 2. Church—History of doctrines—20th century. 3. I. Title. II. Series.

BV600.3 .C87 2015

Manufactured in the U.S.A.   02/05/2015

For Stephanie

Contents

Preface

WHAT IS THE CHURCH? AS THE CHURCH ENTERS THE TWENTY-FIRST CEN-
tury, the church in the West faces internal strife over social issues and core
principles, and a growing culture that is largely indifferent and skeptical to
its purpose and contribution to the wider world. In recent decades, many
theological studies have focused in particular on the field of ecclesiology,
given the fact that ecclesial identity and love for the church can no longer
be assumed within Christian communities, much less within the academic
pursuit of theology. Karl Barth wrote a *Church* dogmatics, yet conventional
theological wisdom asserts that what Barth had to say about the church's
core identity and being was too inadequate, too weak, and too impercep-
tible to endure the challenges and struggles of late modernity. Others believe Barth's major theological contributions lie elsewhere. My own view
is that Barth has a major contribution to make to the field of ecclesiology,
especially Eucharist-centered ecclesiologies and practice-based ecclesiologies. In contrast to such ecclesiologies, Barth seeks to identify the church's
christocentric identity in the gospel proclamation and its aftermath
in mission and action.

This book explores and examines the concept of the threefold Word of
God in the theology of Karl Barth, particularly the third form of the Word
of God, the gospel proclamation, and argues that this tertiary form of the
Word of God is a crucial component of Barth's own theology of the church.
This book argues that Karl Barth revised the concept of the threefold Word
of God in the later volumes of the *Church Dogmatics*, but did not seek to
reject the concept nor reject Christ's presence and God's speech in the
gospel declaration and in the life of the Christian community. This book
argues that the threefold Word of God is a crucial element in Karl Barth's
vision of the church and an important theme for the whole of his theological
project. Disregarded by the field of Barth studies and rejected by modern
ecclesiologists, Barth's description of the gospel declaration and its central
role in the life together of the Christian community offers an important

ecclesiological alternative to carry forward for both Reformed theology and modern ecclesiology.

This study seeks to be the first of its kind to engage comprehensively with Karl Barth's concept of the threefold Word of God and to make clear its later revision. As a result, this study offers a review of the contemporary scholarly literature related to Barth's revision of the threefold Word of God, and addresses the theological and ecclesiological implications of this revision. Finally, this book makes a contribution to the fields of Barth studies and contemporary ecclesiology by arguing for the central place of the third form of the Word of God in Karl Barth's conception of the Christian community.

—TCC

Acknowledgments

THIS PIECE OF WORK IS THE PRODUCT OF MANY YEARS OF LABOR AND EFfort by myself and by the many people who invested in this project. Here it seems I am as indebted to many as I am elsewhere.

I thank my supervisor, David Fergusson, for his wisdom and gentle guidance in overseeing the direction and content of this project from a simple question into book form. More than just individual supervision, David Fergusson offers a fine example of commitment to the life of the church and the broad commitments of the Reformed tradition. He exemplifies good scholarship and leadership, and does it all with class, generosity, and humility. I would also like to register my thanks to my secondary supervisor, Paul Nimmo. Paul also exemplifies all that I admire in a theologian, from his hospitality to students, to his hard work and good humor in the classroom, to his own body of excellent scholarly publications. I would also like to thank my colleague and friend, Dr. Erin Bowers Kesterson, for reading portions of this manuscript and offering valuable suggestions.

I would like to thank William Rikard and the Church in Vocation Group in Charlotte, North Carolina, for their generosity and support. There is no better example of a committed Christian and churchman than William Rikard, and I am grateful for his support of me and his excellent work on the Board of Trustees at Davidson College and as chairman of the Board of Union Presbyterian Seminary. I would also like to thank the Foundation for Reformed Theology for financial support and encouragement. I am grateful to the Scholarship Committee of Covenant Presbyterian Church, Charlotte, North Carolina, Warner Hall and the St. Andrews Society of North Carolina, and the St. Andrews Society of Washington, DC scholarship program, all who supported my studies at the University of Edinburgh.

I have been blessed to serve in wonderful ecclesial communities. For six years, I had the privilege of serving as Pastor of Calypso Presbyterian Church, NC. While in Scotland, my family and I found a wonderful church home in the congregation at Greyfriars Kirk, and I found a challenging and responsive congregation among the staff and prisoners at HM prison Edinburgh. Currently I am grateful to serve as Pastor/Head of Staff at First Presbyterian Church, Shreveport, Louisiana, and to be a part of a loving and vibrant Christian community.

My deepest thanks are reserved for my family members to whom I am most indebted. I thank my parents, Peggy and Tom Currie, for their support and example of Christian discipleship set for me. I am indebted to them for supporting this project when not a word was written, the sea was wide, and my boat was small. I thank my father for reading much of this manuscript and offering helpful insights and suggestions. I thank my children, Thomas, Harrison, and Corinne for going to Scotland and back to see this through, even when it turned their lives upside down. Last, but not least, nothing I say here will express the level of gratitude and awe I have for Stephanie Smith Currie. Her positive attitude, her loving support, her courage and tenacity are scarcely to be believed. She placed things on hold so I could pursue this dream and for that and thousands of other reasons, I treasure each day of life together we share. Therefore, to Stephanie Smith Currie, and to her late father, Franklin Dale Smith, I dedicate this book.

Introduction

A NUMBER OF YEARS AGO, WHEN I WAS FIRST EXPLORING THIS TOPIC AND my interest in the Christian community in Karl Barth's theological project, I shared this interest with a prominent contemporary theologian. "Karl Barth had an ecclesiology?" he responded rhetorically, if not a bit sarcastically. In much contemporary theological discussion, Karl Barth's theology of the church is seen either as a useless dead end or as a topic of little interest or import in favor of more interesting themes in Barth's theological corpus. In addition, Barth's concept of the threefold Word of God is all-too familiar terrain that could not possibly be worth any additional detailed engagement and revisitation. The thesis of this book runs counter to these two commonly held assumptions: that Karl Barth had a weak ecclesiology, and that nothing new or significant can be gleaned from a detailed study of the threefold Word of God in Barth's theology. This book explores in detail the features of the threefold Word of God in the theology of Karl Barth, particularly the third form, the gospel event, as it happens in and to the Christian community and shapes its life in the world. This book is also about the church and argues that the threefold Word of God, particularly the tertiary form, is critical to Barth's theological vision of the Christian community. It is in the church's attempt to proclaim and hear the gospel, that the risen Christ comes and comes again, speaking the Word of God through broken human words, freeing the Christian community to get up and follow in discipleship, and sending the Christian community to engage the world in correspondence to the life and activity of Jesus Christ at work in their midst.

This book commences by comprehensively engaging with Karl Barth's early presentation of the threefold Word of God, from Göttingen to its final form in *Church Dogmatics* I/1 and I/2, including its practical import for the Christian community exemplified in the Barmen Declaration. This book also engages in depth with Karl Barth's revisitation of the threefold Word of God in *Church Dogmatics* IV/3. While Barth revised the concept in his later presentation, I argue that he did not reject the concept or leave it behind. Though Barth admitted that he could not present the concept in exactly the same way, Barth never rejected the claim that God speaks in the life of the Christian community through the gospel declaration nor did Barth reject the conviction that Christ embeds himself in the words and witness of the Christian community.

Beyond engaging and exploring texts within Barth's corpus for theological clarification, I argue for the central role of the threefold Word of God in Karl Barth's vision of the church, something neglected in the accounts that do focus on Barth's ecclesiology. Second, I argue that the gospel proclamation and its impact in the life of the Christian community are integral to Barth's overall vision of the church and the particular characteristics and practices of the Christian community. Throughout this study, I offer a number of examples of how the threefold Word of God is central to Barth's broader ecclesiology and to the particular identity and distinct qualities of the Christian community. Barth's own theology of the threefold Word of God and the Christian community, along with contemporary attempts beyond Barth offering a gospel-centric actualistic ecclesiology, are important ecclesiological alternatives to eucharist-centric ecclesiologies and postliberal practice-based ecclesiologies proliferating in contemporary theology.

While the focus of this book is on the threefold Word of God in the theology of Karl Barth, the second form of the Word of God, Scripture, gets short shrift. This is intentional. While Scripture is the primary witness and foundation for any contemporary proclamation of the gospel of Jesus Christ, and while Scripture is engaged at points in this study, a full blown account of Barth's doctrine of Scripture and the role of Scripture in Barth's theology is not possible in the scope of this study. Instead, the focus of this study is on the tertiary form of the Word of God and its own unique and central role in the life of the Christian community. There have been a number of recent studies on the role of Scripture in the theology of Karl Barth, and many recent attempts to establish and maintain the role of Scripture as a secondary form of the Word of God. Such scholarly endeavors have not extended however to the third form of the Word of God, Christian proclamation, which has been largely limited in scope to the category of "response" to the Word of God. This book argues the other way around: that Christ comes in contemporary church proclamation just as he encountered the early Christian prophets and apostles. To deny Christ's divine reality and presence to the church's contemporary proclamation of the gospel risks denying Christ's divine presence to Scripture and to Christ's humanity. For better or for worse, Christ chooses to encounter human beings through the church's flawed attempts to proclaim his gospel—becoming the third form of the Word of God and shaping the Christian community for distinct discipleship and gospel witness in and for the world.

In the first three chapters of this study, I examine material and draw from sections of the first two volumes of the *Church Dogmatics*. In chapters 4 and 5, I primarily treat materials from the fourth volume. Chapter 1 presents an overview of Karl Barth's early and original use of the threefold Word of God in *Church Dogmatics* I/1 and I/2 and the relationship between the church's proclamation, the gospel event, and the life of the Christian community. Chapter 2 explores the particular role of the Holy Spirit in relation to the threefold Word of God, and traces its activity related to the third form of the Word of God and its activity in the life of the Christian community. Chapter 3 builds on these early themes to argue that the threefold Word of God is a crucial element in Barth's vision of the church and offers the Barmen Declaration as a practical illustration of the threefold Word of God in historical context. Chapter 4 addresses the revision Barth makes to the concept of the threefold Word of God in *Church Dogmatics* IV/3, and explores contemporary scholarly discussion of Barth's use and revision of the threefold Word of God. Chapter 5 argues that the threefold Word of God continues to be relevant today for Barth studies, for Reformed theological expressions of divine and human activity in the life of the Christian community, and for modern ecclesiology. The threefold Word of God serves as a central theological illustration of divine-human encounter and uniting in the church's ongoing life together and witness in the world.

This book is the first of its kind to focus on the role of the threefold Word of God in the larger context of the *Church Dogmatics* and its relation to Karl Barth's vision of the Christian community. This book is also the first of its kind to explore Barth's revisitation and revision of the threefold Word of God and to engage comprehensively with contemporary scholarship related to this revision. Finally, this book seeks to contribute constructively to both the field of Barth studies and to the broader contemporary ecclesiological discussion, all through the lens of the threefold Word of God.

Abbreviations

CD   *Church Dogmatics*

GD   *Göttingen Dogmatics*

KD   *Die kirchliche Dogmatik*

I

The Threefold Word of God and Proclamation

The whole situation in the church suddenly becomes intelligible if it is seen to be the framework of *this* event; the existence of the minister is justified if he makes himself the servant of this event; and the very act which in Protestantism should form the crux of the service, the sermon as the exposition of Scripture, becomes fraught with meaning when it is a preaching of the Word of God.

—Karl Barth in 1922[1]

The Word of God in all its three forms is God's speech to man. For this reason it occurs, applies and works in God's act on man. But as such it occurs in God's way which differs from all other occurrence, i.e., in the mystery of God.

—Karl Barth, *CD* I/1:125

THIS CHAPTER EXPLORES THE CONCEPT OF THE THREEFOLD WORD OF GOD and its origins in Karl Barth's early work, beginning with Barth's dogmatic work in Göttingen (1924), continuing with later revisions and presentations in Münster (1927), and culminating with the form published in the *Church Dogmatics* I/1 (1932) and I/2 (1938). This chapter explores the unity of the three forms of the one Word of God, particularly the divine word and the word of humanity located in the proclamation event. How does proclamation become the Word of God, and what happens in the event of proclamation? This chapter answers such questions and offers illustrations

---

1. Barth, "The Need and Promise of Christian Preaching," in *The Word of God and the Word of Man*, 123.

from Barth about the way the proclamation event shapes the identity of the Christian community, the relationship of Christ to the Christian community, and the divine and human relationships in their differentiated unity.

Beginnings: Origins of the Threefold Word of God

Karl Barth's conception of the threefold Word of God was not his own theological creation. It had its basis and origin in the theology of the Reformation, both in Martin Luther and also in the Swiss Reformers. Indeed, with specific reference to proclamation, Barth's presentation of the threefold Word of God was rooted in Heinrich Bullinger's formulation in the Second Helvetic Confession that, in addition to Jesus Christ and Scripture, preaching is the Word of God.[2] One can survey Barth's early classroom lectures and get a sense of his deep knowledge of and engagement with the earlier theology of the Reformation, particularly in his early lectures on "The Theology of the Reformed Confessions." Barth's own formulation of the threefold Word of God would appear later in the *Göttingen Dogmatics* but Barth's early lectures on the Reformed Confessions indicate that he was not settled as to how to interpret Bullinger's claim. In his classroom reflections on "The preaching of the Word of God is the Word of God," Barth remarks: "it is obvious that this 'is' ['est'] must be understood as 'signifies' ['significat'] . . . Bullinger knows, as the paragraph itself shows, that in the sermon we are dealing only with the 'announcement' ['annunciatio'] of the Word of God."[3]

---

2. Bullinger, "The Second Helvetic Confession (1566)," Article I, *The Constitution of the Presbyterian Church* (USA), Part I, *Book of Confessions*, 53. "The preaching of the Word of God Is the Word of God" is located in the first chapter of the Second Helvetic Confession under the third marginal subheading (5.004). The confession goes on to declare that, as the "Word of God is now preached in the church by preachers, the very Word of God is proclaimed, and received by the faithful." See "The Second Helvetic Confession (1566)," 54. In his study of the relationship between preaching and theology, Kay notes that Bullinger's bold declaration "confesses that the ultimate subject matter of preaching is neither the preacher nor even the sermon, but the Word of God or Jesus Christ, to whom preacher and sermon witness in the company of the church." In Kay, *Preaching and Theology*, 23. Why is preaching necessary? Kay asks. Why not just a twofold Word of God? Kay notes that Scripture has always required interpretation not just recitation in the life of the Christian community, and the work of the Holy Spirit did not end as the Scriptures were written, but continues as those Scriptures are interpreted, proclaimed, and addressed to the life together of the Christian community by the Spirit through contemporary preaching. See Kay, *Preaching and Theology*, 21–23.

3. Barth, *The Theology of the Reformed Confessions*, 54.

Just a year or so later, however, Barth offered a different interpretation of Bullinger's claim. In these classroom lectures Barth proposed that the proclaimed word is God's word, that "the belief that the word proclaimed even by preachers alive today is not just their own word (their own talk about God, though it is this too) but that it is the Word of God that is inseparably bound up with their own word, the same Word of God that speaks in Scripture, the same Word of God that the prophets and apostles heard."[4] In comparing Barth's two classroom reflections both uttered in Göttingen, one gets a sense of the early development of his theology and his attempt to articulate constructively the dynamic life and activity of God in Scripture and in church proclamation. "The preaching of the Word of God is the Word of God."[5] Barth did not qualify this statement as he did earlier in his lectures on the Reformed Confessions. Instead, he provocatively argued, that "either this is an arrogant exaggeration, one of the piously shameless acts that religion is always perpetuating, one of the ecclesiastical formulas that we repeat because they are first told to us, or else it is reality, the wholly new reality of the Spirit of God, which we can only await afresh, understand afresh, and need to seek and find and thankfully receive afresh."[6] Barth's doctrine of the threefold Word of God sought to articulate this dynamic, living, and ever fresh reality, this God who speaks and becomes present in the here and now of the church's proclamation and life.[7]

One of the important elements of Barth's conception of the threefold Word of God, particularly for this study, is his willingness to unite

---

4. Barth, *GD*, 268.

5. Bullinger, "The Second Helvetic Confession (1566)," 53.

6. Barth, *GD*, 268.

7. Barth, *CD* I/1:123. In his most mature presentation of the threefold Word of God in *CD* I/1, Barth would refer to an allegory from one of Martin Luther's sermons on Luke 2 to illustrate the concept of the threefold Word of God. In Luther's allegory, there is the infant Christ (eternal Word/revelation), the baby is wrapped in the swaddling clothes of Scripture (written word), and both the baby and the swaddling clothes lie in the manger (preaching), yet all reveal the one Word of God. Though this use of Luther comes a bit later in his dogmatic work, it is illustrative of how seriously Barth sought to interpret and give voice to the spirit of the Reformers in his own twentieth-century dogmatics. But beyond a modern interpretation of the Reformers, Barth also offered a much needed correction and interpretation of the activity of God in and through Scripture and preaching. Barth's doctrine of the threefold Word of God is far from a repristination of sixteenth-century theology. His concept of the threefold Word of God includes a number of unique elements that point to Barth's theological innovation and his willingness to further clarify and interpret how the preached Word of God is the Word of God and how God remains God in the midst of human activity and life, particularly in the life of the Christian community.

proclamation with Scripture and Jesus Christ as the one Word of God, stressing the unity of the three forms, giving each form a certain continuity of substance, even in their differentiation. While Barth studied and deeply respected Protestant scholasticism (perhaps more than any theologian of his time)[8], he saw in the scholastic theory of Scripture's inspiration, a "freezing of the relation between Scripture and revelation," that equated Scripture directly with divine revelation, fusing them together into one entity.[9] As a result, the Holy Spirit was believed to be contained directly in the written words of Scripture, making God a static possession or prisoner of the written text. In addition, the act of preaching, especially in the here and now of the ecclesial community, was largely overshadowed by the divinization of Scripture.[10] Barth's concept of the threefold Word of God addressed this Protestant "heresy" in two ways: first, by elevating the third form of God's Word, the act of church proclamation, as the central form of revelation in the present,[11] and second, by stressing the dynamic nature of God's life and activity in God's self-revelation. While proclamation remained subordinate to Scripture and to the living Word Jesus Christ, the preached word could also become the living Word of God. If only momentarily, by a miracle of the Holy Spirit, a human word could also become God's Word in the act and event of proclamation in the life of the worshipping community. In such circumstances, a human act and human words could be taken up by God to reveal Godself through the medium of human speech.[12] Such a possibility was not only true for the witness of Scripture, but also true for the weekly proclamation of the gospel in the life of the worshipping community, and such proclamation extended beyond the pulpit to include sacraments, the church's ethical witness and action, Christian education, even theology.[13]

The concepts of Barth's doctrine of the threefold Word of God were uniquely shaped, Bruce McCormack believes, by Barth's "basic orientation towards the revelation-event which occurs in the here and now on the basis

---

8. Barth, Foreword to Heppe, *Reformed Dogmatics*, v–vi. In his introduction to Heppe's dogmatics, Barth credits orthodox scholastics like Heppe and his Lutheran counterpart Schmid with introducing him to the joys and substance of a dogmatics in continuity with Scripture, the Reformation, broader catholic theology, and the early church fathers. Here Barth found himself "visibly in the circle of the Church, and, moreover, in accordance with such prototypes, in the region of Church science, respectable of its kind."

9. Barth, *CD* I/1:124.

10. Ibid.

11. Ibid.

12. Barth, *CD* I/1:137–38.

13. Barth, *CD* I/1:80–81. See also Barth, *GD*, 16.

of God's Self-revelation in Christ."[14] In the ongoing event of proclamation in the life of the Christian community, as well as in Scripture and in the humanity of Christ, Barth sought to uphold the classic Reformed emphasis on the infinite qualitative distinction between God and humanity. Even in their unity, in Christ, in Scripture, and in proclamation, God was God and humanity was humanity without mixture or synthesis. But in spite of such dialectical differentiation, Barth's concept of the threefold Word of God is unique and significant because of his contention that the second person of the Trinity speaks through the witness of Scripture and through Christian preaching, even if we can only make such claims with "fear and trembling."[15] Humanity cannot capture God in human words (the finite is not capable of the infinite), but God speaks to humanity in and through human words (the infinite is capable of the finite). Early in his Göttingen lectures, Barth would describe this action as an event in which God's Word assumes human words, "concealed by the total inability of everything human to attain this object," in such a way that preaching remains a fully human enterprise even as God unites his Word to the preaching event and makes use of it in the event of revelation.[16]

Yet in spite of the infinite qualitative differentiation between divinity and humanity, Barth was so insistent on the unity of these three forms of God's Word with "no distinction in degree or value," that he would claim there could be only one analogy to the doctrine of the Word of God: the Trinity.[17] In the threefold Word of God and in the relationships of Father, Son, and Holy Spirit, God is both one substance and three unique forms. Barth's existential focus on the revelatory presence of Christ in the act of proclamation, Barth's emphasis on the dynamic activity and being of God, and Barth's innovative theological language and use of analogy, while faithful to the theology of the Reformers, were Barth's own unique additions to "unfreeze" the task of Reformed dogmatics in his time.

The Threefold Word of God in Barth's Early Dogmatics

In Bruce McCormack's comprehensive study of Barth's early development, McCormack successfully portrays the consistency between Barth's early dogmatic work in Göttingen and Münster during the 1920s and the early volumes of the *Church Dogmatics* written nearly a decade later.

14. McCormack, *Karl Barth's Critically Realistic Dialectical Theology*, 328.

15. Barth, *GD*, 269.

16. Ibid., 37.

17. Barth, *CD* I/1:120–21.

Though Barth's dogmatic content would develop and expand considerably by *Church Dogmatics* I/1 and I/2, the basic concepts of the threefold Word of God were already in place in Barth's Göttingen lectures.[18] Beginning in 1924 and continuing through the early volumes of the *CD*, the concept of the threefold Word of God served as Barth's way of introduction into God's revelation in Christ, and on the basis of that revelation, the threefold Word of God served as the basis for understanding divine and human interaction, the role of Christ, Scripture, and the church, themes which would continue to be central to Barth's theological vision.

Barth's first dogmatic lectures in Göttingen contain the basic content of Barth's much later and more detailed *Church Dogmatics*. While the content is similar to his later work, his structure and presentation have their own fresh and distinct form in the Göttingen lectures. Barth begins the Göttingen lectures with an introduction as to the problem and goal of dogmatics in the first two paragraphs or chapters. The content or problem of dogmatics is the Word of God and the starting point and goal of dogmatic reflection is the content of the church's proclamation. Though perhaps said with less detail and precision, this material is largely true to the content of the opening sections of the *Church Dogmatics* as well. Not explicitly developed as it would be later in chapter I of *Church Dogmatics*, Barth refers to the concept of the threefold Word of God in the opening introductory chapter in the *Göttingen Dogmatics* "distinguishing the Word of God in a first address in which God himself and God alone is the speaker, in a second address in which it is the Word of a specific category of people (the prophets and apostles), and in a third address in which the number of its human agents or proclaimers is theoretically limited."[19] Yes the Word of God, beginning with revelation, then Scripture, then preaching, comes in three forms, but in all three forms Barth contends, the Word of God abides forever.[20] Barth continues to unfold the threefold Word of God through Chalcedonian terminology to describe their unity in differentiation "neither to be confused nor separated," and in Trinitarian terminology, describing three different

---

18. McCormack, *Karl Barth's Critically Realistic Dialectical Theology*, 343. McCormack writes about the continuity of the threefold Word of God in Barth's thought between 1924 and 1937. According to McCormack, "Each time, no matter how much material expansion took place from one version to the next, the concept of the threefold form of the Word provided the organizing principle." See McCormack, "The Being of Holy Scripture Is in Becoming," 57.

19. Barth, *GD*, 14.

20. Ibid. Barth cites Isa 40:8 and 1 Pet 1:25.

addresses yet "all God's Word in the same glory, unity in trinity and trinity in unity."[21]

While the threefold Word of God may not have been a fully developed formula in Göttingen, it already includes many of its later emphases. The *Göttingen Dogmatics* also reveals a much greater affinity for brevity even as it offers inventive theological analogies and colorful theological language and discussion. As we have already seen, the analogy between the Trinity and the threefold Word of God is made more than once by Barth; he even compares the procession of Christian preaching from Scripture and revelation to the procession of the Holy Spirit from the Father and the Son (filioque).[22] Barth also does not restrict preaching or the church's proclamation to the confines of the pulpit or even the work of pastors, but declares that proclamation includes "whatever we 'preach' to ourselves in the quiet of our rooms" if it is a "mediated addressing and hearing of the Word of God."[23]

Barth's exposition of the threefold Word of God and preaching in the *Göttingen Dogmatics* established two other important features that would be developed more fully in Barth's later work. The first central feature is the central place of proclamation in the church's life. True to the Reformers, Barth believed that the gospel makes the church, not only giving the church its identity, but distinguishing it in this way from all other human fellowships and institutions. The church was distinguished from the rest of humanity through the life of "this very specific hearing and making heard, the Word which it receives and passes on."[24] The church's ecclesial identity and life, its ecclesiology, are grounded in the reception and proclamation of the Word of God. In the act of human speaking (preaching), the church "perceives another address, that is, revelation," and in such human speaking the "divinely posited reality" is concealed.[25]

In addition to grounding the church's ecclesial identity, purpose, and life in the Word of God, Barth lifts up the continuity and unity of the three forms of the one Word of God, especially how the proclaimed form, becomes and is *the* Word of God in the present. Making such a statement is not a synergism of the infinite and the finite. No "humanizing of the divine" is going on. Rather, to take proclamation seriously, as human speech about God "is to take it as *God's Word*, God's Word in the present for the future, grounded in God's Word in the past from which we come (i.e. holy

---

21. Barth, *GD*, 14–15; and *CD*, I/1:121.
22. Barth, *GD*, 16.
23. Ibid.
24. Barth, *GD*, 24.
25. Ibid.

Scripture), and in the eternal Word of God (i.e. revelation)."[26] Nowhere does proclamation carry an air of papal infallibility, Barth cautions. If anything, those who dare preach can only do so in "fear and trembling."[27] Nevertheless, they do so under the presupposition that "preaching is God's Word no less than holy Scripture or revelation—God's Word in the present."[28]

Much of the nucleus of Barth's doctrine of the threefold Word of God was already present in the *Göttingen Dogmatics* even though it would be elaborated and expanded much further in the Münster dogmatics and again in its final form in *Church Dogmatics* I/1 and I/2. While the content of Barth's dogmatic lectures in Münster (*Christliche Dogmatik im Entwurf*) do not differ considerably from the *Göttingen Dogmatics*, Barth develops his content in more depth, and provides more organization and formal structure to the concept of threefold Word of God. Barth spoke in terms of three addresses yet one Word of God in Göttingen, and in the Münster dogmatics Barth further develops this concept, devoting for the first time an entire section (§4) to the threefold Word of God, "Die Drei Gestalten des Wortes Gottes," which discusses the Word of God in its three forms and in its unity. Barth begins with proclamation, the present form of the Word of God which is built upon the prior witness and revelation to the prophets and apostles in Scripture, which is built upon the revelation of God in Jesus Christ, God's eternal Word. In describing the relationship between each form of address, Barth once again employs hypostatic, Trinitarian, and Chalcedonian terminology. He is careful to differentiate and uphold both the fully human and fully divine elements in each form of the Word of God. Each form must not "mix" with the other nor "separate" from the other, but must be apprehended both in their unity and in their differentiation.[29]

Barth's presentation of differentiated forms that do not mix or separate is not confined to his discussion of the three forms of the one Word of God, but is a larger theme that is developed in the other early sections of the Münster dogmatics. Barth differentiates between the Word of God and the word of man in preaching, *§ 5 Das Wort Gottes und der Mensch als Prediger*, Barth differentiates between the Word of God and the word of man in hearing, *§ 6 Das Wort Gottes und der Mensch als Hörer*, and Barth describes the human being becoming known in the Word of God, *§ 7 Das Erkanntwerden des Menschen im Worte Gottes*. In each section, Barth is careful to delimit and make known the fallible and fully human nature that

---

26. Ibid., 35.
27. Ibid.
28. Ibid., 36.
29. Barth, *Karl Barth Gesamtausgabe*, 68–69.

is nevertheless made witness and bearer of God's Word, in a divine and human unity without mixture or separation. The ultimate analogy and ground for such differentiated unity is found in the Godhead, in the triunity of the Father, Son, and Holy Spirit, § *10 Gottes Dreieinigkeit*.[30] In many ways, the material content of the Münster dogmatics is quite similar to the content of the *Göttingen Dogmatics*. However in Münster, Barth further develops the concepts and organization of the three forms of the one Word of God and Barth further develops the unity in differentiation found both in the Trinity and analogously in the threefold Word of God. Such themes would continue to be developed in Barth's third and final dogmatics begun Bonn and completed in Basel.

The Threefold Word of God in the Church Dogmatics

Karl Barth unfolds the concept of the threefold Word of God in the *Church Dogmatics* by beginning with the third form of the Word of God.[31] Rather than beginning with the revelation of Jesus Christ, its repetition in Scripture, and then its ongoing repetition in proclamation, Barth begins his presentation in § 4, "The Word of God in its Threefold Form" (§4 *Das Wort Gottes in seiner dreifachen Gestalt*), first with proclamation, "The Word of God Preached" (*Das Verkündigte Wort Gottes*).[32] He begins with the Word of God in the present, as God speaks and reveals Godself in the life of the church in the here and now. Only after establishing that God speaks in the present and the Word of God comes to be in the life of the church, does Barth then trace the concept back through the Word of God written (*Das geschriebene Wort Gottes*) and the Word of God Revealed (*Das offenbarte Wort Gottes*). Each form of the Word of God has a human element and a divine element that are brought together into a dynamic union in the event of proclamation, in the written words of Scripture, and in the humanity of Jesus Christ. In each form, a fully human element and fully divine element come together to become the Word of God. In Jesus Christ this joining together is the hypostatic union, while in Scripture and proclamation, the Holy Spirit enables God to speak through the written words of the first witnesses (Scripture), and the Spirit makes it possible for God to speak in, through, and in spite of, the speech of the human preacher (proclamation).[33] Such a momentary union of divine

30. Ibid., 199.

31. Barth also begins his discussion of the threefold Word of God in *Die Christliche Dogmatik im Entwurf* in a similar manner.

32. Barth, *CD* I/1:88.

33. Ibid., 166.

voice and human witness only comes about by the power of the Holy Spirit as it lives and moves and speaks in and through the Christian community.

Barth is, however, insistent that in spite of its three forms, there is one Word of God and not three different words of God (*die Einheit des Wortes Gottes*). The church's preaching, Scripture, and the revelation of Jesus Christ are the one and the same Word of God and "there is no distinction of degree or value between these three forms."[34] So unified is the one Word of God in its three forms, the only analogy to the doctrine of the Word of God, according to Barth, is the doctrine of the Trinity. The threefold Word of God is analogous to the Trinity "in the fact that we can substitute for revelation, Scripture and proclamation the names of the divine persons Father, Son and Holy Spirit and *vice versa*, that in the one case as in the other we shall encounter the same basic determinations and mutual relationships, and that the decisive difficulty and also the decisive clarity is the same in both."[35] Just as the Father, Son, and Holy Spirit are three forms of the same being, so proclamation, Scripture, and Jesus Christ are three forms of the one Word of God.

Conceiving of God's activity, presence, and speaking in this way, was not a Barthian invention. Barth referenced Luther and Protestant scholastics to support the mutuality and unity of God's Word in its three forms and as evidence of a continued commitment to the Reformers and the tradition that followed.[36] Barth moved beyond Luther and Reformed doctrine in two distinct ways. First, Barth's actualism kept the doctrine of the Word of God from "freezing" the immediate presence of God in Scripture (his critique of Protestant orthodoxy), or within the sacramental apparatus of the church (his critique of Roman Catholicism), or within the individual and her experience (his critique of modern Protestantism and pietism).[37] Second, in the proclamation event, Barth strongly emphasized the indirect immediacy of the third form of the Word of God, as the encounter between God and humanity that takes place in the here and now through the ecclesial event of proclamation. The centrality of the presence of Christ in the event of proclamation was central to Barth's early theology of the church, and is critical for understanding the roles of Christ, church, and the life of the Spirit in Barth's early dogmatic work.

---

34. Ibid., 120.

35. Ibid., 121.

36. Barth, *CD* I/1:121–24

37. For a greater explanation of Barth's critique of modern Protestantism and its origins, as well as his appraisal of Roman Catholicism, see Barth, *Protestant Theology in the Nineteenth Century*, 107–21.

In themselves, Scripture and proclamation are not the Word of God. When Scripture and proclamation are actualized and become the Word of God, God's speech and written human words are united in such a way (Scripture), or God's speech and the spoken proclamation in the life of the church are united in such a way, that "God does reveal Himself in statements, through the medium of speech, and indeed of human speech."[38] Yet revelation is never frozen or static, God becomes a human person in Jesus Christ uniting divinity and humanity in the flesh of Jesus Christ. In the here and now, through the work of the Holy Spirit, the risen Christ comes into humanity's own time and space momentarily through Scripture and proclamation. Because God's revelation in Scripture and proclamation cannot necessarily be anticipated or guaranteed,[39] both Scripture and proclamation have an all too human aspect, just like the humanity of Christ in the hypostatic union.

Scripture and proclamation can only become the Word of God. Trevor Hart illustrates Barth's delineation of this concept by making use of christological categories. According to Hart, Barth describes the relationship between humanity and divinity in Scripture and preaching, not in terms of a permanent union and a union of identity, but a temporary and momentary union, "more of a Nestorian union than a Chalcedonian one," in which Scripture and proclamation are momentarily taken up by God through the work of the Holy Spirit to speak in our own space and time in the life of the Christian community.[40] God continues to speak in Jesus Christ, through Scripture and proclamation, as the Holy Spirit makes Jesus Christ contemporaneous in the words of Scripture and through the voice of the preacher.[41] A temporary union occurs as the Spirit makes it possible for God to speak in and through and in spite of the fallible words of Scripture and the fallible words of the human preacher.[42] In the event of the Word of God, "these two different things become one and the same thing."[43] In the event of the Word of God, the actualistic union of divine and human elements brought together by the work of the Spirit, become one without losing their distinct and separate elements. Even as they dynamically come together, they are united but remain two different things that "become one and the same thing in the event of the Word of God."[44] Still, before, during, and after the event,

38. Barth, *CD* I/1:137–38.

39. Barth, *CD* I/1:137.

40. Hart, "The Word, the Words, and the Witness," 35.

41. Ibid., 36.

42. Barth, *CD* I/1:166.

43. Barth, *CD* I/1:113. See also, Hart, "The Word, the Words, and the Witness," 39.

44. Barth, *CD* I/1:113.

the human elements, words, and voices, remain entirely human, even as they are taken up and used by God to do something and reveal someone quite beyond themselves.[45]

One development that does occur between the *Göttingen Dogmatics* and the *Church Dogmatics* has to do with the form and nature of proclamation. In the *Göttingen Dogmatics*, Barth does not define proclamation solely in terms of pulpit activity, but proclamation includes "whatever we all 'preach' to ourselves in the quiet of our own rooms."[46] Proclamation is broadly defined as the transmission of the gospel, "a speaking, a mediated addressing and hearing of the Word of God from revelation and scripture."[47] Proclamation extends beyond the pulpit and the clerical office, and beyond the event of the Sunday sermon to include any speaking and hearing of the Word of God in the life of the Christian community. Later in *Church Dogmatics* I/1, Barth defines proclamation more formally, differentiating proclamation from other forms of Christian activity like social work or the education of youth. What distinguishes proclamation, Barth insists, is that it seeks to bring to a decision, to direct the claims of the gospel toward specific fellow human beings in a specific moment of life, with the expectation that the Word of God is being declared to them.[48] While proclamation is still not defined as a clerical activity alone or even restricted to the pulpit, it is defined more narrowly in terms of purpose and intent as the particular ecclesial activity which seeks to declare God's Word.

Still, there is a danger, Barth believes, in too directly equating the Word of God with the pulpit address in Sabbath worship. Might sung praises, acts of love, Christian education, and ethical acts of witness be better and more genuine forms of proclamation? Is it possible, Barth continues, that God's Word might be revealed by God outside the apparatus of ecclesial proclamation?[49] Of course the Word of God is not confined to the church's existing proclamation. Barth answers, famously, that God is free to "speak to us through Russian Communism, a flute concerto, a blossoming shrub, or a dead dog,"[50] enabling even the stones to shout out.[51] Still, Barth describes

---

45. Ibid., 165–66.
46. Barth, *GD*, 16.
47. Ibid.
48. Barth, *CD* I/1:51.
49. Ibid., 53–54.
50. Ibid., 55.
51. Luke 19:40, Matt 3:9.

and defines proclamation as the specific divine commission laid upon the church: proclamation is preaching and proclamation is sacrament.[52]

The Bible as the Word of God

While this chapter and this larger study focus particularly on the threefold Word of God and the role and significance of its third form in Karl Barth's theological *corpus*, the third form of the Word of God is only made possible by its second form. The gospel does not come apart from its third, second, or first form. Therefore, the role of Scripture is central to the church's existence, worship, and proclamation of the gospel. According to Barth, the Word of God is "God Himself in Holy Scripture," and the Bible serves as the primary witness to the divine revelation by which the church's own attempts to proclaim the Word of God are measured, confronted, and empowered.[53] The second form of the Word of God is not made unnecessary, redundant or less important by the reality of the third form of the Word of God. As Barth makes clear, that the "Bible is the witness of divine revelation is not, therefore, limited by the fact that there is also a witness of the Church which we have to hear," rather that there is a Word of God for the church at all is because the church "receives in the Bible the witness of divine revelation."[54] While God is to be found in and through the written words of Scripture (both as a source of past revelation and as an instrument of revelation that is to come), Barth also wants to distinguish Scripture from divine revelation. From beginning to end, written human words are the content of Scripture, even in their unity with divine revelation. Divine revelation, the Word of God, is found and revealed in the humanity of the written words of Scripture, not the other way around.[55]

---

52. Barth, *CD* I/1:56. See also Guretzki, *Karl Barth on the Filioque*, 95. In a section on the threefold form of the Word of God, Guretzki notes the narrowing of proclamation from the *Göttingen Dogmatics* to the *Church Dogmatics*. He correctly observes that Barth defines proclamation broadly (in *GD*) to include an outward or inward mediated addressing and hearing of the Word of God through revelation and Scripture (*GD*, 16), whereas Barth restricts proclamation in the *Church Dogmatics* as a exposition of the biblical witness and the attempt to bear witness to revelation in one's own words in the here and now to gathered human beings (*CD*, I/1:56). Guretzki does not note that Barth also includes the sacraments in his restricted and more developed definition of proclamation in *CD* I/1.

53. Barth, *CD* I/2:458–59.

54. Ibid., 462–63.

55. Ibid., 463.

In relating Scripture to the divine revelation, Barth is careful to note that we cannot have revelation except through the biblical witness in expectation (Old Testament) and in recollection (New Testament) of Jesus Christ, and that in the Bible we cannot have revelation (Jesus Christ) "in itself."[56] What we "have" instead is no direct identity between the human words of Scripture and the Word of God, but in an indirect identity "in a decision and act of God to man."[57] As Scripture serves God's revelation, like the humanity of Jesus Christ, "it stands in that indirect identity of human existence with God Himself," and though it is not itself Jesus Christ, Barth declares that it must be called the Word of God, or in Barth's more precise definition: "The Word of God in the sign of the word of man."[58] And even when Scripture becomes the Word of God, bearing witness to God's revelation, it does so not as a "book of oracles" or as an "instrument of direct impartation,"[59] but as the presence of the Word of God "comes to us in this or that specific measure," when it is "taken and used as an instrument in the hand of God."[60]

Barth's portrayal of Scripture as the Word of God elicits further points that will be relevant to the course of this study. First, the freedom and presence of God, is something humanity cannot possess, create, or anticipate, even in the realm of Scripture. According to Barth, the biblical text in the hands of humanity does not automatically lead to the presence of the Word of God nor can humanity make God present through Scripture or any other special devices. Rather it is precisely as the church faces and reads the biblical texts in all their humanity and fallibility, as the text is allowed to speak as it stands, and as humanity stands at the door of the Bible and knocks and hopes, that the infallible Word of God miraculously comes and speaks.[61] The second important theme to carry forward in regard to Scripture as the Word of God is the slight distinction Barth gives the scriptural witness in relation to the third form of the Word of God. While Scripture and proclamation are both signs of revelation and sacramental instruments of revelation, "Holy Scripture is the original form of its attestation," as it attests revelation "in its uniqueness and temporal limitation," and as such has a certain priority,

---

56. Ibid., 492.

57. Ibid., 499.

58. Ibid., 500.

59. Ibid., 507.

60. Ibid., 530.

61. Ibid., 530–33. Barth again uses the water in the Pool of Bethesda as the image of Scripture in which the text is taken up and used by God himself to do something miraculous in the life of humanity.

authority, and precedence over the third form of the Word of God.[62] However, Barth also adds that there cannot be a two-fold word of God, that Scripture "cannot stand alone as the Word of God in the church." Instead, as the Word of God attested and heard in Scripture wills to have actuality in the contemporary church's own words, proclamation, and witness, so the Word of God requires a secondary witness in contemporary context alongside its original witness.[63]

The final theme worth mentioning in Barth's excursus on Scripture as the Word of God is an ecclesial one. Repeatedly, Barth rejects notions that either the church or Scripture can serve as an extension or continuation of the Incarnation. However, it is important to note that Barth does depict some indirect identity between the church's life in the world and the divine life and activity in the world. As the biblical witness is read and proclaimed in the concrete life of the Christian community, "the eventuation of the presence of the Word of God in the human word of the prophets and apostles, can only be regarded as a repetition, a secondary prolongation and continuation of the once-for-all and primary eventuation of revelation itself."[64] So while the church is distinct from Jesus Christ in his contemporary manifestation, the church lives as it is united to Jesus Christ (the primary eventuation) and through Scripture and proclamation, the church serves as a contemporary form and sign of Christ's presence on earth in the time between the times.

Proclamation Becomes the Word of God

How does a contemporary human word become God's Word? Barth maintains that the human words of Scripture and the human words of the church's proclamation are taken up by God to address human beings in the event of proclamation and the life of the Christian community. Bruce McCormack traces this development in Barth's thought to his early writings on the threefold Word of God in the *Göttingen Dogmatics*.[65] The result of this divine action is the impossible possibility that human words can become

62. Barth, *CD* I/2:500.

63. Ibid., 501.

64. Ibid., 534.

65. McCormack, *Karl Barth's Critically Realistic Dialectical Theology*, 340–41. McCormack writes that "God's act of taking up a creaturely reality and revealing Himself in and through it was no longer restricted to the event of the cross, and not even to the incarnation," but "God was seen by Barth as taking up human language, and bearing witness to Himself in and through it," specifically as the gospel is declared in the life of the Christian community.

"bearers of revelation."[66] Just as the human nature of Christ is not divinized in the hypostatic union, McCormack reminds us that Barth has not set aside "the complete inadequacy of human language for revelation."[67] Rather in the reading of Scripture and the event of proclamation, the "Word of God conceals Himself in human words, a relation of correspondence is established, an analogy between the Word and the words."[68] Not only does such an event (miracle?) create an analogy between the Word and the words, but such an analogy is produced and actualized by the dynamic union and momentary uniting of God's act and speech together with human hearing and proclaiming in the life of the Christian community.

Attempting to articulate how revelation reaches human beings through creaturely media (Scripture and proclamation) is always a risky and mysterious venture; Barth admits: "all that we know is that God Himself does really avail Himself of this medium."[69] To be taken up into the event of revelation, for human words and human speaking to become the Word of God, God's speech in the here and now, "is the work of the Holy Spirit or the subjective reality of revelation."[70] This activity of the Holy Spirit is not a secondary or subsequent action, but a continuation, an actualization, "an impress, (and) sealing of objective revelation upon us."[71] The Holy Spirit is not God's second act, but the "work of the Spirit is nothing other than the work of Jesus Christ."[72] Perhaps this is why Barth maintains that the three forms of the Word of God are also still the one Word of God. It is the Holy Spirit who proceeds from Jesus Christ and "unites men closely to Him *ut secum unum sint* (that they may be one)," and it is the same Spirit who joins Jesus Christ together with human words in the event of proclamation so that they may dynamically become one, one Word of God.[73]

Apart from the Spirit of Christ, apart from the power of the Holy Spirit, human words have no hidden potential or abilities in themselves to become anything more than human words. Theology cannot explain or logically make sense of the event of proclamation. Barth believed that human attempts to locate the potential for revelation or union with God somewhere within humanity were futile, not to mention sinful, dangerous, and idolatrous.

66. Ibid., 341.

67. Ibid.

68. Ibid.

69. Barth, *CD* I/2:233.

70. Ibid., 238.

71. Ibid., 240.

72. Ibid., 241.

73. Ibid.

Nothing in human experience or in the range of human possibilities can account for or explain the new reality that confronts the creature and addresses the creature in God's act of revelation through the creaturely media of proclamation. All the possibilities for God's Word to be heard and proclaimed in human words come from the side of God. Barth makes clear that only "Jesus Christ creates the fact that we believe in Jesus Christ."[74]

And so human preaching cannot try to become the Word of God and human attempts that do try and trust in their own potential to become the Word of God, according to Barth, always end disastrously. Rather, human preaching is grounded upon the trust, by both the preacher and the gathered Christian community that God can and does speak in and through human preaching and is received in human hearing by the work and power of the Holy Spirit. Through the Spirit of Christ, Christ speaks through the voice of another. In the event of proclamation, the voice of Christ comes and joins together with human proclamation and such proclamation becomes, not just human speaking, but the Word of God, in a particular place in a particular time. Yet even as proclamation becomes the Word of God, it does not remain so. Even in their momentary union in the event of the Word of God, divinity and humanity are not co-mingled and synthesized. In a lecture delivered to a meeting of ministers in 1922, Barth declared that the "word of God on the lips of a man is an impossibility" and yet "nothing else can satisfy the waiting people and nothing else can be the will of God than that he himself should be revealed in the event."[75] We must trust, Barth emphasizes, "that what is God's is also man's," or put in more actualistic terms, what is God's also *becomes* humanity's in the event of the Word of God.[76]

According to Eberhard Jüngel, in Barth's description of the event of the Word of God, the Creator and creature distinction remains, even in the event of union. As God allows himself to be perceived in God's Word and human beings know that they stand before God in faith, God remains God before the human person and the human person remains human before God.[77] But, Jüngel adds, God is able to transcend what seems to be an ontological standoff in this event, and as these two qualitatively distinct relations give themselves to each other, "God becomes speakable as God," and the human being "brings this God to speech as the God who has become speakable."[78]

74. Barth, *CD* I/2:247.

75. Barth, "The Need and Promise of Christian Preaching," in *The Word of God and the Word of Man*, 124–25.

76. Ibid., 124.

77. Jüngel, *God's Being is in Becoming*, 59–60.

78. Ibid., 60.

Without this speech event, Jüngel adds, there would only be a "*unio mystica* of *silence*."[79] Instead, though there is a permanent distinction between God and humanity, the Creator also differentiates himself from the creature at the very point where God gives Godself to be known.[80] In this context and sense, Jüngel believes Barth could then talk of the union of humanity with the God who remains distinct from humanity.[81] Walking the dialectical tightrope is tricky in describing this union-in-distinction in the divine speech event. At least at this point, Jüngel believes Barth is trying to hold both union and differentiation together. The question remains whether and to what extent Barth would always maintain that creaturely realities, human speech and proclamation in the life of the Christian community in particular, are commandeered for the purposes of God's self-manifestation.[82]

The Sacramental Nature of Proclamation

Sacramental references to the theology of Karl Barth have the potential to become controversial given Barth's revision of infant baptism in 1943 and his later alteration of sacraments to ethical responses in *Church Dogmatics* IV/4. Whether Barth's later theological decisions called into question some of his earlier dogmatic endeavors and foundations,[83] and whether his sacramental revision was part of a much larger theological and ecclesiological revision that significantly altered the threefold Word of God and the place of proclamation, all remains to be seen. While Barth himself would later be more reticent in discussing divine and human unity outside the life of the hypostatic union,[84] it is difficult to ignore the sacramental role of proclamation in Barth's theological project. In the essay and lecture, "The Need and Promise of Christian Preaching," given in 1922, Barth made clear in his presentation that the Reformation was not just an attempt at deconstruction. The Reformers, Barth argued also wished to "see something better substituted for the mass it abolished, and that it expected that the better thing

79. Ibid.

80. Ibid.

81. Ibid.

82. This question will be fully addressed in chapter 4: "What Happens to the Threefold Word of God?"

83. Yocum, *Ecclesial Mediation in Karl Barth*, 171–75. See also, Jüngel, "Karl Barths Lehre von der Taufe," in *Barth Studien*, 175–180; and Jüngel, *Karl Barth: A Theological Legacy*, 47–51.

84. Webster, introduction to *God's Being is in Becoming*, by Jüngel, xvi.

would be—our preaching of the Word."[85] The visible Word, "the objectively clarified preaching of the Word," Barth provocatively asserted, "is the only sacrament left to us."[86]

In the event of proclamation, Barth describes the dynamic unity of God's activity and human activity in world occurrence. Just as Scripture is not God's Word frozen in time, neither is proclamation God's Word frozen in the present. Rather, proclamation must again and again become the Word of God, not by extra human effort, but in and through human proclamation and effort, by the activity of God. In *CD* I/1 §4, "The Word of God in its Threefold Form," Barth describes how human proclamation becomes God's Word. It happens "in the sacrament and in preaching and in the whole life of the Church" as the "earthly body acquires a new form from the heavenly Head that it becomes the actuality of revelation and faith."[87] And it does so all the while maintaining its same form as human preaching; it does not undergo an ontological alteration, but in the event of reading Scripture and proclaiming its gospel content in the life of the Christian community, the "earthly reality acquires this new *nota* by the Word of God."[88]

The content of preaching, Barth continues, is not just a human enterprise.[89] The humanity of the event, the humanity of proclamation, and the "human talk, with its motives and themes and the judgments among which it stands as human talk, is there even while God's Word is there."[90] Proclamation becomes the Word of God as "the new robe of righteousness (is) thrown over it," and human proclamation is united with the Word of God in the "event of God's own speaking in the sphere of earthly events, the event of the authoritative vicariate of Jesus Christ."[91] In the course of this event, something new happens in "man's talk about God," and in this act of proclamation, "God speaks about Himself."[92] While the presence of God, the voice of Christ, and God's divine activity can never be confused or reversed with the human talk about God and the church's proclamation, in the event of the Word of God, far from being set aside or bypassed, human talk about God becomes the very medium in which God speaks to humanity about Godself.

85. Barth, "The Need and Promise of Christian Preaching," 114.

86. Ibid.

87. Barth, *CD* I/1:89.

88. Barth, *Church Dogmatics* I/1:89.

89. Ibid., 94.

90. Ibid., 93–94.

91. Ibid., 95.

92. Ibid.

Momentarily, a human word becomes an intersection, a union, a new creation, of divine activity and human activity, unleashed by divine action and initiative, which includes and incorporates and never happens without creaturely activity, speaking, and hearing. God speaks, Jesus Christ is revealed, and the Spirit is poured out, not because of human proclamation, but in the event of the Word of God, the event in which God speaks about Himself. This event, however, does not happen without human proclamation. Indeed, in the contemporary context, it happens through it.[93] This divine event includes human proclamation; it is a dynamic union of the Word of God with human proclamation in which God speaks to his creatures through creaturely media and it is also the event and movement in which the creature is exalted by God and set free by the Spirit to be a witness and to correspond to Jesus Christ. Barth describes this proclamation event in terms of mediation,[94] in terms of divine sign-giving,[95] in terms of secondary objectivity,[96] and in sacramental language.[97] Any reference to sacrament does not begin with the Lord's supper or baptism, Barth maintains, but begins with Jesus Christ and his ongoing presence in the life of the Christian community through the work of the Spirit. This broader view of sacramental presence, not only includes Scripture and preaching, but renders baptism and the Lord's Supper dependent on the gospel, on the proclaimed and heard Word of God. This sacramental understanding of Scripture and preaching in the church's life is why Barth maintains that preaching grounded on the witness of Scripture, "is the only sacrament left to us."[98]

In an essay on Barth's ontology of Scripture, Bruce McCormack argues that the word "sacramental" can be rightly applied to Scripture as it becomes a "sacramental union of the divine Word with the sign that is the prophetic and apostolic witness."[99] Just as the human nature of Jesus Christ remains fully human in the divine and human unity of the hypostatic union, so do the human words of the prophets and apostles (Scripture) remain human in the "sacramental union by which God joins them to the Word of God," as they become the Word of God.[100] Though McCormack does not extend

93. Barth, *CD* I/1:94–95.

94. Barth, *CD* I/2:233

95. Ibid., 233–34.

96. Barth, *CD* II/1:52–53.

97. Barth, *CD* I/2:227–33; II/1:53–54; and see also McCormack, "The Being of Holy Scripture Is in Becoming," 68–69.

98. Barth, "The Need and Promise of Christian Preaching," 114.

99. McCormack, "The Being of Holy Scripture Is in Becoming," 69.

100. Ibid., 70.

the sacramental union to proclamation, it seems just as possible to use the same language to describe the sacramental union of the human words of proclamation and the Word of God that together become the one Word of God in the event of proclamation in the life of the church. If a case can be made for an actualistic ontology that includes a divine and human sacramental union in Scripture, then might such a union be applicable to the proclamation event in the life of the Christian community? In his study of the threefold Word of God, Trevor Hart makes the case that for Barth, both Scripture and preaching stand and fall together both as human witnesses to God and as the Word of God. [101] To deny any divine reality to proclamation risks denying it to Scripture and to Jesus Christ. Indeed, Barth's doctrine of the threefold Word of God sought to be faithful to the theology of the Reformers by identifying contemporary gospel proclamation, no less than the human words of Scripture, with the Word of God.[102] Fallible human beings speak the Word of God in fallible human words in Scripture and fallible human beings speak the Word of God in fallible human words in the event of proclamation.[103]

Divine-Human Relations in Proclamation and Beyond

In this exploration of the threefold Word of God in Karl Barth's theology, a number of important themes and concepts within Barth's theological framework have been identified. First while Barth is careful to maintain God's sovereignty, lordship, freedom, and transcendence, he also believes a central feature of God's triune identity is to create, nurture, and actualize fellowship with human beings. The divine act of speaking in the course of human events and in the midst of human speaking about God *is* how God chooses to address humanity, draw near to humanity, and unite human beings to Godself. Second, Barth believes God's existence in the world is not that of some grand static being, but instead is a life of dynamic movement and action. There is no static union of divinity and humanity, but rather ongoing opportunities in the present and future for such union and fellowship to occur. Third, in spite of the fact that God is God and humanity is humanity, in spite of the infinite ontological distinction between divinity

101. Hart, "The Word, the Words, and the Witness," 38–39.

102. Ibid., 37.

103. Barth, *CD* I/2:529. To put it another way: the God who took human form and who spoke in human form in first-century Palestine, speaks in and through the witness of the prophets and apostles, and speaks presently in the life of the Christian community through Scripture and the church's proclamation.

and humanity, Barth affirms that "the Word of God is God Himself in the proclamation of the Church of Jesus Christ."[104] These continuous theological themes are not relegated to Barth's early work and the first volume of the *Church Dogmatics,* but are found elsewhere in the *Church Dogmatics* and his shorter theological essays and lectures.[105]

In *Church Dogmatics* I/2 Barth continues to develop and expound upon the threefold Word of God, particularly in relation to the church and its life (§22–24). Barth is very clear in maintaining that God's presence in the life of the church, in Scripture, and in proclamation is not diminished, diluted, nor weakened, but all three forms together constitute the life and foundation of the church.[106] Proclamation, he insists again, is not just a human enterprise but is integral to who God is, such that "preaching is not merely a proclamation of human ideas and convictions, but, like the existence of Jesus Christ Himself, like the testimony of the prophets and apostles on which it is founded and by which it lives, it is God's own proclamation."[107] And at the same time, Barth insists that only God can speak about God. To think otherwise, he adds, is to forfeit the miraculous nature of human proclamation, and it is to descend instead into a presumptive clericalism where "miracle ceases to be miracle, grace to be grace, and venture to be venture."[108]

In addition to early volumes of the *Church Dogmatics,* a very clear summary of the doctrine of the threefold Word of God, particularly the third form, proclamation, can be found in lectures from Barth's seminar on preaching held at Bonn in 1932 and 1933. Barth offers a new definition

---

104. Barth, *CD* I/2:743.

105. Ibid., 233. In this exploration of objective revelation and divine sign-giving, Barth describes Scripture and preaching as central instruments of God's sign-giving. Though Barth does not describe how divinity unites with humanity in detail, he writes that, "when we are asked how objective revelation reaches man, we can and must reply that it takes place by means of the divine sign-giving. In this sign-giving objective revelation is repeated in such a way that it can come to man in genuinely human form. But the presupposition still remains a mystery." All that we can maintain and confess, Barth continues, "is that God Himself does really avail Himself of this medium," and it is always by God's grace that one can see God through such means (*CD* I/2:233). Still, Barth believes Scripture along with the church are the present arenas of God's revelatory activity where in the event of proclamation, the sovereign and free God speaks in and through human beings and creates hearers (thus doers) of the Word of God and the unity that exists between the revelation of Jesus Christ, the witness of Scripture, and the proclamation of the church, must not be dissolved "however sharply the distinction between the servants" is stressed (*CD* I/2, 744). See also Webster, *Barth,* 57.

106. Barth, *CD* I/2:745.

107. Ibid., 746.

108. Ibid., 756.

of proclamation in which "preaching is the Word of God which he himself speaks," through the exposition of Scripture in free human words, and "preaching is the attempt to serve God's own Word," by proclaiming a biblical text and applying it to the present congregation as a word from "God himself."[109] Both the interaction between divine and human activity and the freedom and creaturely activity of preaching are maintained. From strictly the human perspective, preaching can only be an attempt to serve the Word of God, to bear witness to it, to "announce it."[110] Barth even prefers "announcement" over "proclamation" because if preaching is to be any thing more than pointing or signifying or bearing witness, it is so only as God works in and through it.[111] Barth depicts the human and divine event of proclamation in this way: "God is the one who makes himself heard, who speaks, and not we, who simply have the role of announcing what God himself wants to say."[112]

These lectures offer a clear presentation of the threefold Word of God in distilled form. Articulating the fully human and fully divine aspects of proclamation, Barth insists that the preacher is not tasked with bringing about the kingdom through his own rhetorical efforts or presenting Christ by her own persuasive powers or giving the "impression that the preacher has a corner on Christ and the Spirit."[113] Rather, Barth continues, while preaching differs historically from the immediacy of the prophets and apostles to revelation, "who saw and touched Christ," it does not differ "qualitatively."[114] God speaks through the voice of a simple pastor and the prophets and apostles are there too, Barth adds, and yet, "we should not be self-conscious about this, nor listen for our own prophetic booming, for even though Christ be present, it is by God's own action."[115] The preacher can only serve the divine commission, the preacher can only bear witness, yet it is through this particular way of witness that God seeks to make Godself known. Both the preacher and the congregation are commissioned to look for and to look forward to God's own self-presentation in the event of proclamation. For Barth, this is the central point of all preaching.[116]

109. Barth, *Homiletics*, 44.

110. Ibid., 45.

111. Ibid., 45–46.

112. Ibid., 46.

113. Ibid., 48.

114. Ibid.

115. Ibid., 49.

116. Ibid., 51.

Barth's theology of proclamation presents a provisional union between divine activity and human activity in the preaching event that is not a completion of nor a complete fulfilment of humanity in the event of the Word of God. Rather, the dynamic union establishes, makes possible, and propels forward hearers and doers of the Word as witnesses. Members of the Christian community are brought into a union with God in order to be set free through this event to look for and to look forward to the next event of God's speaking. They are also set free through this provisional union to move toward the second Advent, when all provisionalities and tears will be wiped away, and God and God's people will live in full union and communion together. Until the Second Advent, the suspect and provisional nature of proclamation will always remain. "Its sheer impossibility," Barth continues, "will always remain, but it has now pleased God to present himself in and in spite of this human action."[117] A better summary could not be found of what Barth means that proclamation becomes God's Word. Wherever and whenever human speech and preaching becomes God's Word, in that place and to that particular people in that dynamic moment, it is God's Word, God speaks.[118]

Barth's theology of proclamation presented in these lectures display a sacramental kind of reality in the sense that the divine Word is united to the human word in the singular event of the Word of God. At the same time, these lectures also maintain the free and dynamic movement of God that can never be bound to or imprisoned by the proclaimed Word. From creation to redemption, from incarnation to resurrection, from parousia to eschaton, God remains Lord of the universe and the Lord of this event of proclamation and it is never in humanity's power "that our human word should be God's Word."[119] That such an event occurs can never be guaranteed or become an automated mechanization of the church's life. The next to last words of John of Patmos, "come, Lord Jesus," are crucial for Barth's sacramental understanding of proclamation.[120] Proclamation and preaching must never put their confidence in their own powers and the success of their own actions, Barth maintains, but must "become prayer," meaning they must acknowledge their own provisionality, incompleteness, and lack of finality and certainty, and "remain open to God, so that God himself can now come to us and give us all things richly."[121] Conceived in this way, proclamation is sacramental, not mechanically sacramental, but dynamically

117. Ibid., 69.

118. Ibid., 78.

119. Ibid., 90.

120. Rev 22:20.

121. Barth, *Homiletics*, 90.

and eschatalogically sacramental. As Trevor Hart makes clear, the presence of Jesus Christ, the Word in "human words cannot be guaranteed, coerced, pinned down or held on to,"[122] rather Christ's presence is an eschatological hope and promise that is prayed for and received in, with, and never without the church's all-too-human proclamation.[123]

This sacramental theme of dynamic and momentary union through proclamation is also taken up in later volumes of the *Church Dogmatics*. In *Church Dogmatics* II/1, §25, Barth describes God's ability to give Godself to be known in the limitation of creaturely objectivity. While the basic reality and substance of the sacramental reality of God's revelation is brought together once and for all in Jesus Christ, a one time only occurrence, there are sacramental attestations and continuations, Barth maintains, beginning with Jesus and extending backwards into Israel's life and forward into the church's life.[124] The humanity of Jesus Christ is the first sacrament, the fullness of God's revelation and the reality and "substance of the highest possibility of the creature," but Barth adds, "the existence of this creature in his unity with God does mean the promise that other creatures may attest in their objectivity what is real only in this creature."[125] In this section, Barth uses terms like secondary objectivity, sacramental reality, and divine sign-giving, all of which speak to a number of themes related to the threefold Word of God. First, Barth believes that in God's own self-giving to humanity in and through Jesus Christ, God permits his creatures in temporal moments and places to "speak for Him."[126] In other words, God's speech and action in Jesus Christ has a sacramental continuity that extends beyond the humanity of Jesus Christ to the life of Israel and the life of the church. Barth refers to Jesus Christ as the first sacrament and the only creature taken up into unity with God, yet nevertheless, God's objectivity extends secondarily to other creatures who may serve momentarily as the "temple, instrument and sign of God as He is."[127]

That such an event happens is not a given or a guarantee, but a promise for the creature and for all creation. Such an event is not a freezing of the sacramental union nor is it a dissolution of the infinite qualitative distinction between Creator and creature. It is not a permanent or complete union. While God chooses to use such a sacramental reality and medium "to expose

122. Hart, The Word, the Words, and the Witness," 44.

123. Ibid.

124. Barth, *CD* II/1:53–54.

125. Ibid., 54.

126. Ibid., 53.

127. Ibid., 54.

Himself and make Himself known," Barth warns that just as often such a reality cannot serve God's will and "can even hinder and prevent it."[128] The joining together of the Word of God with the word of man is by no means a given. Barth declares that "the blindness of man can continue in face of the work and sign of God," and the words of the creature can be left unused or can even oppose and contradict the Word of God.[129] That the proclaimed Word of God becomes the Word of God is never a certain outcome; it cannot be expected to come easily. That proclamation may become anything more than human talk about God, can only be hoped for and prayed for, but never guaranteed or possessed.

In Barth's discussion of the divine accompanying, the *concursus Dei*, in *Church Dogmatics* III/3, Barth describes God's activity and the creature's activity, particularly the union of their actions in ways that also correlate to the threefold Word of God. While this section deals primarily with Scripture, the theological framework put forward in this section offers another way to see the interaction between divinity and humanity in their differentiated unity. In describing the divine accompanying in the life and activity of the creature, though the activity of God and the activity of the creature are two separate actions, Barth's first point is that "we have to understand the activity of God and that of the creature as a single action."[130] Barth's description of God's activity in the life of the creature is not only one of transcendence, but God is "so present in the activity of the creature, and present with such sovereignty and almighty power, that His own action takes place in and with and over the activity of the creature."[131] Barth then provides a brief scriptural exegesis that offers a vivid interpretation of God's activity in, with, and over the activity of the creature:

> It is He Himself who does what Moses and David do. It is He, Yahweh, who thunders out of Sion when the prophet speaks. It is He who judges when the Assyrians capture Samaria and the Babylonians Jerusalem. It is He who speaks to the Church when Paul composes His Epistles.[132]

And perhaps, in the interest of this study, one might add that it is the same One who speaks as the Scriptures are read, proclaimed, and heard in the life of the worshipping community.

128. Barth, *CD* II/1:55.
129. Ibid.
130. Barth, *CD* III/3:132.
131. Ibid.
132. Ibid.

This event of union occurs in the event which proceeds "from God by His Word; and subjectively, (moves) towards man by His Holy Spirit."[133] Every time God acts and this event of union occurs, Barth adds, it comes to pass in the same way: God's Word comes to particular people in a particular time and place, and is received by them in the power of the Holy Spirit, and God's Holy Spirit empowers people in a particular time and place to receive God's Word.[134] Through this event a union, a divine-human communion and relationship is established so that human beings are enabled to become the "means," "instrument," and "organ" of God's work to such a degree that Barth warns against laboring vigorously to draw too distinct a line between the freedom of God and the freedom of the creature. "Who," Barth asks, "can mark off the boundary where the freedom of God ceases and the freedom of the creature begins?"[135] Or who can mark off the boundary where the Word of God ceases and the word of humanity begins?

Signs and themes of Barth's threefold Word of God continue to appear in the fourth volume of the *Church Dogmatics*. For instance, as Barth begins his fourth volume excursus on justification through the biblical theme of "God with us," he describes the presence of God through human proclamation in the life of the Christian community. As the gospel is proclaimed, "where between man and man there is a real communication of the report of what took place in Him and through Him, He Himself is there and at work, He Himself makes Himself to be recognised and acknowledged."[136] In the gospel, the Christian message that is passed on from one human being to another in the life of the Christian community is only gospel, only truly the Christian message, as Jesus Christ "speaks through it and is received in it,"[137] as the "One who proclaims Himself."[138] In the present time, Barth asserts that the prime way God comes to humanity and speaks to humanity is in and through the proclamation of the Christian community. Later in this volume (*CD* IV/1), in describing the relationship between Christ and the church, Barth writes that wherever the Christian community lives by the Holy Spirit, Jesus Christ lives on in the world.[139] Here as well, one could easily substitute the language of the threefold Word of God and say that

---

133. Ibid, 142.
134. Ibid.
135. Ibid., 148.
136. Barth, *CD* IV/1:17.
137. Ibid.
138. Ibid., 18.
139. Ibid., 353.

wherever the Christian community proclaims the Word of God by the Holy Spirit, Jesus Christ himself speaks on earth, in the world and in history.[140]

The Centrality of the Threefold Word of God

The themes and concepts of the threefold Word of God and the proclamation event that are so prevalent throughout the initial volumes of the *Church Dogmatics* do not recede completely in the later volumes of Barth's work. There is a conjunction between the divine word and the human word, not in terms of a syncretistic union of grace and nature, not in terms of an ecclesiastical possession of the divine, and not in terms of pre-fabricated ecclesiastical mediums. Rather, the union in the event of proclamation occurs more organically and accurately as "a divine victory concealed in human failure."[141] In the event of proclamation, God's Word does not negate the human word, nor does it fuse together or freeze the divine Word in the proclamation, but instead, by the Holy Spirit, God's Word joins the fully human words, in, with, and over humanity's proclamation,[142] so that in and through humanity's proclamation God is "in its midst as the Lord of its speaking, (and) the Lord who in and through its speaking bears witness to Himself."[143] Barth describes the effects of this union as God making good what we do badly and God manifesting his presence and life in spite of human frailty and limitation.[144]

Proclamation becomes the Word of God in our own time and place, in and through fully human proclaimers, and yet it does not remain the Word of God. The union and conjunction of divine speech and human speech that occurs in proclamation is a momentary happening and event, but never a "freezing" or syncretism of divinity and humanity into a third thing. The event of proclamation, the dynamic and momentary union that occurs in and through that proclamation is never the fulfilment of divine and human relations, but sets the relationship on a new plane and propels it in a new direction, strangely rendering humanity evermore dependent on the divinity that pursues it. Barth describes the church's incomplete eschatological reality in this way: it "has the promise that Jesus Christ wills to be present in its midst and to speak through it, that this presence and voice of His is to be his life, and that living in Him and through Him it is to be the light

140. Ibid., 353.

141. Barth, *CD* I/2:752.

142. Barth, *CD* III/3:133

143. Barth, *CD* I/2:749.

144. Ibid., 752.

of the world."[145] And yet, this event must occur ever again, this gospel must always be heard afresh, Jesus Christ must come over and over again, and his presence must be prayed for over and over again "in the Church and by the Church, if it is to find fulfilment."[146] To claim possession of Jesus Christ or to seek to freeze Christ's presence in the biblical witness or in the Eucharistic host or in the pious human heart, or even in the church's proclamation, denies the eschatological reality of the church's life. And here Barth's language cannot be clearer or more severe. To deny the eschatological reality of the church, to endeavor to secure and possess the divine in the act of proclamation, is to "fall back onto something without first having had to hear it again," it is to cease to be the church of Jesus Christ and to become something else.[147]

Summary

Much of Karl Barth's early dogmatic work is a theological exposition of the threefold Word of God. For Barth, proclamation in the here and now, grounded upon Scripture and the eternal Word of God in Jesus Christ, is the one Word of God. Proclamation becomes the Word of God in an ecclesial event and a momentary uniting of divine and human speech and action. Even in this dynamic union, there is no mixture or synthesis of divine and human subjects, but a divine accompanying and joining with creaturely speech and action in one single event. In this event, proclamation and Scripture share in Jesus Christ's sacramental reality, even as this sharing is only provisional and momentary, never final. Nevertheless, this sacramental event is a real uniting of humanity and divinity together so that humanity may be set free to correspond and respond to God's speaking in and through the church's proclamation. This event is dynamic but also eschatalogical, setting humanity free to pray for and to look with anticipation toward God's future coming and speaking, in and through the life of the Christian community, for the sake of all creation.

The event of the threefold Word of God has a distinct christological content, but it does not happen apart from the presence and activity of the Holy Spirit. The next chapter will explore the integral role the Holy Spirit plays in relation to the threefold Word of God, and the particular character of the Spirit as it manifests Christ's presence, enables the church's proclamation, and shapes the church's life and witness in the world.

145. Barth, *CD* I/2:806.
146. Ibid.
147. Ibid.

2

The Threefold Word of God and the Holy Spirit

> The Holy Spirit, at least according to the Western understanding
> of the divine Triunity, cannot be separated from the Word, and
> his power is not a power different from that of the Word but the
> power that lives in and by the Word.
>
> —Karl Barth, *CD* I/1:150

KARL BARTH'S CONCEPT OF THE THREEFOLD WORD OF GOD HAS A CHRIS-
tological emphasis, but also a pneumatological dimension. It is the Holy
Spirit that is the bond of union in the event of proclamation, dynamically
uniting the voice of God to the voices and ears of the Christian community, and it is the Holy Spirit that confirms as God's own work "the work of
faith which is proclaimed in words of human thought and expression on
the lips of the preacher and in the ears of the here and now, thus turning
the preached promise into the event of real promise that is given to the
Church."[1] It is the Holy Spirit who enables the voice of Christ to traverse
time and space to speak in the present life of the Christian community and
it is the Holy Spirit whose eschatological reality breaks into the present enabling human words of hope and expectation to become God's Word.

This chapter examines the activity of the Holy Spirit in relation to the
threefold Word of God, especially in regard to the church's proclamation,
drawing from Karl Barth's early theological writings in the 1920s and in
his more mature presentation in *CD* I/1 and I/2 in the 1930s. This chapter
argues that the work of the Holy Spirit is integral to the threefold Word of
God, as the contemporaneous form of Christ, the "real presence" of Christ in
Scripture and proclamation and the Christian community. In conversation

1. Barth, *CD* I/1: 60.

with contemporary scholarship, this chapter engages some of the problems with Barth's eschatological emphasis on the coming event and the coming Spirit as opposed to present possession of the Word of God. Finally, this chapter argues that the Holy Spirit is the bond of union between the divine voice and the human voice in the event of the Word of God.

The Holy Spirit and Proclamation

Just as things were calming down after World War II, legend has it that Karl Barth got himself involved in a dispute over the stained glass windows in the Basel Münster. At the onset of World War II, the windows were removed for fear of destruction, and after the war when the attempt was made to restore the windows to their former positions, Barth resisted the effort.[2] Barth resisted the restoration of the stained glass windows because of his insistence that "the gospel came to the church only through the Word proclaimed," and needed no crutches or assistance even in the form of vivid depictions of the gospel story in stained glass.[3] Later in his life, Barth again articulated these themes in an article on church architecture. Other than an ordinary communion table, a simple pulpit, and a baptismal font all located at the center of the church building, Barth argued that all images and symbols had no place in a Protestant church building, as they would only distract and create confusion from the central focus of the church's life and activity: "the preaching of the Word of God and the prayers of the assembled congregation."[4] Ostentation, decoration, and ornamentation, even the choir and organ, could all be distractions for a congregation whose primary duty in worship should be to hear the Word proclaimed and respond in prayer, praise, and faithful witness.[5]

Barth was not just displaying an allergy to high church liturgy. Rather his vision of the ecclesial community was underscored by his very Reformed insistence that the essence of Christian faith is more an aural faith than a visual faith. The gospel of Jesus Christ is transformative as it is heard and received in the life of faith. The church lives and walks by faith, not by sight,[6] and thus can only see as it hears and is transformed by the voice of Christ. Even Jesus Christ's own life was not self-evidently revelatory except through the power of the Holy Spirit and the eyes and ears of faith, so too in the con-

2. Achtemeier, "Relevant Remembering," 109.

3. Ibid.

4. Barth, "Protestantism and Architecture," 272.

5. Ibid.

6. 2 Cor 5:7.

text of the particular worshipping community, grace is not simply mediated by hands or by ingesting it by the mouth or even through delightful visual images. Rather by the work of the Spirit, grace reaches human beings through the ears. For Karl Barth, perhaps the ultimate sacramental medium was not an inanimate object, but the human ear. The Word proclaimed must also be heard, and it is the Holy Spirit that unites human speaking and hearing with the living God and makes them one in the event of proclamation.[7]

In his 1925 "Church and Theology" address given in response to Erich Peterson, Barth described the Spirit as the "Spirit of the Word," which works equally along with the Word, "neither of the two is greater or lesser," to speak and mediate Christ's authority in the life of the church.[8] Though there seems to be an equal division of labor between the revelation of Jesus Christ and the outpouring of the Holy Spirit, or objective revelation and subjective revelation, Barth would later interpret the work, role, and power of the Spirit in light of the *filioque* clause of the Nicene Creed pointing out that the Spirit is the Spirit of the Father and the Son, "not a spirit side by side with the Word, but the Spirit of the Word itself who brings to our ears the Word and nothing but the Word."[9] In other words, the Spirit does not work independently from Jesus Christ. Far from being a second revelation, the Spirit is the creative power of the one Word of God, Jesus Christ, that becomes present through Scripture and proclamation in the life and activity of the Christian community.[10]

7. Barth, *GD*, 271.

8. Barth, "Church and Theology," in *Theology and Church*, 296. Though Barth speaks in terms of Word and Spirit together working equally, the pneumatocentric to christocentric shift McCormack describes may have been taking place earlier than Barth's adjustment to the doctrine of election.

9. Barth, *CD* I/2:239.

10. McCormack, *Karl Barth's Critically Realistic Dialectical Theology*, 328. McCormack characterizes the period of Barth's thought, roughly 1924–1937, as pneumatocentric. Though the centrality of God's self-revelation was in Jesus Christ, his focus was on the here and now of God's self-revelation rather than the there and then of Christ's own life history in the first century. According to McCormack, Barth then seeks to read his doctrines from the starting point of the revelatory event in the present making it a christologically grounded pneumatocentric theology. After his deeper articulation of the doctrine of election, McCormack argues that Barth would read all doctrines off the self-revelation of Christ in history making it a christologically grounded, christocentric theology. Though Barth speaks in terms of Word and Spirit together working equally, the pneumatocentric to christocentric shift may have been taking place earlier than Barth's adjustment to the doctrine of election. As we see in *CD* I/2, Barth is already describing the Spirit not as a Spirit "side by side" with the Word, but as the power that emanates from the Word, the "Spirit of the Word." See *CD* I/2:239.

As the Spirit of the Word, the creative power that brings to human ears nothing but the Word,[11] the Holy Spirit is the distinct power within God that makes the ontologically distinct, wholly other, sovereign and incomprehensible God knowable, recognizable, and capable of being loved and acknowledged in the life of the Christian community. How is this activity of the Holy Spirit and this event of revelation specifically related to the third form of the Word of God? In relation to proclamation in particular, Barth describes the Spirit's ability and activity uniting human proclamation of the gospel to Christ's own voice. Reflecting on the significance and work of the Spirit in the New Testament, Barth describes the Spirit as God's ability to empower humanity to evoke an affirmative response to the gospel, God's ability to guide and instruct human beings in ways they could never do for themselves, and most central to proclamation, the Spirit empowers human beings to "speak of Christ in such a way that what they say is witness and that God's revelation in Christ thus achieves new actuality through it."[12] Here Barth clearly articulates the unity and continuity of the third form of God's Word with the first form through the activity of the Spirit. The Spirit not only establishes human witnesses and a faithful response to God's Word within humanity, but the Spirit empowers human witness and speech about Christ to be annexed by God's own self-revelation in Jesus Christ so that "revelation now is not only Jesus Christ," but extends to and is actualized in the here and now, among and through particular human beings.[13]

Even as God makes human beings active participants in revelation, Barth cautions that humanity always remains humanity, the sinner always remains the sinner, and the outpouring of the Holy Spirit always remains God.[14] In this revelatory event and union, the creature does not lose her nature and become transformed into the Holy Spirit, nor does the Spirit dissolve into the creature. God remains God, Barth maintains, "even and precisely when He Himself comes into our hearts as His own gift, even and precisely when He 'fills' us."[15] And yet, God is able, through this activity of the Spirit, to enable finite human beings in the proclamation of the Word, to become "enclosed in the act of God."[16]

11. Barth, *CD* I/2:239.

12. Barth, *CD* I/1:453–54.

13. Barth, *CD* I/2:235–36.

14. Barth, *CD* I/1:462.

15. Barth, *CD* I/1:465.

16. Ibid., 462. See also, Barth, *CD* I/2:245–47. Barth writes that in the Holy Spirit "we know the real togetherness of God and man," but from the side of man there is no freedom or capacity or human possibility that attains revelation. Rather the Word

Real Presence

Bruce McCormack's study of Barth's early theological development presents Barth's theology of the Word, articulated in Göttingen, Münster, Bonn, and Basel, as christocentrically grounded, but argues that the basic orientation or focus was chiefly on the revelation event as it happens in the present through God's self-revelation.[17] Instead of reading all doctrine in light of the event of election and its actualization in Jesus Christ's life, death, and resurrection, which McCormack believes represents Barth's later view, in this period, Barth sought to read doctrines in light of the event of Christ's self-revelation in the contemporary life of the Christian community.[18] Mc-Cormack refers to this period of Barth's development as a christologically grounded, pneumatocentric theology.[19] Perhaps a more practical outcome of Barth's earlier christologically grounded pneumatocentrism is exhibited in Barth's confidence in theology's ability to identify the presence of the Holy Spirit in and through Scripture, proclamation, and the church's life together. Where in his later theological work Barth might draw clearer distinctions, Gabriel Fackre argues that "his earlier language was sometimes interpreted as a fusion" of the historical event of reception with the "moment of its reception."[20] Thus the Word of God is not only Jesus Christ, but by the present power and activity of the Holy Spirit in the life of the Christian community, Scripture and proclamation become God's Word, so that "the one who proclaims the gospel, preacher or theologian, proclaims

---

of God reaches human beings as the outpouring of the Holy Spirit brings the Word of God to human hearing. See also, *CD*, I/1:186. As Barth replies earlier to the question of how the Word of God is the same Word of God in three forms: "It is on our lips and in our hearts as the mystery of the Spirit who is the Lord."

17. McCormack, *Karl Barth's Critically Realistic Dialectical Theology*, 328.

18. Ibid.

19. Ibid. After modifying the doctrine of election, McCormack argues that Barth's theology would become a "Christologically, grounded, christocentric theology." Others also argue that Barth shifted from a concern with and a present focus on existential realization (the Word of God becoming the Word of God in the present through the dynamic activity of the Holy Spirit), to an eschatological theology of expectation (we pray and call on God to become present and unite his life and speech to our human speech and action), but Barth will exhibit a much greater wariness of any claims of the "present possession" of God in any form. What we possess is the hope that God will speak and become present through Scripture and proclamation. See also, Wood, *The Comedy of Redemption*, 49; and Fackre, "Revelation," 11–12. Jenson hints that this shift from pneumatocentrism leads to a binatarianism in Barth that subordinates or dissolves the independent person and work of the Spirit from the word and work of Christ. See Jenson, "You Wonder Where the Spirit Went," 296–304; and Jenson, *America's Theologian*, 187.

20. Fackre, "Revelation," 9.

what God in person is saying presently to the church and to the world" in the particularity and dynamic reality of the present moment.[21]

Though Barth does not specifically refer to the unity of the threefold Word of God in terms of "real presence," the Word of God in its three forms, Jesus Christ, Scripture, and proclamation, does seem to indicate a "real presence" of God in Christ that also extends provisionally, temporarily, and dynamically to Scripture and proclamation in the life of the Christian community. Barth discusses this mysterious presence of God through the Holy Spirit in relation to the event of faith on and in humanity (I/1), through an extended discussion of divine sign-giving (I/2), and through an extended excursus on the secondary objectivity of Israel and the church's life (II/1). Indeed, Barth believes that the possibility of faith itself is the sign within humanity of the real presence of Christ which opens up humanity from above, but "remains just as hidden for us as the event itself or God Himself."[22] The event of faith, the event of Christ's presence opening up the ears and heart of the hearer through the Word, reveals the divine ability to enclose humanity in an act of God.[23] This event occurs in the present and the particularities of the Christian community, where in the event of faith, "the event of the presence of the believed Word in man, (and) the union of man with it," the Holy Spirit enables the inadequacy of human possibility to "become the adequate divine possibility."[24]

The work and the presence of the Holy Spirit in the life of the Christian and in the life of the Christian community, is the life and activity of God, "after He has become man in Christ for us," in which God also adopts particular human beings "in such a way that He Himself makes us ready to listen to the Word, that He Himself intercedes with us for Himself, that He Himself makes the speaking and hearing of His Word possible among us."[25] The Word of God is actualized in its reception by the Christian community and particular hearers within the community by the power of the Holy Spirit.[26] Not only do Scripture and proclamation become the Word of God as the

---

21. Richardson, "*Christus Praesens*," 141.

22. Barth, *CD* I/1:243.

23. Ibid., 462.

24. Ibid., 243.

25. Barth, *CD* I/2:221.

26. Fackre, "Revelation," 9. Again, Fackre makes the point that fulfilment or actualization is more of an existential reality than an eschatological one as the Word of God is actualized as it is received by the believer in the community by the Holy Spirit, which makes it possible for the Bible and proclamation of Scripture to become God's Word in the present as the Spirit enables God's voice and presence to be revealed in and through the speech and reception of the Christian community.

Spirit makes Christ's voice contemporaneously present as the Scriptures are read and proclaimed, but Barth also describes the movement of the Spirit as mediating the present reality of Christ, and as imparting the knowledge of Christ into the life of the Christian.[27] Barth illustrates this dual activity of the Holy Spirit in a quotation he takes directly from Eduard Thurneysen: "The statement of revelation that God speaks is identical with the statement that man hears."[28]

As we have already seen, Barth describes the work of the Holy Spirit in the life and activity of the Christian community, by way of an extended discussion on divine sign-giving, the way Jesus Christ reaches man[29] and the way "real revelation puts man in God's presence."[30] The work and role of the Holy Spirit, works in and through divine sign-giving to address human beings and to take them up into the event of revelation in which they are made to see themselves not only as sinful creatures but as children of God, as those who are in Christ by Christ, whose lives are hid with Christ in God, those who have become hearers and doers of the Word of God.[31] Without the Holy Spirit, without the Spirit's life and activity of making Christ present and known in and through Scripture and the church's proclamation, without the Holy Spirit's ongoing activity, there would be no threefold Word of God, and Scripture and proclamation could not become the Word of God.[32] In and through the secondary forms of the Word of God, the Spirit is the source of union and the bond that unites the presence and voice of Christ to the life and activity of particular human beings in the Christian community. The Spirit enables God's revelation to penetrate humanity in the present; the Spirit enables finite and broken human beings to be instruments and receptors of God's revelation in and through Scripture and proclamation.[33]

27. Richardson, "*Christus Praesens*," 142.

28. Barth, *CD* I/1:242. See also Thurneysen, *Das Wort Gottes und die Kirche*, 222.

29. Barth, *CD* I/2:232.

30. Ibid., 237.

31. Ibid., 236–40.

32. Ibid., 241. Barth writes that just because the Spirit belongs to Jesus Christ, "the work of Christ is never done without Him. Nor is it done except by Him. The grace of our Lord Jesus Christ does not exist except in the fellowship of the Holy Spirit (2 Cor. 13:14), and the love of God is not poured out into our hearts except by the Holy Spirit (Rom. 5:5)."

33. Even so, that God's speaks in and through the witness and proclamation of the Christian community is never less than a miracle. "To receive the Holy Spirit means an exposure of our spiritual helplessness, a recognition that we do not possess the Holy Spirit. For that reason the subjective reality of revelation has the distinctive character of a miracle, i.e., it is a reality to be grounded only in itself." Barth, *CD* I/2:244. See also, Webster, *Barth*, 56.

Bruce McCormack's description of Barth's christological pneumato-centrism appears to be an accurate depiction, especially when focusing on the here and now of Barth's theological work. Though Barth describes the Holy Spirit in various ways as the Spirit of the Father and the Son, as the Spirit of Jesus Christ, the present activity of Jesus Christ, the contemporaneous presence of Christ Himself, the activity of the Spirit is perhaps the primary mode of divine revelation and activity in the here and now, and seems to function as the particular divine capacity to become the Word of God in and through Scripture and proclamation.[34] According to Barth, it is the power and bond of the Spirit that is able to overcome the infinite qualitative distinction between divinity and humanity, to unite finite sinful human beings to Jesus Christ[35] and to enable God's speech to be received by human beings through human speaking. In the present, it is the Holy Spirit that mediates Christ's presence and enables human beings to proclaim and to hear what God is saying in the here and now to the Christian community and to the world.

The Holy Spirit and the Second Form of the Word of God

As Scripture is the foundation and content of the church's proclamation, the Holy Spirit plays an integral role uniting God's self-revelation with the biblical account of Israel's life and the life, death, and resurrection of Jesus Christ. While this study is focused primarily on the third form of the Word of God and its importance in the formation and identity of the Christian community, the third form of the Word of God derives from and does not come without the second form of the Word of God. Barth does not maintain a doctrine of scriptural infallibility, but the concept of the threefold Word of God serves to illustrate how the one infallible Word of God, the living Jesus Christ, incorporates fallible witnesses into his own self-revelation through the biblical witnesses primarily, but also secondarily through the church's particular attempts to proclaim and live out the gospel for the sake of the larger world.

In relation to Scripture, the Holy Spirit has a multiform role to play as God speaks through the written word. First, in terms of inspiration, Scripture is the account of Israel's life with and before God, from the patriarchs to Moses to Israel's worship and prayers to Israel's prophets, a written record of God's past encounter with this people and their response and witness to the presence of the Lord in their midst. While the inspiration of the Holy Spirit

34. Barth, *CD* I/2:239–42.
35. Ibid., 241–42.

led to the recording of this written word in the first place, Barth interprets the inspiration of Scripture "as a divine decision continually made in the life of the Church and in the life of its members."[36] Scripture therefore serves as a record of God's past faithfulness and inspiration, past evidence of the Holy Spirit at work in the history of Israel and the church. Yet in the contemporary life of the Christian community, Scripture can only again become the Word of God, something more than a record of God's past history with Israel and its fulfilment in Jesus Christ, by the present power of the Holy Spirit.

As the church returns to these eyewitnesses, who are not self-evidently revelatory even in their written form, the Holy Spirit enables these witnesses of Christ's humanity to speak and to again become witnesses of divine revelation in the present.[37] Such past accounts of inspiration are apprehended as revelatory in the present life of the Christian community as the Holy Spirit enables the revelation that was apprehended by Israel and the early church to also be apprehended as revelation by the contemporary church.[38] This happens not by human processes or determination or by right interpretation of Scripture alone, but as "the work of God is done through" the text and a "miracle of God takes place in this text formed of human words."[39] While Scripture serves as a record of God's past inspiration, Barth declares that "we are not bound to imagine the Word of God is present," nor is the Christian community called upon to make it present, but in thankfulness and hope, the church trusts that God will take up this text and use it and speak through it in spite of its human infallibility.[40] In so doing, the divine Word does not stop by speaking again through the biblical witness, but seeks to speak in the particular context of the Christian community through the gospel proclamation, as the mystery of God manifests itself in the contemporary words and witness of the Christian community.[41]

Proclamation, Illumination, and Union

In an address given in 1922 titled "The Word of God and the Task of the Ministry," Barth makes the point that ministers of the gospel are tasked to preach the Word of God. That being the case however, Barth's second point

---

36. Barth, *CD* I/2:534–35.

37 Ibid., 537.

38. Ibid.

39. Ibid., 532.

40. Ibid., 533.

41. Ibid., 532.

is that it is impossible for human beings to speak the Word of God, and so if the third form of the Word of God ever becomes the Word of God it can only become so by an act of God. All the proclaimers and hearers can do is acknowledge that we should speak and hear the Word of God, yet finite human beings who are infinitely qualitatively distinct from God are incapable of doing just that, and so human beings can only acknowledge this impossibility before God and "by that very recognition give God the glory."[42] And yet, while humanity may not be able to offer more than an acknowledgement of human frailty and the mortal incapacity to contain the Word of God on the lip or heart, Barth argues that from the side of God, God's transcendent sovereignty does not exclude but includes God's fellowship with humanity.

The divine and human relation is not ultimately defined and lived out in infinite distance and qualitative distinction, God is not a prisoner of his deity, Barth often remarks, but the Holy Spirit unites divinity and humanity without creating a permanent fusion or synthesis. Barth acknowledges that the sharp line that separates humanity from divinity is never "expunged or removed," but through "the Holy Spirit we know the real togetherness of God and man."[43] Echoing his address given more than a decade earlier, Barth acknowledges that everything one can say about humanity from the standpoint of revelation refutes the possibility that God can be made known to human beings, "but the work of the Holy Spirit is in favor of that possibility."[44] The only reason proclamation can become something other than human talk and human talk about God, the only reason gathered humanity in the life of the Christian community hear anything besides human talk and human talk about God, is because the Word of God is brought to humanity's hearing in the Holy Spirit.[45] The Word of God creates the possibility that human beings proclaim and hear the Word of God.[46]

To receive the Holy Spirit is never to possess the Holy Spirit or to have the Word of God on humanity's terms or to engineer the event of human proclamation becoming the Word of God. That such an event and miracle may ever occur is only possible as humanity's own spiritual helplessness and utter dependence are exposed. That exposure and acknowledgment of human emptiness of the Spirit, Barth indicates, is perhaps the very way the Holy Spirit makes it possible to place the Word of God on humanity's lips

---

42. Karl Barth, *The Word of God and the Word of Man*, 186.

43. Barth, *CD* I/2:245–46.

44. Ibid., 246.

45. Ibid., 247.

46. Ibid.

and hearts.[47] Part of the Spirit's work renders human beings lacking in self-sufficiency, completely helpless, and fully dependent on God's grace. In the midst of such circumstances, does the work of the Holy Spirit make the impossible possible, enabling the Word of God to be spoken and heard in the life of the Christian community. Only as the Holy Spirit cuts away from human beings all other possibilities and means of possessing and speaking for God, only as human beings are exposed as completely dependent and spiritually helpless to help themselves, only when there is no other possible way for God's Word to be on human lips and in human hearts, only then is the Holy Spirit able to complete God's work and bring Christ, the Word of God to human hearing and Christian life together.[48]

Before the Scriptures are read and proclaimed, the minister and the community together pray for illumination, *Veni Creator Spiritus*. Barth is bold enough to say that one cannot proclaim the gospel without praying.[49] Even humanity's calling on God can only take it so far; there is a limit to what human beings can say and "the Spirit himself must represent us with sighing that cannot be uttered."[50] Though the presence of the Holy Spirit does not come because humanity asks, though the proclamation of the Word of God does not become the Word of God because of prayers for illumination, Barth cautions that it is "impossible to abstract the divine reality of the Holy Spirit from the prayer for the Holy Spirit in which it is acknowledged and accepted as a divine reality."[51] Here too divine and human distinction and togetherness are held together and enclosed in an act of God.[52] Here too the Holy Spirit creates both the distinction between the free grace of God and the adoration of humanity as well as their union and unity, as the free grace of God, the Word of God, Jesus Christ, in the power of the Holy Spirit, encloses humanity's adoration and petition.[53]

In and of itself, humanity does not possess nor is it capable of bearing the Word of God; rather it is the activity of Jesus Christ through the power of the Holy Spirit who determines and makes it possible for God to speak in and through human speaking and hearing. God's speaking in the life of the Christian community, Kurt Anders Richardson writes of Barth, "is the miraculous and continuous activity of God by his Spirit to actualize

47. Ibid., 244.
48. Ibid., 246–49.
49. Barth, *Homiletics*, 86.
50. Ibid.
51. Barth, *CD* I/2:768.
52. Barth, *CD* I/1:462.
53. Barth, *CD* I/2:245.

the words of Scripture as his own."[54] Such actualization does not end with Scripture, but extends to the third form of God's Word as the Spirit actualizes proclamation and the gospel message in the particular hearts and lives of the Christian community. It is the Word of God, by the power of the Holy Spirit that dynamically and provisionally contains, embraces, and exalts humanity's own words, so that God may again and again speak in the present particularity of the Christian community, and so that human words and proclamation in the life of the church are never assumed to be the Word of God, but must always seek and hope to become God's Word.[55]

It is the Holy Spirit that is the source of unity between the one Word of God and its secondary forms. Without the presence and work of the Holy Spirit, human words, whether in Scripture or proclaimed in the life of the Christian community, cannot become the one Word of God.[56] Because this work of the Spirit is dynamic and not static, the Spirit momentarily makes use of these fallible human words and creatures, enabling those words to retain their identity yet to become the way God addresses the community. The unity, illumination, and inspiration the Spirit creates are not permanent. Human words in proclamation, from beginning to end, are human words. They may become something more "when they are inspired and used by God Himself by the Holy Spirit," but they will still remain quite human words throughout the dynamic activity of the Spirit.[57] While human words may be shot through with God's grace or enclosed in an act of God, they are not so permanently.[58] In the presence of divine activity, Barth argues, humanity is still humanity.[59] Yet the Holy Spirit enables the Christian community to speak about God in human words and in so doing, to proclaim God's own words.[60] The Holy Spirit maintains the differentiation between God and humanity without creating a third thing or synthesis between the two, even as the Holy Spirit unites these two disparate partners in the church's own speaking and hearing in the event of the Word of God.

54. Richardson, "*Christus Praesens*," 138.

55. Barth, *CD* I/2:775.

56. Ibid., 768. See also Hart, "The Word, the Words, and the Witness," 44–45. Hart writes that the event of the Word of God, proclamation, is a miraculous event in which Jesus Christ speaks to human beings through the event; Hart stresses that this event is created by the Word and Spirit together.

57. Ibid., 756.

58. Ibid.

59. Ibid., 758.

60. Barth, *CD* I/1:757.

Proclamation and Consummation

After World War II, Karl Barth returned to the University of Bonn where he had been expelled from teaching more than a decade earlier. In this place of reconstruction and rebuilding, not unlike the exiled prophet returning to Israel, Barth referred to the present time, "our time," as the "time of the Word," or the time of abandonment, "in which the Church is united with Christ only in faith and by the Holy Spirit."[61] In this interim time, this time of the Spirit, Barth made clear that God does not seek to transform the Christian community and the Christian into a completed and finished state, but God makes room and leaves room for humanity's own participation and response to the work of the Spirit.[62] The work of the Spirit is not complete when Scripture and proclamation become the Word of God, not even as faith is created and gratitude offered. Barth presses forward, making the case that Scripture proclaims the Christ who has already come in the flesh but Scripture likewise proclaims the Christ who will one day come again. Rather than creating a personal possession and static security for the Christian and the Christian community, the work of the Holy Spirit between the first and second Advent creates an expectation and hope that what has been given (actualized) will be given again.[63] When human words become the Word of God in the event and life together of Christian community, they do not become the possession of the Christian or Christian community. As the preached word becomes God's Word, rather than reaching a state of fulfilment or a permanent possession of grace, the work of the Spirit creates a longing to hear the gospel afresh again, a yearning for future redemption and consummation, a movement forward in expectation and hope.[64]

Perhaps the most important and distinctive work of the Holy Spirit in Barth's account of the threefold Word of God and proclamation, is that the work of the Spirit is not finished or complete even as the words proclaimed become the Word of God. Beyond making the Word of God contemporaneous by revealing it amidst the human words and activities of the Christian community, the Holy Spirit frees the Christian community and Christians to correspond in their own decisions to the decision made about them in Jesus Christ.[65] While Barth argues that the proclamation of the Word of God and the written Word of God become the Word of God in

61. Barth, *Dogmatics in Outline*, 128.

62. Ibid.

63. Barth, *Homiletics*, 53–54.

64. Ibid., 54–55.

65. Barth, *CD* I/1:240.

the Christian community, to believe this, he maintains, is not to treat God's Word like capital at one's disposal or to regard the Word of God as one's own possession or the community's ecclesiastical property.[66] Christ's presence in the church's proclamation, Barth argues, also implies the possibility of absence.[67] Christ's power is never ceded over to the Christian community to be perpetuated and maintained as a human possession.[68] Rather the Spirit comes and is at work in Scripture and proclamation as the Christian community looks forward in anticipation of Christ's reign and Christ's return. Only as the Christian community surrenders all human assurances and claims and falls back in dependence on the free grace of God alone, does the Spirit of the Word enable Scripture and proclamation to again become the living Word of God.[69]

Far from making the third form of God's Word into a human possession under the auspices of the Christian community, the role of the Spirit is open-ended, ongoing, future-oriented and eschatological. The gospel after all is not for the Christian community, but for the world. And Christ's presence and action in and through the event of proclamation cannot be guaranteed, assumed, or possessed by human beings, but only prayed for in hopeful expectation. Human talk about God in the context of the church's proclamation fails in its striving to become anything more than prayer and expectation. It can only become the Word of God as the church prays in expectation and hope, "thrown back completely on free grace," and "trembling assurance," that God's Spirit alone will be able to make God's infinite Word heard in the midst of a finite community.[70] As a result, the church's gospel proclamation can never rest on its laurels or believe that it possesses the kingdom of God by its mere stature and ability and commission. It must always humbly pray, expectedly wait, struggle, and longingly hope, that God will come again, and by the power and activity of the Holy Spirit, speak in and through the words of Scripture and proclamation and make them God's own. Preaching and proclamation that rests secure in its own office or preaching that seeks to represent God's interests to the rest of the world, Barth cautions, is like a "majestic Gothic arch that shelters us from the gaze of heaven, for we are truly sheltered only when we are

66. Ibid., 225.

67. Ibid., 98.

68. Ibid., 225. See also, Barth, *CD* I/1:97–98. Here Barth suggests that Roman Catholic theology too easily transfers or collapses the Lordship and presence of Christ directly into the church where he argues it is simply self-evidently present and is not distinguished from the power exercised by sinful human beings in the same sphere.

69. Barth, *CD* I/1:225.

70. Ibid., 99, 225.

exposed before God."[71] Triumphalistic confidence in human proclamation and human ecclesial action impede and prevent such a posture before God. Such a view of preaching does not need prayer or the work of the Holy Spirit that comes in asking, but instead trusts in its own rhetorical powers and achievements. Only as preaching finally becomes a prayer for help, "the seeking and invoking of God," that trusts and hopes expectantly and dependently on God to speak, may it also become God's own Word in the life of the Christian community.[72]

In his only seminar held on the topic of preaching, Barth writes that "the proper attitude of preachers does not depend on whether they hold on to the doctrine of inspiration but on whether or not they expect God to speak to them here."[73] Proclamation is never a completed act, but an ongoing submission and active expectation that moves forward with the hope and expectation that God will speak in and through the sinful preacher by the power of the Holy Spirit, and that a Word from the Lord will be heard in the life of the Christian community by the same activity of the Holy Spirit.[74] In the becoming of the Word of God, the presence of God and God's speech in the life of the Christian community is never something the church has or possesses. The church is always on the way, from event (Easter) to event (parousia), and never has Jesus Christ on its own. And so while Barth claims that the Word of God becomes Scripture and proclamation in a secondary way, it happens in a dynamic event and encounter in the presence of the Holy Spirit, not through a permanent transaction that infuses human beings with the contents of grace. Scripture and proclamation are not the Word of God in all times, places, and circumstances, but only as Christ appears and speaks in and through them by the power of the Holy Spirit.

Proclamation of the gospel is practiced with expectation, hope, and understanding that its own proclamation and speech must be ever afresh enclosed by an act of God. Therefore, in the present time or interim time or time between the times, the work of the Spirit is never completed nor finished in the act of proclamation, but is always empowering the Christian community to look back in trust and confidence at past revelation, even as the same Spirit beckons the community forward with hope and expectation toward God's future revelatory event. Scripture and proclamation do not exist statically as the Word of God but by the ongoing work and outpouring of the Holy Spirit, they become the Word of God, dynamically, momentarily,

71. Barth, *Homiletics*, 79, 90.

72. Ibid., 90.

73. Ibid., 78.

74. Ibid., 79.

and ever again in the life and witness of the Christian community. The proper posture of the Christian and the Christian community is one of expectation not possession, one of empty outstretched hands not clutching, controlling fingers, one that does not contain the presence of the One it signifies, but one that expects, hopes, and trusts that it will be embraced and contained by the One it signifies, as the Spirit unites such disparate elements together and encloses them in an act and event of God. As those who live between Christ's Ascension and Christ's return in this interim "time of the Word," time of the Holy Spirit, a time between the times, the Christian community can never have or possess the word completely in this time. Still, even though Scripture and proclamation are not the Word of God in its original form, the Christian community is a field of divine activity where these derivative forms, Scripture and proclamation, become instruments of divine communication by the ongoing activity of the Holy Spirit in which human beings are brought into an encounter with God.[75] Though proclamation and Scripture are derivative forms of the Word of God, they are nevertheless forms that point to the reality of God's presence and self-revelation in Christ, and in their witness as herald and witness of past revelation, they become part of the one event in which God continues to speak to the world through the life and witness of the Christian community. In spite of his qualifications, in both Scripture and in the church's proclamation of the gospel, Barth believes the Holy Spirit truly gives humanity the Word of God to speak.

Only at the consummation, as the work of the Spirit reaches its goal, will it be self-evident and clear to all that Scripture, proclamation, and the life together and witness of the Christian community were anything more than human talk about God, anything beyond strange self-deferential worship and action. In the interim time, Christ speaks and is made known in and through the Christian community as the Holy Spirit makes Christ present and unites human voices and ears to his voice in the event of Scripture and proclamation in the life of the Christian community. The work of the Holy Spirit in relation to the threefold Word of God makes the present reality of Christ known, enabling human beings to say and to hear what "God in person is saying presently to the church and to the world."[76]

75. Webster, *Barth*, 55–56.
76. Richardson, "*Christus Praesens*," 141.

Critical Reflection and Appraisal

The purpose of this chapter has been to unfold the particular role of the Holy Spirit in relation to the threefold Word of God, specifically as the presence of the Spirit manifests Christ in the church's engagement with the biblical witness and in the church's attempt to proclaim the gospel. In the act and event of proclamation, it is the Holy Spirit that makes Christ present in the contemporary life together of the Christian community, and it is the Holy Spirit that annexes Scripture and proclamation enabling them to become the Word of God. Becoming is never a completed act or static existence though, so it is also the Holy Spirit that creates both presence and absence in the life of the proclaiming and hearing community, giving the Christian community the freedom and desire to move from Advent to the Second Advent, waiting and hoping and praying, for Christ to come again.

Even though proclamation becomes the third form of the Word of God as God speaks to the life of the world through the proclamation event in the Christian community, neither the proclaimer nor the hearer of the Word ever possesses the Word of God. The proclaimer of the Word is always reliant on a new act of the Holy Spirit for the Word of God to come through human speech, and the hearer of the Word continues to pray and call upon the Holy Spirit if the Word of God is ever to become proclamation in the life of the Christian community and the life of the hearer. The gift of the Spirit in relation to the Word of God is not so much the permanent bestowal of the Word of God upon the Christian or Christian community; rather, as the outpouring of the Holy Spirit enables God's Word to be proclaimed and heard in the Christian community, the Spirit creates a deeper longing and greater hunger for God to speak again in and through the life of the Christian community. And so the Christian community is never defined by what it possesses, but is a community that is on the move and always reliant on God. For Barth then, the Christian community lives in hope for the coming Word by the power of the Holy Spirit rather than living in a static confidence and assurance of its ongoing and continuing presence.[77]

While Barth's presentation of the outpouring of the Holy Spirit (subjective revelation) and the role of the Holy Spirit in relation to the threefold Word of God is lucid and clear, it is not above critique. Gabriel Fackre offers a few stumbling blocks and challenges in regard to the relationships between proclamation, the Holy Spirit and the threefold Word of God in Barth's thought. Fackre believes Barth at times speaks interchangeably about future revelation as both future reception and actualization of the Word in

---

77. Fackre, "Revelation," 9.

the Christian community and as the final eschatological consummation.[78] While Barth does speak in eschatological terms about future revelation as Bible and proclamation become the Word of God in the present life together of the Christian community, even in *Church Dogmatics* I/1 and I/2, Barth has a healthy sense of the distinction between actualization of the Word and final eschatological disclosure. Though Barth speaks in less inhibited language about "future revelation as the actualization of the Word," he does not do so at the expense of the Second Advent, but maintains that there is some sense of present realization and actualization of the Word of God as it is proclaimed, heard, and lived out in the life of the Christian community. There is some sense of realization in terms of eschatalogy. Still, there is a danger in Barth's description of the event of the Word of God, that where God's Word is actualized in human words, that this point or event in the life of the Christian community is idealized and treated as the termination point and goal of the Christian community's life and witness in the world rather than as the beginning of the life of discipleship. Barth's theology of the Word has been read in this way. As a result, existential realization in the present tends to overtake any sense that the event of the Word of God produces a new creation which moves forward in eschatological expectation.

Not unrelated to this theme of the present realization of revelation is the issue of the have-ability and grasp-ability of the Word of God within the life of the Christian community. Here, Fackre compares Dietrich Bonhoeffer's own exploration of this theme in contrast to Barth. Coming out of the Lutheran tradition, Bonhoeffer was less cautious about equating God's Word with the Word proclaimed and uttered in the life of the church.[79] While both Barth and Bonhoeffer believed that in the human form of the church's proclamation, the Word of God is present,[80] Barth's Reformed commitments led him to distrust ecclesial attempts to claim continuity of divine presence in Word, sacrament or any other ecclesial media. Attempts to control and possess the dynamic and divine presence of Jesus Christ only ended in sin and failure, and such claims sought to place human limitations on the sovereignty of God.[81] According to Fackre, Bonhoeffer believed God is always "haveable" and "graspable" in the Word and in its ongoing life in the Christian community. In contrast, though Barth could also refer to the event of the Word of God as the union of the Word of God and the human word, the event in which the Holy Spirit enables human words to become

78. Ibid.
79. Ibid., 19.
80. Barth, *CD* I/1:250.
81. Fackre, "Revelation," 17–18.

instruments of divine revelation,[82] Barth still sought to maintain the divine and human distinction. Barth sought to retain and emphasize both the continuity of Christ's presence and activity in and through the activity of proclamation *and* the discontinuity of Christ's distinction from strictly human actions and signs, including proclamation. To Lutherans like Dietrich Bonhoeffer and later Robert Jenson, such *extra Calvinisticum* qualifications risked an unnecessary separation and severing of sign from thing signified.[83] And while Barth would agree that the Christian community should hope and trust and pray that we are really given the Word of God to speak, that it is not so un-possessable that it is never received, he nevertheless refuses to directly identify it or automatically equate it with every ecclesial reading of Scripture and every proclamation of the gospel in the life of the Christian community, not only on ontological grounds, but on pneumatological grounds as well. If the gospel proclamation so assuredly contains the Word of God, then why pray for the Holy Spirit at all?

Barth resisted all theological attempts on the church's and Christian's behalf to possess the presence of Christ in Scripture, preaching, or sacrament. Still Gabriel Fackre argues that Barth could have emphasized the once and for all nature of Christ's deity and humanity in union together without denying the "present possession of the glorious presence" of Jesus Christ in the life of the church.[84] Even so, John Yocum believes Barth's description of the union between the divine Word and human words and their union in differentiation is made most clearly and appropriately in *Church Dogmatics* I/1 and I/2. The event of the Word of God is not separate from or beyond human words, but takes place "in the conjunction of the Word of God and

---

82. Yocum, *Ecclesial Mediation in Karl Barth*, 7.

83. Fackre, "Revelation," 19. See also, Bonhoeffer, *Act and Being*, 81, 83, 90–91; Jenson, *God After God*, 189–92. In his study of Jonathan Edwards, Jenson levels a general critique of Reformed theology that I believe nicely summarizes his reservations about Barth's doctrine of the Word of God and the particular work and union the Holy Spirit makes possible between divine and human action. Jenson remarks that while the Holy Spirit may certainly blow where it wills, Scripture witness portrays such "unpredictable dynamism" through the church's life in proclamation and sacraments. Does the gospel/proclamation contain the grace it signifies or does it not? Jenson pointedly asks. At this point in the *CD*, I am not sure Barth would sit comfortably on either of these options, instead arguing that the Word of God contains, embraces, and exalts human words, i.e., the gospel, through the power of the Holy Spirit. While the gospel may not contain the grace it signifies, the Holy Spirit makes it possible for the grace signified to embrace and contain the gospel.

84. Fackre, "Revelation," 18.

the human word," where the Holy Spirit enables the human word to be enclosed and embraced in an act and word of God.[85]

It is the precise role and identity of the Spirit in this conjunction that is not clear. In his essay the "Mediator of Communion," George Hunsinger writes that in *Church Dogmatics* IV (Christology), Barth preferred to speak primarily in terms of Christ (the agent) making himself present through the Spirit, whereas one would expect if Barth had gotten to a doctrine of redemption, the agential language for the Spirit, where the Spirit makes Christ present, would figure more prominently.[86] By a similar pattern, would the unity of the three forms of the Word of God figure differently or more prominently as well? Or perhaps Barth's later modification to the threefold Word of God sought to offer a greater distinction between a free and authentic human response and the one Word of God. In a theological seminar with English speaking students in the early 1950s, one of the students asked Karl Barth why the Holy Spirit did not appear more explicitly in relation to the "revealed Word."[87] Barth responded that his main concern in that period of the dogmatics was the avoidance of subjectivism. If starting today, he remarked "I would speak more of the Holy Spirit."[88] And perhaps if we do speak more of the Holy Spirit, Scripture and proclamation can more easily be united with the Word of God in the life of the Christian community.[89]

In the later volumes of the *Church Dogmatics,* it remains to be seen whether Barth's earlier theology of the threefold Word of God could cohere with a later emphasis on human witness and attestation as the principle purpose of gospel declaration. But perhaps one example of how such a union of divine and human speech happens is found in his account of the Holy Spirit and the threefold Word of God. The preacher and hearer of the Word can do no more than seek to be a human witness. The words and lives of the Christian and the Christian community only seek to signify and bear witness to the life, death, and resurrection of Jesus Christ. Yet, through Christ's ongoing activity and presence in the Holy Spirit, more, it seems, is possible.

85. Yocum, *Ecclesial Mediation in Karl Barth*, 7.

86. Hunsinger, "The Mediator of Communion," 161n13.

87. Barth, *Karl Barth's Table Talk*, 27.

88. Ibid.

89. Rosato, *The Spirit as Lord*, 159. In Rosato's study of Barth's pneumatology, he writes that, while Barth set out to place the life of the church under the sign of the Spirit, he "so invariably presents the Christian's life in the Spirit as a reflection of the life of Jesus, that the poignancy of the church's on-going 'now' is severely relativized by the uniqueness of Jesus' 'then.'" The question is whether the Spirit acts beyond recognition toward occurrence and completion, not to mention mediating Christ's presence, in the here and now.

The Holy Spirit is that person of the Trinity and that dimension of God's life that enables God to "be present himself in and in spite of" the human action of proclamation.[90] God remains God and humanity remains humanity, but in the event of the Word of God, in the event of proclamation, God's own presence is able to make room for and include humanity's words and witness. In the event of the Word of God, God acts in conjunction with human action and humanity's own words and actions are enclosed by God's own words and actions.

Perhaps Barth would later question whether true human response would be negated by such a mode of union and action, but in these early volumes, the threefold Word of God represented the here and now "union of the divine and human possibility," where the divine word and human word were at once distinct and united in the one event of the Word of God.[91] Though Christ remains Christ and stands at the door and knocks, and humanity remains humanity and must open the door, Barth described the union and the work of the Holy Spirit in this way: while it is true that humanity must open the door and it is true that that Christ does not remain outside the door, it is also true that "the risen Christ passes through closed doors."[92] It is the Holy Spirit that enables the risen Christ to pass through closed doors, to be seen and heard in fallible human words, and to contain and embrace human proclamation in an act of God, in the event of the Word of God.

Summary

The first two chapters of this book offer a detailed depiction of the threefold Word of God, the role of Christ and the Spirit in relation to the church's proclamation and contemporary life together. This chapter in particular has sought to build on these themes and to explore them in a pneumatological context. In the present time, the time between the times, it is the Holy Spirit who enables the Word of God to be spoken through human speech in the event of the Word of God. While the divine and human distinctions remain in the union of this event, it is a union that propels the Christian community toward the next event of the Word of God, and it is an event that sets the Christian community free to correspond to Jesus Christ in the context of their lives. The next chapter will explore the importance of the threefold Word of God as a central feature of Barth's vision of the Christian

90. Barth, *Homiletics*, 69.

91. Barth, *CD* I/1:246.

92. Ibid., 247.

community. The concept of the threefold Word of God is crucial to Barth's understanding of the church and serves a principle role in defining the life of the Christian community. The next chapter explains how Barth's concept of the threefold Word of God serves as a *nota ecclesiae* and a concrete ecclesiological vision for life together in Christian community.

3

The Threefold Word of God as Ecclesiology

> The Church is held together as a single whole, from Jesus Christ
> at the right hand of the Father down to the humblest of those
> who by the word of His witness have been called to faith. But
> this connecting link consists in the one Word of God, which
> in these three different forms, in none of them less than in the
> others, in none of them diminished and weakened, but in all
> three remaining the selfsame Word, constitutes the life and the
> foundation of the Church.
>
> —Karl Barth, *CD* I/2:744–45

THIS CHAPTER EXPLORES THE CONCEPT OF THE THREEFOLD WORD OF GOD
in relation to Barth's theology of the church in his early theological writings in the 1920s and 1930s. The second section of this chapter will explore the relationship and development of Barth's theology of the church and the threefold Word of God in the early volumes of the *Church Dogmatics,* I/1, I/2, and II/1. The theology of the church forged out of Barth's concept of the threefold Word of God offers a variety of images of the Christian community as it is actualized and takes visible form in its life in the world. Particular attention will be given to the various descriptions Barth uses to describe the conjunction of divine and human activity in the gospel declaration and in the church's life together. The theology of the church set forth by the threefold Word of God has had a powerful impact when put into practice through the church's witness to the world, whether in Nazi Germany or in apartheid South Africa or in our own time.[1] This chapter will discuss the importance of the threefold Word of God as ecclesiology, especially as it has

---

1. Smit, "'. . . The Doing of the Little Righteousness,'" 142.

shaped Christian witness in particular times and places, even as it is later revised and possibly recedes in Barth's own later work.

Karl Barth's theology of threefold Word of God also includes a theology of the church. Though Barth's ecclesiology is most fully articulated throughout the doctrine of reconciliation, volume IV of the *Church Dogmatics* in paragraphs §62, §67, and §72 respectively, Barth's doctrine of the threefold Word of God serves as a theology of the church that should be read alongside the ecclesiology later developed in his doctrine of reconciliation. In his study of Barth's ecclesiology, Nicholas Healy argues that the placement of ecclesiology within theological inquiry should follow the same logic and structure that Barth uses to describe the place of theological ethics within theological inquiry, first with general ethics, a discussion of God's action, and then a special ethics that considers the directions of human action in light of God's action.[2] General ethics looks "upward" to divine action as it enfolds and makes it claims upon humanity while special ethics looks "downwards" to concrete human action as it is lived out under the command of God and in light of God's own action.[3] Healy acknowledges that Barth does not explicitly describe a general theology of the church and a special theology of the church, but it could be argued that the theology of the church developed in the early volumes of the *Church Dogmatics* functions precisely as general ethics functions in relation to special ethics.[4]

The church made possible by the Word of God in three forms is the account of God's being-in-action in the life of the church. Only then can there be a special ecclesiology that seeks to trace the human possibilities for ecclesial life and action in light of God's action in and through the life of the Christian community. Barth's early theology of the church emerges from the concept of the threefold Word of God and is not simply made redundant by the later special ecclesiology found in the doctrine of reconciliation, rather the two overlap, complement each other, and serve different functions, much in the same way as general ethics and special ethics. Rather than reading Barth's later ecclesiology as a departure or contradiction from the general theology of the church articulated through the threefold Word of God, these two accounts, while not always in complete accord, should be read together in order to capture Barth's fullest expression of the theology of the church.

In his introduction to Karl Barth's thought, Joseph Mangina argues that what distinguishes Barth's theological project and vision from other

2. Healy, "Karl Barth's Ecclesiology Reconsidered," 294.

3. Barth, *CD* III/4:4–5.

4. Healy, "Karl Barth's Ecclesiology Reconsidered," 294.

Reformed and Protestant contemporaries, was not just his dialectical adherence to the ontological distinction between divinity and humanity, but his insistence that God distinguishes himself from all other idols, not ultimately in transcendence, "but by becoming incarnate in Jesus Christ."[5] The church becomes an event and shared life that is both a divine and human possibility because it arises out of the activity of the God who refuses to be God apart from fellowship with human beings.[6] While Barth's account of the church in relation to threefold Word of God is not an exhaustive description of the church's life, activities, and purpose, the threefold Word of God does serve as a general theology of the church which complements and supplements Barth's later ecclesiology. Particularly central to the ecclesiology of the threefold Word of God is Barth's description of the particular presence, activity, and speech of God through gospel proclamation in the church's own life and activity. This contemporary speech and activity of God shapes all surrounding reality, empowering human freedom and activity in the service of God.[7]

5. Mangina, *Karl Barth: Theologian of Christian Witness*, 177.

6. Barth, *CD* II/1:*The Doctrine of God*, 276.

7. I am not aware of any study that makes the case that Barth's theology of the threefold Word of God serves as a general theology of the church in relation to special ecclesiology that appears in the doctrine of reconciliation (IV/1, IV/2, IV/3). O'Grady's study of Barth's ecclesiology does have a brief section that explores the church in Barth's theology of the Word, but goes on to present Barth's definitive theology of the church beginning with *Church Dogmatics* II/2: *The Doctrine of Election*, § 34, "The Election of the Community," which also has a role to play as well in a general theology of the church. See O'Grady, *The Church in the Theology of Karl* Barth, 50–58. Bender's recent in-depth study of Barth's ecclesiology moves from the theology of the church presented in the *Göttingen Dogmatics* to Barth's doctrine of election, *CD* II/2, altogether passing over Barth's account of the church in *Church Dogmatics* I/1 and I/2. While Bender does cite sections from *CD* I/1 concerning proclamation and the church in his presentation of Barth's mature theology of the church, *CD* I/1, *CD* I/2, and *CD* II/1 are largely bypassed. One could argue that the election of the community (§34) is Barth's presentation of a general theology of the church as well as the beginning of Barth's mature ecclesiology, but one must also come to terms with the theology of the church that is expressed in Barth's doctrine of the threefold Word of God in the early volumes of the *Church Dogmatics*. Bypassing the larger sections of material on and about the church in *Church Dogmatics* I/1, I/2, and II/1 offers an incomplete account of Barth's theology of the church. See Bender, *Karl Barth's Ecclesiology*, 95–96. Healy does discuss the possibility of a general theology of the church that engages "doctrines of the trinity, creation and Christology and pneumatology which are the condition of the possibility for the being-in-action of the church," but points out that Barth "does not explicitly draw the analogy between ecclesiology and the two forms of ethics." It is true that Barth does not explicitly draw this analogy; however, the account of the church in relation to the threefold Word of God serves this very purpose in the first volume of the *Church Dogmatics*. See Healy, "Karl Barth's Ecclesiology Reconsidered," 294.

The Threefold Word and Barth's Early Vision of the Church

Before Barth set about his own dogmatics in Göttingen, he engaged, along with his students, Calvin, Zwingli, the Reformed Confessions, and the father of modern theology, Friedrich Schleiermacher. Such historical faithfulness and theological care of those who had gone before him would become a hallmark of Barth's future theological work. In his own serious engagement with Calvin, Barth explored the 1536 *Institutes* in depth, and in a passage from his lectures, he would describe Calvin's theological dilemma in this way:

> Can we succeed in simultaneously saying the two things as one, that the church is God's work and yet that as such it is also a human reality? From the outset we must say that even Calvin could not succeed in really establishing and upholding both aspects, at least as one and the same. As everywhere, so here too, he had to be content to put the two alongside one another and to show how they are interrelated and affect one another . . . But if Calvin's undertaking did not and could not succeed—the person who has found the right word in this predicament has not yet been born."[8]

One wonders whether Barth's modest refusal to offer an easy solution to Calvin's dilemma was also an admission that modern attempts at Reformed theology must continue to come to terms with Calvin's struggle to articulate the church as a fully human enterprise but also a divine one. Barth concludes his assessment of Calvin's early theology of the church by remarking that what Calvin wanted to profess "deep in his heart was a church that can honour God in the world, a church that has the advantages of a sect without the disadvantages, a church that knows what it wants and does not want, a church that knows its people, a church militant that could be compared to the Jesuit order in external power if not perhaps in inward organization because after all it is not an order or society but in spite of everything a church."[9]

Perhaps this is at least one reason why the threefold form of the Word of God was so central to Barth's theological vision of the church, especially as it appeared in his work in Göttingen, again in Münster, and its final form in *Church Dogmatics* I/1 and I/2. The concept of the threefold form of the Word of God was not peripheral to the central theological themes in Karl Barth's theological project. As Bruce McCormack has pointed out in depth, Barth's doctrine of the "threefold form of the Word" was central to

8. Barth, *Theology of Calvin*, 177–78.
9. Ibid., 186.

his dogmatic efforts from 1924 to 1937.[10] Originally presented in classroom lectures, the threefold form of the Word of God did not seek so much to move beyond the simplification of the *Römerbrief* that "God is in heaven and you are on earth,'" but to further develop the ontological truth of God being "wholly other" while at the same time articulating the equivalent truth of God's self-giving "real presence" incarnate in Jesus Christ, and God's contemporaneous "real presence" in the Spirit's activity in the ecclesial community, specifically through Scripture and proclamation.[11]

While the threefold Word of God appeared in dogmatic concepts in the classroom and in theological volumes, Barth was already presenting the same material prior to 1924 and was doing so in more informal settings outside the classroom and lecture hall. The threefold Word of God was more than a Protestant answer or Barthian reaction to the Roman Catholic synthesis between Creator and creature that Barth believed was the misguided principle of Roman Catholicism (i.e., *Analogia Entis)*. As seen in Barth's lectures on Calvin, Barth sought to find a way to articulate the existence of the Christian community as both a work of God and a fully human reality. The doctrine of the threefold form of the Word of God was a modern construal of classical Reformed theology, guided by the Reformers who "wished to see something better substituted for the mass (they) abolished."[12] As the ecclesial community was gathered by the Word, as the Scriptures were read and proclaimed, the Lord who became flesh also became present in this context, uniting his act and being to the words of Scripture and the act of proclamation, becoming through them a living event and an encounter. In this event and encounter, the God who became flesh and would also come to speech through human words, and the very same God would be heard by human ears, all the while remaining Lord of heaven and earth. This was the miracle of the event, this was the content of the doctrine of the threefold Form of the Word of God, and this was the appropriate intended consequence of Reformed Theology, as Barth put it, the *"verbum visibile*," the only sacrament the Reformers left us.[13]

Such a way of describing Word and church was not a new innovation but a traditionally Reformed and Reformation way of articulating the role of the church and its relationship to Christ and God's divine agency. What

10. McCormack, "The Being of Holy Scripture Is in Becoming," 57.

11. Thurneysen, "Part I: The Beginnings," in Barth and Thurneysen, *Revolutionary Theology in the Making*, 17; and Barth, "The Need and Promise of Christian Preaching," in *The Word of God and the Word of Man*, 106.

12. Barth, "The Need and Promise of Christian Preaching," in *The Word of God and the Word of Man*, 114.

13. Ibid.

was new in the doctrine of the threefold Word of God, what sought to hold together Calvin's somewhat schizophrenic conceptions of the relationship between Christ and the church, was the dynamic unity between Christ and church that took place in the living encounter between the incarnate God and the ecclesial community through Scripture and proclamation. In this way, Barth sought to move Reformed theology beyond the problem of two separate ecclesial realities: the church where God's presence dwells on the one hand, and the wretched, corrupt, human gathering of sinners on the other. The doctrine of the threefold Word of God did not seek to fuse these two realities into one synthesis (i.e., *Analogia Entis*), but did seek to overcome the tendency towards ecclesial dualism by articulating the real if only temporary unity and possibility that takes place in the ecclesial community when God's Word (Jesus Christ) unites to human words (Scripture and proclamation) in the event and life of the Christian community.[14]

Through his careful reading of Romans in light of world events, Barth grew ever more certain that only God could bring about the kingdom of God on earth.[15] This growing conviction also led him to think differently about the true substance of the church as well. He began to describe and view the church, not as a static ongoing creation founded at Pentecost and extending indefinitely into the future, nor as a sociological gathering

14. Bender, *Karl Barth's Christological Ecclesiology*, 90–91. In his detailed and comprehensive study of Karl Barth's ecclesiology, Bender also believes that Barth's analysis of Calvin was an admission and a window into Barth's own theological thinking in regards to the church. According to Bender, Barth's assessment of Calvin revealed Barth's own struggle to conceive of the church in light of modern Protestantism and its vacillation between religious individualism and nation-state advancement on the one hand, and Roman Catholicism and its unassailable ecclesiological claims on the other. Bender argues that Barth's insight into Calvin reveals the very "principles that would guide his own ecclesiological development," and even more, Bender believes that Barth's summary of Calvin could serve as an apt summary of his own ecclesiology. Barth began his own theological project then, not to recover the sixteenth-century Calvin or to return to the Calvinist orthodoxy of the seventeenth century; rather, he began with God and God's ultimate encounter with humanity in Jesus Christ, but also in Christ's subsequent encounters with humanity through the Spirit, as Scripture and proclamation become God's word in and through the life of the Christian community. As Barth sought to address the situation of the preacher in the pulpit and the people of God who sought to hear a word from the Lord through the voice of the sinful preacher, the threefold form of the Word of God served as Barth's way of describing how such an impossibility was indeed possible.

15. Busch, *Karl Barth: His Life from Letters*, 100–101. While part of Barth's break with the Protestantism liberalism of his forebears had to do with his teachers' unqualified support for the Kaiser and the war, his larger concern was a theological one. Barth rejected the theological aid and comfort given to Germany's war effort and the absolute belief held by his socialist friends that their human attempts at reform could bring about something new, God's very kingdom on earth.

of religious individuals, but as the ever new creation of God's revelation and God's Word. Already in his commentary on Romans, Barth sought to describe the integral relationship between God's Word and the church by referring to the church as "the fellowship of men who proclaim the Word of God and hear it."[16] What is important to see in this early period of Barth's theological development is the ongoing encounter between God (Word) and humanity (church) even when it is often portrayed in terms of a so-called negative ecclesiology where the "Church is condemned by that which establishes it, and is broken in pieces upon its foundations."[17]

Still, Barth sought to describe the church's existence in terms of God's activity alone. As Kimlyn Bender rightly points out, "the church differed from the world only in that it was the site where the revelation event occurred."[18] But by describing the interior life of the church in this way, Barth was introducing another problem in the realm of theological ethics. What difference does the church make if it remains just as unfaithful and disobedient as it was prior to the event of God's Word? These questions would follow Barth throughout his work and are often critiques of his work today, and these questions may offer at least one clue as to why Barth later modified the concept of the threefold Word of God in *Church Dogmatics* IV/3. The fact that Barth describes the church as the locus of God's judgment and thus also God's revelation is an important feature of Barth's theology that begins with Romans and is further developed in the *Göttingen Dogmatics* and the *Church Dogmatics*. Throughout the *Römerbrief* Barth consistently describes the church as weak, its life and activities only related to God's revelation as a crater is related to a shell that explodes and creates in it, "a void in which the Gospel reveals itself,"[19] and yet the very same church is a direct consequence and creation of God's self-revelation. In spite of the church's derivative and negative status, Barth argues that a "non-ecclesiastical relation between men and God is no more a reality in this world than is the innocence of paradise."[20]

---

16. Barth, *The Epistle to the Romans*, 341.

17. Ibid. See also McCormack, "A Scholastic of a Higher Order," 377. In his comprehensive reading of Barth, McCormack warns against reading Barth's early theology as only negative and his mature theology as only positive. Even as Barth's material doctrinal work takes on a greater christological emphasis and he undergoes "a shift in attitude" toward the church, McCormack maintains that Barth's use of dialectical method remains intact throughout his work.

18. Bender, *Karl Barth's Christological Ecclesiology*, 35.

19. Barth, *The Epistle to the Romans*, 36.

20. Ibid., 334–35.

While the *Römerbrief* does not describe a material role to the church's life and activity, from the Romans commentary onward, Barth did develop a fairly central role for the church as the specific location in the world and medium where God addresses humanity. Because the church is the place or medium of God's self-revelation, it is differentiated from the rest of the world.[21] What would develop over time and take fuller shape in Barth's mature thought is a Christology which could more directly identify God's revelation with the historical person of Jesus, and more closely describe an ecclesial community that participates in the revelatory event through the witness of Scripture and proclamation (the one Word of God). The three-fold form of the Word of God served Barth's attempt to express the unity of divinity and humanity in Jesus Christ, and the provisional union and shared life of divinity and humanity in the life of the church. Barth would not express this fuller understanding of the church until the *Göttingen Dogmatics*.

Kimlyn Bender believes, especially early on in Barth's thought as the Romans commentary and the *Göttingen Dogmatics* took shape, that Barth treated the church primarily as the initial problem in theology (i.e., where is God revealed?), around the issue of revelation in particular. Bender writes that "the church for Barth serves as the locus of the preaching event, and therefore the locus of revelation in the present."[22] The church is the place where the event of God's Word happens in the present, but the church is also the community gathered together by Word and Spirit where revelation is actualized in Christian life together and witness. Barth's early theology of the church defines church more in terms of event location in the world, not in terms of a particular people in a particular place in time whose life and activity are enclosed and shaped by the life and activity of God in their midst.

As he began his work in Göttingen, Barth sought to articulate more fully the role, purpose, and content of the church's life together in relation to the Word of God. In the opening sections of the *Göttingen Dogmatics* Barth describes the essence of the church's existence not in terms of fellowship or practices or apostolic succession, rather what makes the church the church, Barth argues, what makes it a distinctive community, "what

---

21. Bender, *Karl Barth's Christological Ecclesiology*, 20–23. Though Barth rejected the theological direction of Harnack, Herrmann, and Schleiermacher, Bender wonders whether Barth's description of the church in the *Römerbrief* was not similar to his teacher Wilhelm Herrmann's description of the church, which sought to retain a formal if undeveloped place for the church in his own theological work. Even in the Romans commentary Barth's theological direction was vastly different from Herrmann's, but Bender wonders whether the *Römerbrief* exhibited some of the problematic and ambiguous elements that were also evident in Herrmann's own ecclesiology.

22. Ibid., 62.

distinguishes it from any other fellowship of faith and spirit and distinctive orientation and sacrament, is the vital link between this very specific hearing and making heard, the Word which it receives and passes on."[23] In short, the gospel makes the church; the Word of God constitutes the church. So in a way, Barth's theological starting point is a theology of the church made possible by the Word of God, whereby God speaks and is heard in the present through Scripture and proclamation. Liturgy does not make the church. Apostolic succession does not make the church. The infallibility of Scripture is not the basis of the church. Nor is the human experience of the divine. What makes the church is the event of union between divine speaking and human speaking (Jesus Christ and the act of proclamation) on the one hand, and on the other hand, the union of divine reception and human hearing (Holy Spirit and faith).

Bruce McCormack describes this more positive role for the church as a "shift in attitude."[24] According to McCormack, Barth grew in appreciation for the church and sought to listen for the voice of the church through his new teaching responsibilities, in his own inner struggle with preparation and historical mastery of the subject matter, and in the critical and deep theological engagement he found in Roman Catholic theology.[25] Part of the reason Barth's theological work was leading him into deeper engagement with earlier church tradition had to do with the fact that Barth believed Roman Catholicism, not modern Protestant theology, was interested in many of the questions (perhaps not the same answers) that Barth believed were critical for theology and the church in modernity. For instance, as Barth prepared his own dogmatics in Göttingen and struggled with a faithful way to describe the hypostatic character of the incarnation, he acknowledged that with the exception of the Catholics, he was probably the only professor of theology "racking his brains over it."[26] Barth's polemical engagement with and theological appreciation for Roman Catholicism would also shape the place of the church in his work during this period and beyond. And Barth's ongoing desire to hear the voice of the church in the past, would lead to a greater appreciation for the life of the church in the present and the predicament of the church amidst the challenges of modernity.

When Barth began to teach theology for the first time, his work led him into the prior labours of the Protestant scholastics, the Reformers, medieval theologians, and the early church fathers. As Eberhard Busch

---

23. Barth, *GD*, 24.

24. McCormack, "A Scholastic of a Higher Order," 374–75.

25. Ibid., 375.

26. Busch, *Karl Barth: His Life from Letters*, 172.

notes, "Barth not only began to listen to 'orthodoxy,' but also developed a positive interest in the Fathers of the early church and even to some extent in Catholic scholasticism."[27] Perhaps this would lead him to make the surprising remark in 1924 that "one ought not to place himself too securely on the 'base' of 'Protestantism.'"[28] Yet Barth maintained that theological and ecclesial substance were not things a Protestant theologian had to go looking for in Roman Catholicism, but were integral to Protestant and Reformed theology as well, even if neglected and difficult to articulate at times. Indeed, in a series of lectures at pastoral and theological conferences in the middle of the 1920s, Barth sought to articulate Protestant and Reformed ecclesial substance shaped by and in direct engagement with its Roman Catholic ecclesial counterpart. Perhaps he did this most fully in his lecture "Roman Catholicism: A Question to the Protestant Church," given three different times in 1928. In this lecture, Barth made the case that Roman Catholicism posed two fundamental questions to the Protestant Church: to what extent was Protestantism a church, and to what extent Protestantism was still Protestant.[29]

On the first score, Barth argued that the theological purpose of the Reformation was not "to cast doubt on the real and primary presence and action of God in his Church rather to assert both in a more compelling form."[30] While Barth believed the Reformers were right to question Roman Catholicism's efforts to institutionalize divine revelation, the solution was not, Barth maintained, to be found in modern Protestant attempts to "by-pass Church, Word, and sacrament, and to fly at once to the Unmediated and Absolute in pure spirituality and inwardness."[31] Instead, Barth believed the Reformers sought to restore and strengthen the "interrelation between the divine reality of revelation and the equally divine reality of faith."[32] What was at stake in the Reformation, Barth believed, was not an attempt to remove the mediatory functions of church, but to reject all attempts to make Christ's once-and-for-all life, death, and resurrection, a work that must be made present *again* by the sacrificing priest or the activities of the Roman pontiff as Christ on earth.[33]

27. Ibid., 154.

28. Barth and Thurneysen, *Revolutionary Theology in the Making*, 168.

29. Barth, "Roman Catholicism: a Question to the Protestant Church," in *Theology and Church*, 315, 319, 323.

30. Ibid., 316.

31. Ibid., 318–319.

32. Ibid., 318.

33. Ibid.

In addition to the problem of mediation, Barth believed Roman Catholicism challenged the Protestant identity of modern Protestantism. "Are we still Protestants?" Barth bluntly puts it.[34] To be a Protestant, in Barth's view was to see the church as a divine reality and also as a sinful reality, the "Church of sinners."[35] Sin could not be removed by sacramental infusions of grace, for even in the church, we find ourselves "sinners from head to toe."[36] Barth then pointedly asks whether modern Protestantism really offers an alternative to the Roman Catholic relationship between sin and grace, when it replaces "God's Word of grace with the work and exaltation of men, either in the inner regions of the soul or in cultural and social activity?"[37] Barth challenged modern Protestantism's efforts to supplement that grace alone with "religious-ethical virtuosity," or a "Protestant cult of saints" or a thinly veiled religious version of human success and progress?[38] If modern Protestantism seeks such a fusion between humanity and divinity, grace and nature, Christ and Christian, Barth wondered whether Roman Catholicism might offer a more responsible, more beautiful and simpler ecclesial form already. If that is the substance of our ecclesiology, then why are we still Protestants, Barth asks.[39]

Barth's critical engagement with Roman Catholicism was both ecumenical and polemical. It was ecumenical in the sense that few if any of his Protestant contemporaries saw either the threat or the opportunity for conversation that Roman Catholicism posed to Protestantism.[40] Due to geography (Münster), but also due to the fact that Barth could only find conversation partners interested in the church's received theological traditions within Roman Catholicism, Barth became a serious ecumenical theologian during this period. Barth's engagement with Roman Catholicism was also polemical. He was not seeking theological compromise, but in trying to

34. Ibid., 326.

35. Ibid., 327.

36. Ibid., 327–29.

37. Ibid., 332.

38. Ibid., 331–32.

39. Ibid., 332.

40. McCormack, "A Scholastic of a Higher Order," 381. McCormack describes Barth's engagement with Roman Catholicism in terms of a "tendency to subsume polemic against (Protestant) liberalism under his critique of Catholicism." I would only add that Barth's critical engagement with Roman Catholicism was not just critique, but also a critical appreciation for Roman Catholicism's willingness, in spite of its theological flaws and Barth's theological objections, to confess that the church was the central sphere of divine activity and the particular location of God's ongoing activity in the here and now.

represent the best thought and practice of Reformed theology, he wanted to remind both modern Protestantism and Roman Catholicism of the deep theological differences that still existed between the two ecclesial bodies.[41]

We return to the earlier question of the paradoxical nature of the church, a problem with which Barth struggled as he read Calvin, and a theology of the church that Barth sought to address and build upon. Though many of the problems and questions about the reality of God in the here and now were presented by Barth as ecclesiological problems, he found the solution to his ecclesiological questions in the form of a christological answer. Bruce McCormack explains this development in Barth's thought as a material change in Barth's Christology that took place between the second Romans commentary and the *Göttingen Dogmatics*. In *Romans*, God could only be present, though completely veiled, in the event of the cross. As he prepared for the Göttingen lectures, Barth adopted the *anhypostasis* of Reformed and patristic theology, and could then say much more, that God is fully unveiled in the veil of his humanity, and revelation could be historical without becoming a historical possession or a static deposit in the church and world.[42]

This christological move allowed Barth to say that Jesus Christ is fully God and also fully human without confusion, without change, without

41. Barth, "The Concept of the Church," in *Theology and Church*, 273. Barth's style of ecumenism was not first and foremost an attempt to forge theological compromise between Roman Catholicism and Protestantism In his own words, he called it a full engagement with one's opponent and a willingness "to take upon ourselves the whole burden of opposition between us as our burden and as a mutual burden of opposition on both sides." In this vein, Barth sought to express a theology of the church, not by backing away from the theological claims and traditions grounded in the Reformers' valid protests and convictions, but by articulating them afresh in light of modernity and in light of the on-going differences with Roman Catholicism. To see each other, even in the midst of deep theological divisions, to not gloss over real theological differences, Barth thought, will not dismantle ecumenical convergence, but in the very manifestation of contradictions and differences, would prod the ecclesial bodies to truly be homesick for the peace that unites all Christians in Jesus Christ. First through a debate with Erik Peterson, and later with Erich Przywara, Barth would carry out this way of ecumenism, not seeking compromise as much as a clearer understanding of the conflicting standpoints between the two ecclesial bodies. Seeking to understand and articulate the confessional position of the Reformed church as thoroughly as possible did not inhibit Barth's engagement with Roman Catholicism, it enhanced it. And it led him to pursue a modern ecclesiological alternative, true to the theological tenets of Reformed Protestantism, but ecumenically open to the serious theological and ecclesiological questions and challenges posed by Roman Catholicism. See also, Busch, *Karl Barth: His Life from Letters*, 183.

42. McCormack, "A Scholastic of a Higher Order," 374.

division, without separation,[43] and it allowed Barth to base the church's life and existence on God's ability to disclose Godself in the one Word of God, revealed in Jesus Christ, but also in Scripture and the church.[44] Barth's innovation of the Chalcedonian formula did not conceive of God, Scripture, or the church in static terms, but rather in terms of action. While the Word of God could never be directly identified with the life and witness of the church in a static existence, God could reveal himself in the words of Scripture and through Christian proclamation in the event and gathering of the worshipping community. The church, therefore, could be fully sinful, yet fully the sphere of God's self-revelation, if only from moment to moment, through the being and activity of God.[45]

Did Barth's christological and actualistic innovations allow him to overcome the problematic tendency towards dualism (divine/human, faithful/sinful, visible/invisible) he himself read in Calvin? During the period of Barth's teaching at Göttingen and Münster until the beginning volumes of the *Church Dogmatics,* Barth's work and the doctrine of the church that emerged from his labours, was defined by the threefold Word of God, where in the life of the Christian community a present encounter between God and humanity took place, an encounter where the Word of God that became flesh in Jesus Christ was also made manifest through Scripture and in the church's proclamation. Such a unity of divine activity in the midst of human activity could only be a momentary event. Human creatures were always in danger of mistaking the provisional union of this event for a more permanent union. Only in the eschatological union at the consummation, would the Holy Spirit hold together God and humanity in a permanent unity for eternity. For Barth any divine and human union in the life of the church could only be described in provisional and actualistic concepts. The event

43. Phrasing from the Chalcedonian Creed.

44. Barth, *GD,* 14–15.

45. Hunsinger, *How to Read Karl Barth,* 31. Hunsinger describes Barth's ability to hold together the *simul iustus et peccator* nature of the church as a consequence of his actualism: "[T]he church, the inspiration of scripture, faith, and all other creaturely realities in their relationship to God are always understood as events." Never self-initiating or self-sustaining, the church, and through the life of the church each individual Christian, can only truly come to be "as they are continually established anew according to the divine good pleasure." This allowed Barth to describe the church as a divine reality and an instrument of God's revelation, without turning God into a possession of the church or institutionalizing divine revelation, both of which were dangers Barth saw in Roman Catholicism and in some strands of modern Protestantism. This actualistic method allowed Barth to account for the divine and human freedom, their unity and their differentiation, in the divinity and humanity of Jesus Christ, but also in the divine and human intercourse in the here and now of the church's life.

was not a completion of divine and creaturely union, only a momentary unity. The event occurred from moment to moment by the divine initiative, not by any human initiative, but only in God's sovereign freedom and by God's good grace. Such an event was not an aberration or accident, nor did it occur by God's capricious or erratic will, but did happen and would happen; it could be both promised and expected in the particular being and activity of the church's life together.

In Barth's later theology, specifically regarding the church, descriptions of provisional unity brought about in the life of the church would be severely strained, possibly to the breaking point.[46] Yet at this point in his introductory theology of the church, Barth could describe a particular pattern of divine activity that incorporates and integrates human life and activity into its life and work in the world, a real union of activity but always a unity in differentiation. In the church's encounter with Scripture and the gospel address, divine speaking and human speech and hearing would be joined together momentarily by the work of the Spirit. This unity would be fragile and provisional, never static, always actualistic, but nevertheless a real unity, that was, is, and would become a possibility in the Christian community, in its worship and corporate life together, and in its ethical witness in the world.

The Threefold Word of God: A General Theology of the Church

While Barth does not always refer to the church and its life specifically, Barth's account of the church that emerges from the doctrine of the threefold Word of God attempts to describe the divine presence and activity in the event of the Word of God as it enters into contemporary time and space.[47] In the event of the Word of God, people become "bearers and speakers of the Word of God as it becomes a word spoken by them in the form of their human word,"[48] and the church becomes the specific place in the world where God speaks, where divine grace meets human faith, where the vertical line of revelation meets the horizontal, temporal line of worldly existence. Barth continued to describe the church in *Church Dogmatics* I/2 by place and particularity. The church could be described as the place in the world where God and God alone makes humanity recipients of revelation.[49]

46. Barth, *CD* IV/4; and Webster, *Barth's Ethics of Reconciliation*, 173.

47. Barth, *CD* I/1:133.

48. Barth, *CD* I/2:744.

49. Ibid., 210.

In this section, Barth would add further particularity to the church by defining the area of the church according to the witness of the Old and New Testaments in which the church includes both Israel and the church inaugurated by Christ.[50] Under the heading of his doctrine of revelation (§16), Barth delineated the form and shape of the church beyond the vague conceptual descriptions like sphere of revelation or arena of God's grace so often found in Barth's earlier theological descriptions of the church. Ultimately Barth concludes, the church can only take on flesh and bone, so to speak, when it is described as the place or realm of the world where "Jesus Christ is present as the real acting subject, as the head of all the members gathered in the Church with their definite tasks and functions," the particular area in the world where God and God alone turns human beings into recipients of revelation who become God's witnesses in the world.[51] God's activity does not take place in a vacuum or everywhere in general, but in the particular life of Israel and the church. And Israel and the church were never just empty concepts, but particular people in particular places encountered by and bound to God's Word revealed to them in the particularity of time and place through an encounter and event. As Barth's work progressed, the church took on content as a location and people of dynamic life and activity. The church was more than an undefined space of reality. The church included a meeting and encounter between two dynamic living realities, a fellowship where God encounters human beings in an act of grace.

Though much of Barth's description of the church in *CD* I/2 occurs in §16.1, "The Holy Spirit the Subjective Reality of Revelation," Barth grounds the church's life and existence in the reality and presence of Jesus Christ, apart from whom the church cannot exist or function in any real form or way. According to Barth, the church lives and has its origin in Jesus Christ. On this basis and foundation, Barth then proceeds to define what such a claim implies. First, it means that as a result of the Incarnation, the Word that was in the beginning, in which all things were created, the Word before all things and in all things, is also spoken and heard in this world.[52] What this means for the church is that it becomes the subjective reality of Jesus Christ's revelation, the meeting of the Word of grace with the children of God for the sake of the whole world.[53]

Barth would continue to define the life of the church as one of complete dependence on the Word. The church has no independent existence,

50. Ibid., 211.
51. Ibid., 210.
52. Ibid., 214–15.
53. Ibid., 215.

but only truly lives when it lives in total dependence on its head (Ephesians 4:15) from whom it receives "its whole existence, comfort, and direction from Him and only from Him."[54] Barth describes the third identification of the church's life as communal. Life lived in dependence upon the Word of God is a life together, a common life. It is a common life not defined exclusively by brotherly love or certain spiritual characteristics of Christian togetherness and piety, not on the basis of certain commonly held Christian virtues, but in relationship to the presence and activity of Jesus Christ in the midst of the community. What this means in the here and now of the church and its common life is that "by belonging to Christ we belong to all who belong to Him," and the church has no other existence in its common life apart from the Word.[55] Barth's final point about the church is that the church is both divine and human, eternal and temporal, invisible and visible, hidden in God and a historical reality in time and space.[56]

According to Barth, the divine and human elements of the Christian community are held together in a momentary unity in correspondence to the reality of Jesus Christ. Just as God is at one in the same time God in Godself and God with humanity, so Jesus Christ is both an eternal and historical reality. Similarly, the church is invisible by virtue of election, illumination, justification, and sanctification, it is "invisible by virtue of the invisible Word spoken to it" and yet it is simultaneously visible as an event and gathering in which the subjective reality of revelation "is fulfilled in a temporal encounter and decision, an encounter and decision which can be seen and thought and experienced."[57] This description of the reality of the church in relation to the reality of God and Jesus Christ begins to point us to the way the threefold Word of God serves as a foundation for Barth's theology of the church. After describing the church as the particular area in the world where God's revelation occurs, Barth moves beyond the "empty crater" images that characterized the ecclesiology of the Romans commentary. One cannot speak of the area of revelation, Barth now argues, without also speaking of the reality itself.[58]

54. Ibid., 216.
55. Ibid., 217.
56. Ibid., 219.
57. Ibid., 220.
58. Ibid., 221.

Threefold Word and Church: Miracle and Mystic Vision

From the side of God, or looking upward,[59] God is the content of the Word, God intercedes with human beings for the sake of God's own abundant grace, enabling the gospel to be heard, so that from beginning to end, the content of the church's life is God's dynamic activity and presence enabling the speaking and hearing of the Word to become a reality for qualitatively distinct and sinful human beings.[60] What does this look like in the concrete life of the Christian community? Perhaps Barth's fullest expression of the way the threefold Word of God, specifically, the third form of the Word of God is central to his theology of the church occurs in §22 "The Mission of the Church." Barth describes the object of the church's preaching and authority as the witness of the prophets and apostles (Scripture), but believes that the need of each present moment demands that there be "bearers and speakers of the Word of God as it becomes a word spoken by them in the form of their human word."[61]

The church's existence, therefore, comes to be as its own human words and witness become the Word of God in the particularity of Christian life together for the sake of the gathered community and the world. Or put another way, the church is actualized in the here and now when through the mystery of grace, the living presence of Jesus Christ is revealed in and through the human words and witness of the church's proclaiming and hearing of the gospel. Barth puts it in even more concise terms: "The Word of God is God Himself in the proclamation of the Church of Jesus Christ."[62] The church may not be the exclusive meeting and confrontation between God and humanity, but the church is established by the "self-communication of Jesus Christ to his followers" which sets it in motion to witness and conform to Christ in the larger world.[63]

Barth's doctrine of the Word of God, particularly the threefold Word of God, allows Barth's vision of the church to take on content and not just form. And there simply is no content of church apart from the claim that human beings who are not God are permitted to speak the Word of God in the midst of their own human words.[64] Apart from this miracle, life together

59. Barth uses this term "looking upward" to distinguish general ethics from special ethics, which would be a "looking downward" toward specific human and ecclesial forms of action and witness.

60. Ibid.

61. Ibid., 744.

62. Ibid., 743.

63. Ibid., 744.

64. Ibid.

in Christ is unintelligible and incomplete. The church lives by and trusts the commission that Jesus Christ is present in the here and now of the church's life as the "Lord of its speaking, the Lord who in and through its speaking bears witness to Himself."[65] Whatever else the church may do or strive to be, it is only fully the church when "Jesus Christ in the power of his resurrection is present" wherever human beings speak of God.[66] Barth describes the content of the church's life in terms of preaching and the sacraments by characterizing them as the church's most formal attempts to speak of God, but Barth is quite open to describe the sphere and activity of the church's proclamation beyond the Sunday sermon or communion table to include the church's "prayer and worship, its confession and instruction, pastoral activity and, not least, of theology itself."[67] In all of these ways and activities, Christians attempt the impossible, Barth believes, by trying to speak of God with the intent that others will hear the gospel.[68]

The challenge of the humanity and the divinity of the church that challenged Barth as he read Calvin is also echoed in Barth's own vision of the church. In spite of the Christian community's "incapacity and unworthiness," the church is in Christ, Barth maintains and "there, in Him, (the church) is not unworthy and not incapable of speaking about God."[69] As Christ becomes present by the power of his resurrection, the church has all it needs to speak of God and for God to speak. In Christian life together, as human beings are drawn out of themselves and into the mysterious presence of Jesus Christ in their midst, in their broken attempts to speak about God in human words, Barth maintains, they proclaim God's own Word. And in doing so, truly become the church of Jesus Christ.[70]

While the church's life happens in the human attempt to speak of God and in the human attempt to hear a Word spoken by God in the life together of Christian community, what ultimately makes the church the church is God's own presence in and through such human attempts and ventures. The church is what happens when God speaks. The church is what happens when the Word of God's third form is actualized. When human words proclaim God, they proclaim God's own Word.[71] This vision of the church emerges out of Barth's concept of the threefold Word of God, and it is also serves as

65. Ibid., 749.

66. Ibid., 752.

67. Ibid., 750.

68. Ibid.

69. Ibid., 757.

70. Ibid.

71. Ibid.

a general theology to Barth's vision of the church.[72] It is a theology of the church that seeks to ground the church's life and existence by the voice and presence of Jesus Christ in the time and space of Christian life together. It is not a theology of the church that makes the church a constant possessor of grace or a human receptacle of God's constant presence. The church has the Word of God in virtue of God's promise, not in terms of human possession or self-justification.[73] Only "according to the promise," Barth declares, does "the Church live in the presence of Jesus Christ."[74] To refer to "having" the presence of Jesus Christ or the Word of God or even faith, Barth argues, like capital at one's disposal, is to not have Christ at all. The church "has" the presence of Christ not in presumptuous claims of ownership, but precisely in the church's dependence, hunger, thirst, and expectation that what has come in Jesus Christ will come again.[75] The church is and lives and happens as Christ's presence through the Spirit comes, divinely empowering human beings to speak the Word of God, and propelling them into the strange new world of possibilities and opportunities to conform to Jesus Christ.[76]

Later in the *Church Dogmatics* Barth would dismiss concepts of mystical communion and *unio mystica*, believing they created more problems than they offered theological explanation.[77] Yet in the context of the

72. Fackre, *The Doctrine of Revelation*, 132, 138. Fackre reminds us that the life of the church is the location and event of God's giving (grace) and humanity's receiving (faith), where the "Word has 'happened,' and ever again will happen." Fackre argues that Barth's dialectic requires him to affirm both the sovereignty of God over and against the church, but also the solidarity of God in and with the church in the presence of Christ by the Spirit's power. In his presentation of the threefold Word of God, Barth holds these two divine movements in equal dialectical tension with each other. For instance, he writes that while it is true that God alone can speak about God, he also claims that God "gives the church the task of speaking about Him, and in so far as the Church fulfils this task God Himself is in its midst to proclaim His revelations and testimonies." Still, Barth adds, this does not lead to self-assurance, presumption, and possession of grace on the part of the church, but the question remains how to order God's solidarity and God's sovereignty in the event of the Word of God. See Barth, *CD* I/2:756.

73. See Matt 28:20: "Lo, I am with you always, even to the end of the age."

74. Barth, *CD* I/2:849. See also, Fackre, *The Doctrine of Revelation*, 133, 138–139. Fackre notes Barth's wariness about claims of "present" possession of Jesus Christ, but also wonders whether Barth is able to hold together the two theological claims of the sovereignty of God and the promised continuous presence of God in the life of the Christian community.

75. Barth, *CD* I/1:225.

76. Rosato, *The Spirit as Lord*, 80.

77. Barth, *CD* IV/3:539–40. Barth rejects any descriptions of union with Christ as psychical or experiential or in terms of human self-consciousness. Barth also rejects descriptions of union with Christ that seek to blur the distinctions between Creator

threefold Word of God, the union and ecclesial event that occurs, at least from the side of God certainly suggests a mystical dimension.[78] As the work of the Holy Spirit makes Christ present in temporal form in and with human beings, faith occurs from the human side of the event which propels humanity forward, opening up a new direction from this encounter, and enabling humanity to correspond and conform to Jesus Christ in freedom and obedience.[79] Likewise in the very same event, from the side of God, the Holy Spirit makes it possible for God to draw near, to speak and be heard in temporal reality by finite human beings. Such a happening is a human occurrence and activity like any other, and yet such an activity and life take place with the expectation that the work and speech of God takes place within it.[80] The event of the grace of the Word of God is not magic, Barth cautions, but nor can its action on and in human beings be fully explained.[81] It is an inexplicable phenomenon, a miracle.[82]

---

and creature. Whatever union with Christ may be, one can only describe it only after safeguarding the sovereignty of God and the freedom of the human partner in the relationship and event. I do not think this position represents a radical departure from Barth's earlier theology of the Word, especially his concept of the threefold Word of God, and the theology of the church in relation to the threefold Word of God. Later, as we will see though, Barth becomes more reticent about any descriptions of divine and human activity united in communal or ecclesial activity, preferring instead first and foremost to mark the distinction between divinity and humanity, describing their two distinct being-in-acts alongside each other in the church and in the Christian life. See also Bender, *Karl Barth's Christological Ecclesiology*, 280n24.

78. Traces of this mystical dimension of Barth's theology of the Word can be found in Barth's early essay and address, "The Strange New World within the Bible." In this address, Barth refers to the event and encounter of reading Scripture in the midst of the spirit and living river that inhabits the Bible, a spirit and river "that carries us away, once we have entrusted our destiny to it—away from ourselves and to the sea." God speaks to us through the Scriptures, Barth claims, in spite of our human limitations, and we "need only to follow this drive, this spirit, this river," as it sweeps us out of ourselves and into the presence of God. See Barth, "The Strange New World within the Bible," in *The Word of God and the Word of Man*, 34.

79. In *Church Dogmatics* III/4, in reference to the mystical elements in Calvin's discussion of God's work in and on humanity in the midst of human rest on the Sabbath day, Barth remarks that if such a description is mysticism, then Paul was a mystic along with Calvin and that "if this is mysticism, then mysticism is an indispensable part of the Christian faith." See Barth, *CD* III/4:58–59. Clearly Barth is against any mysticism that originates out of human experience or human faith, but does seem to allow for a responsible christocentric and pnuematological mysticism that does not collapse the Creator/creature distinction and speaks of God's actions in and with humanity's, rather than the other way around.

80. Barth, *CD* I/2:758.

81. Ibid., 765.

82. Ibid., 847–50.

This encounter with God does not deify humanity or permanently bring about a static union between human beings and Christ, rather, the event of Christ's presence in Scripture and proclamation enables human beings to act as those who have heard the Word of God in faith and so act in such a way that one's own sinful existence and limited humanity could never account.[83] In the gospel event, God's grace kills and makes alive, the sinful disobedient human being is destroyed, and a new creation and creature is resurrected. The activity and event of the gospel are actualized throughout the life of faith by the miraculous and mysterious work of the Holy Spirit.[84] Through the Spirit's work, Christ's temporal presence in the world, momentary divine and creaturely union occurs in the gospel speech event. Talk of a Barthian mysticism or the mystic aspects of the threefold Word of God must be qualified. Human experience and human religious experience cannot ultimately be equated with faith. The difference between faith and mysticism, Barth argues, is that faith respects the mystery of God's veiled unveiling while mysticism believes proclamation, Bible, and Christ are dispensable once communion with the unveiled Deity occurs. A true event of the Word of God, Barth believes, will not lead to self-fulfilment or religious ecstasy or static communion, but instead will lead one again and again to the church, the Scriptures, and Jesus Christ in all their veiled and worldly secularity. Rather than receiving a clear mystic vision, the person of faith is set in motion, set on the way where again and again she will return to the church and Scripture and proclamation with the expectation of an encounter with God.[85]

Nothing in human experience or human knowledge can account for or bring about the miraculous event of the Word of God. All that can really be said about the "How" of the threefold Word of God, Barth concludes, is that "it is on our lips and in our hearts as the mystery of the Spirit who is the Lord."[86] In this way, the strange new world of church, the kingdom of God, the death and resurrection of the sinner, all become an event and

83. Rosato, *The Spirit as Lord*, 71.

84. Neder, *Participation in Christ: An Entry into Karl Barth's Dogmatics*, 13–14. Neder picks up this strand of mysticism of the Word by arguing that in the Word event Barth offers an "actualized conception of the divine-human communion," and union while maintaining the ontological distinction between Creator and creature. In the event of the Word of God, rather than speaking in terms of what the *finitum* is capable of, one speaks of the particular *homo peccator*, who in the encounter with the Triune God, becomes not capable of *infiniti*, but capable of the *verbi Domini*. See Barth, *CD* I/1:221.

85. Barth, *CD* I/1:178–79.

86. Barth, *CD* I/1:186.

occurrence in the life of the Christian community. Moving forward from this event, a new creation, a resurrected human being, a "regenerate" person arises from this event as one whom God has addressed, one who has heard the voice of Jesus Christ in the midst of Scripture and the gospel, one who is set in motion into a new reality and possibility "that lies in God's Word and nowhere else."[87] This miraculous event occurs, not in a "Cloud of Unknowing," but in the ordinary life of encountering Scripture and gospel proclamation in Christian worship and Christian community, where a miracle occurs "before the eyes of every man, secular and religious, Greek and Jew."[88]

Barth also describes the relationship between the Word of God and the church by using concepts such as sign-giving, instrumentality, and secondary objectivity. Though the specific three forms, proclamation, Scripture, and Jesus Christ are not always replicated verbatim, the differentiated union of being-in-action in the life of the church that Barth describes certainly has its basis in the already developed concept of the threefold Word of God. While the church is not a place in the world where God's grace continuously flows through Scripture, proclamation, or other means, Barth argues that because God's presence is a dynamic reality, the church is the place in the world where an encounter with God is possible through the witness of Scripture and the witness of the Christian community as the Spirit confronts human beings and draws the community into the presence of Jesus Christ. The church of Jesus Christ, Barth contends, is not a vessel that continuously contains and dispenses grace,[89] rather the church exists and lives by the promise that "Jesus Christ wills to be present in its midst, to speak through it, that this presence and voice of His is to be its life, and that living in Him and through Him it is to be the light of the world."[90]

There is no Word of God at all, Barth maintains, "without a physical event."[91] Even from below, from the human side of the event, Barth can describe the church as a sign and token and witness to the contemporaneous presence of God in the life of the world.[92] While such signs and tokens and instruments can never be confused with the being-in-action of God, the being-in-action does not occur without or apart from these signs.[93] Barth describes Israel and the church as two of the most visible and lucid signs of

---

87. Ibid., 222.
88. Ibid., 223.
89. Barth, *CD* I/2:224.
90. Ibid., 806.
91. Barth, *CD* I/1:133.
92. Barth, *CD* I/2:855.
93. Barth, *CD* I/1:224.

God's revelation in the witness of Scripture. Much as he does in his description of the threefold Word of God, Barth compares the humanity of these signs, not in terms of hammers or shears in the hands of a worker, where the sign and instrument have no true freedom of activity, but in the hands of God, the signs become a possibility that they could not become before. To use proclamation as the central example, God enables a human creature in his own creaturely way and words, not to be diminished, not to be set aside, but to be exalted, to speak the Word of God in and through a creaturely reality.[94]

In a similar union of divine activity and creaturely activity, the church is the place and reality in the world where the subjective reality of God is made visible through sign-giving and visible signs. Even though signs are full creaturely realities, the activation and manifestation of the sign are the direct activity of God, which means the church's life and activity in the world cannot be separated from objective revelation in Christ.[95] Indeed, Barth asserts boldly that "the church, the body of Christ, and therefore Christ Himself exists and exists only where there are the signs of the New Testament, that is preaching, baptism, and the Lord's Supper."[96] Barth continues these themes again in *CD* II/1. In this context, Barth refers to this divine way of action as God's secondary objectivity.[97] In his doctrine of God and the discussion of secondary objectivity in *CD* II/1, §25 *The Fulfilment of the Knowledge of God, 2) God before Man*, Barth maintains the once and for all occurrence of the incarnation, but also argues for a "sacramental continuity," that extends backwards in and through the life of Israel, and forwards into the life of the Christian community. Here Barth refers to Jesus Christ as the "first sacrament," through whom God continues to become present in creaturely reality through the Spirit. By the ongoing presence of Christ in the life of the Christian community, God's grace enables the creature to become a "temple, instrument, and sign," of the reality of God.[98] Just as God speaks once and for all in Jesus Christ, God continues to speak through the witness of the prophets and apostles, and the proclamation of the Christian community.

Barth describes God's secondary objectivity as God making Godself known to human beings through media and signs which God takes up and uses in creaturely reality but which remain creaturely reality before, during,

94. Ibid., 95.
95. Ibid., 224.
96. Ibid., 227, 233–34.
97. Barth, *CD* II/1:53.
98. Ibid., 54.

and after the divine impartation.[99] Building again upon the concept of the threefold Word of God, Barth maintains that when God "raises us to Himself through the speech of the creature, He lowers Himself to us."[100] While Jesus Christ is the one supreme sacrament, the first sacrament, the permanent union of divinity and humanity, there exists in God's very life and activity, Barth says, the promise that by grace other creatures and signs and creaturely realities will be used by God to impart Godself to humanity.[101] And through this secondary objectivity, Barth declares, there is the church: "the self-witness of God in the sphere and time of the world created by Him."[102]

Barth's theology of the church does not emerge in one designated location in these early volumes, but can be located in the number of the themes that have been surveyed here. Divine sign-giving, the limits and possibilities of instrumental media in the church's life, secondary objectivity in the church's witness, the differentiated unity-in-action between divinity and humanity, all cohere and seem to be built upon the threefold Word of God and the conception of the church that emerges from this concept. Christological, pneumatological, and ecclesiological themes are all central to the concept of the threefold Word of God, but Barth's theology and description of the church is by far the most dependent on the three forms of the Word of God for a concrete depiction of its life and activity. The commission of the church rests in the assurance, Barth declares, that the church has Jesus Christ "Himself in its midst as the Lord of its speaking, the Lord who in and through its speaking bears witness to Himself."[103] Apart from this third form of the one Word of God, which comes on the basis of the first and second forms, it would seem that the content of the church's life would be incoherent and unintelligible.

---

99. Jüngel, *God's Being Is In Becoming*, 60–65. Eberhard Jüngel believes this section of Barth's doctrine of God is crucial for interpreting how God gives Godself to be known by human beings while maintaining the permanent distinction between Creator and creature. God's secondary objectivity, contemporaneous presence, and sacramental reality are a reiteration of God in that which is not God, but through which the power and reality of God enable created reality to speak for God. Most fully and centrally in the humanity of Jesus Christ, but also indirectly through Israel and the church, through Scripture's witness and the gospel proclamation of the Christian community, God brings Godself to speech in and through the surrounding reality. Jüngel interprets and defines the church in this section of Barth as the event and activity in which God speaks with us in a human way.

100. Barth, *CD* II/1:55.

101. Webster, introduction to Jüngel, *God's Being Is In Becoming*, xvi.

102. Barth, *CD* II/1:54.

103. Barth, *CD* I/1:749.

Threefold Word of God and Church in Historical Context

In his Gifford lectures given in Aberdeen in 1937 and 1938, Barth declared that while Jesus Christ is not a prisoner of the church's proclamation and sacramental activity, while Christ is not dependent on or in need of the church to complete his action or transmit the gospel, he has not rendered himself superfluous, "but it is his good pleasure to glorify Himself in the human nature of the church."[104] While Christ does not need the church to so love the world, by God's own good pleasure, Christ's ongoing presence in the world wills to make itself known to all in and through the witness of the Christian community. The church is not truly and fully the church if its content is only Christian piety and morality, Barth contends. What makes the church truly and fully the church in the world, "the most important, momentous, and majestic thing" on earth, is that its "primary content is not the work of man but the work of the Holy Spirit" in and through humanity's proclamation, prayers, and praise.[105] The church is a distinctly human and distinctly visible sign in the world, and it is by the freedom and good pleasure of the Holy Spirit, that God chooses to speak and declare his will for the entire world, not apart from, but through the life together and the visible signs of the Christian community.[106]

The concept of the threefold Word of God in Barth's vision of the church allows Barth to describe the life of the Christian community in human and divine terms. Not only does the presence of God come in spatio-temporal form to join and exalt human speech about God, but God's speaking through human words enables a response of gratitude and makes possible true human becoming. In short, the church can only be the church in faith. The church of Jesus Christ is always and at all times a human community and institution situated in history, yet in relation to Jesus Christ more is always possible. Barth does not deny the divine dimension of the church's life and activity. What Barth does seem unwilling to concede is a direct correlation between so-called mediation or sacramental mediation of the church and the present and ongoing activity of the Holy Spirit. Human proclamation never stops being human proclamation; in and of itself, it can only attest, point, and signify; in and of itself, it cannot mediate divine revelation. But Barth believes, with God, with Jesus Christ, more is possible. The coming of the Word of God in the speech and life of the Christian community is always a possibility because it rests on the actuality of what

---

104. Barth, *The Knowledge of God and the Service of God*, 201.

105. Ibid., 198.

106. Ibid., 201.

God has already done in Jesus Christ, and what God promises to do until the consummation of all creation. Just as the water in the pool of Bethesda never becomes anything other than water, it is moved by a living hand that enables the water to become and do more than was humanly thought possible, so does the church rest and rely and pray that God will move through its own life and words, enabling human witness and attestation to be and to become more than is perceived to be humanly possible.[107]

Barth is clear that the miraculous presence of Jesus Christ at work in the Christian community cannot be miraculous if it is contained by the church as its ongoing possession. It is a miracle we can only recollect and hope for,[108] a possibility which seems a bit far-fetched and improbable, except that for Barth, the church lives and rests on the axiom that "where the actuality exists, there is also the corresponding possibility."[109] So while the church's recollection and hope do not seem to indicate a continuous, unbroken presence of Jesus Christ in the words and activity of the Christian community, the church's recollection, witness, and hope, have become, do become, and can become the very signs of Christ's presence and the means by which the Spirit mediates Christ in the present. Though the community is never assured of a static presence of Jesus Christ as its possession (this would not be miraculous), it can always expect and trust that God will keep God's promises, and that God will manifest Godself through human words offered in service to the one Word of God. The God who spoke once and for all in Jesus Christ, continues to come to speech through the witness of Scripture and the church's attempts to bear witness in every corner and context of creation.

Perhaps the best expression of the threefold Word of God in concrete historical context comes from the Barmen Declaration. In the Barmen Declaration, in a time of ecclesial and national crisis, a clear theological confession was publicly affirmed in opposition to the German-Christians' theological and ecclesiological fusion of divinity with nation, blood, and soil. The historical witness of the Barmen Declaration serves as an expression of the church under threat, an ecumenical declaration agreed upon by Lutheran, Reformed, and United churches, and an attempt to call the church to faith and obedience to the living Christ.[110] In relation to the church and the concept of the threefold Word of God, the Barmen Declaration offers a

107. Barth, *CD* I/1:111.

108. Ibid., 247.

109. Jüngel, *God's Being Is In Becoming*, 63.

110. Weinrich, "God's Free Grace and the Freedom of the Church: Theological Aspects of the Barmen Declaration," 405, 413.

particular historical exhibition of Barth's theology of the church in concrete space and time, and it offers an example of the threefold the Word of God in historical praxis, particularly as its third form becomes the Word of God in "contemporaneous self-attestation."[111] While Karl Barth was not the sole author of the Barmen Declaration, the document emerged from theses Barth had earlier written for a confessing fellowship. The declaration was then prepared and edited in partnership with Lutheran theologians Thomas Breit and Hans Asmussen in Frankfurt ten days before the meeting of the Barmen Synod.[112] Though some minor changes were made to the third article to accommodate Lutheran sacramental concerns, Barth professed to be the principle author of the declaration.[113]

Among the many things that the Barmen Declaration affirms in relation to the church is that the church cannot be the church without a life and self-involving (even life-costing) decision of faith, and without the present activity of Jesus Christ in the church's words and action. Such a declaration might sound as if it is a cocksure assertion, but Michael Weinrich observes that despite what seems to be a bold proclamation, the Barmen Declaration was not an expression of the church's strength and power, but a confession of its own weakness and inability to produce a source of proclamation or have a source of life and identity apart from the one Word of God.[114] In retrospect, while the frailties and failures of the Confessing Church in Germany are certainly lamentable, in his own commentary on the Barmen Declaration in *CD* II/1, Barth declared that the Barmen Declaration was a miracle precisely in its unified confession of the power of the church's weakness as it "lost all counsellors and helpers," and was thrown back upon the "one Word of God, called Jesus Christ," in whom it still had its comfort and hope.[115]

---

111. Barth, *CD* II/1:177.

112. Busch, *Karl Barth: His life from letters and autobiographical texts*, 245. See also Busch, *The Barmen Theses Then and Now*, 7.

113. Ibid. See also Busch, *The Barmen Theses Then and Now*, 56. According to Busch, the original text of article three, described the church as the community where "Jesus Christ is proclaimed as Lord." In a synod meeting, Lutheran delegates sought to amend the wording to read that Christ was present in the Christian community "in Word and Sacrament," to which Barth and his fellow Reformed delegate William Niesel agreed if it also included reference to the presence of the Holy Spirit. The final version described the church as the "congregation of brothers and sisters in which, in Word and Sacrament, through the Holy Spirit, Jesus Christ acts presently as Lord." See Busch, *The Barmen Theses Then and Now*, 51.

114. Weinrich, "God's Free Grace and the Freedom of the Church," 409.

115. Barth, *CD* II/1:176.

The Barmen Declaration offers a theology of the church grounded in the dynamism of the Word of God. This point is illustrated not only by the theological confession and language of the Barmen Declaration, but by the very movement and actions of those who sought to call the church back to its only true life and identity in Jesus Christ. The theology of the church presented and lived out in and through the Barmen Declaration was not an ecclesiology as an independent academic discipline. It was not a theoretical self-investigation of the church in order to establish a good understanding and clarity in describing what the church is and does in the world.[116] Rather the Barmen Declaration was, in a particular place and time, the church's "reassessment of its basis in God, something which always has to be done anew."[117] Perhaps this is how theological reflection on the church is and must be for Barth. Not an account of particular practices and internal ecclesial self-investigation, but the opportunity that space, time, and history present the Christian community to witness in its own particular historical circumstances and challenges, to the "one old revelation of God in Jesus Christ."[118]

Thus the Barmen Declaration illustrates the ongoing challenge presented to the church in every time and place to confess its faith in Jesus Christ and to proclaim Christ's gospel to the world. The Barmen Declaration is also an attempt to describe the church's life together in light of God's action in Word and Spirit.[119] And the Barmen Declaration represents why theological confessions and creeds are never just abstract enterprises, stating doctrinal assertions about God, but they are always attempts to describe the life of God in its dynamic movement in one's own time and place. In the case of Barmen particularly, it is a declaration and confession that attempts to call the church to conform and to bear witness to the self-attestation of God in its midst. The Barmen Declaration is not abstract metaphysics, but the careful attempt to bear witness to the one Word of God, Jesus Christ, attested in the witness of Scripture, acting presently in the church as Lord, by Word and Sacrament, through the Holy Spirit.[120] Just as God is not a static entity, neither is the life together of the Christian community. Because the church's life together is not a static thing that can be fully depicted and dissected and made sense in and of itself, a theology of the church must rely on Christology and Pneumatology for a significant portion of its content

116. Perhaps this is a bit of a caricatured description of what modern attempts at ecclesiology seek to do.

117. Weinrich, "God's Free Grace and the Freedom of the Church," 408.

118. Barth, *CD* II/1:177.

119. Healy, "Karl Barth's Ecclesiology Reconsidered," 296.

120 "The Theological Declaration of Barmen (1934)," 53.

and form. Still, article three and article six of the Barmen Declaration both set out clearly to describe the church's life and the church's responsibility in the world in light of Jesus Christ.

The form and content of the Barmen declaration put the principles and convictions of the threefold Word of God into practice, into a concrete ecclesiology.[121] Barth begins article one with the Jesus Christ, the one Word of God, but also includes the second form of the Word of God as Christ is attested in Scripture. The second article proclaims Christ's claim upon the whole of a human being's life, while the third article seeks to describe the particular pattern and movement of the presence of Jesus Christ in the contemporary life of the Christian community. After asserting the one Word of God in the first article of Barmen, it is the third article that offers a theology of the church in light of the third form of the Word of God. The third article describes the promised rather than the possessed activity of Jesus Christ in the temporal life of the church. The church is always on the way, never static and never fully consummated, but also never without the possibility and promise that Christ is "really present" as Lord in Word and Sacrament by the power of the Holy Spirit.

The latter articles seek to confess the church's freedom and commission in relation to the state and in relation to the entirety of God's dominion, in which both church and state have a role to play. The Barmen Declaration offers, in a shorthand but practical and concrete form, a description of the church's identity and role in Christ's on-going activity of the world. While the church is not the entirety of Christ's life, activity, and dominion in the world, the Barmen Declaration offers a distinct vision and description of Christ's life made manifest in the Christian community, while at the same time acknowledging the larger realm and more vast dominion of God's reign and kingdom.[122] In addition, the Barmen Declaration distinguishes the voice, role and identity of the church from the world and defines the church's central contribution to the world as its encounter with Jesus Christ as recorded in Scripture, the church's contemporary proclamation of Jesus Christ, and the church's free commitment to Jesus Christ in the ordering of its life and its engagement with the world at-large.[123]

---

121. Barth, *Letters 1961–1968*, 150. In a letter to Pastor Arnold Bittlinger inviting Barth to give a lecture on the third article of the Barmen Declaration at a church event recognizing its thirtieth anniversary, Barth declined for a number of reasons, one of which was "that the Barmen Declaration should be put into practice and not brought out like an old flag every five years or so, waved a little before not very interested young people, and then carefully preserved in a chest again."

122. Fergusson, *Church, State, & Civil Society*, 124.

123. Ibid., 125.

The Barmen Declaration offers a theology of the church grounded by the conviction that the activity of Jesus Christ in its midst produces the church's faith and obedience, even its own bold attempt to offer a confession of faith to the surrounding world in 1934 Germany. Reflecting on the Barmen Declaration in 1940, Barth wrote that the publication and production of such a public statement by the churches in Germany was a miracle.[124] One of the ways it bears a miraculous quality is the clear articulation of trust in the one Word of God's ability to enact witnesses in a time of ecclesial and national crisis. It might also be derivatively miraculous in its insistence that this Word of God chooses to address and encounter humanity and the world through the particular life and witness of the church's proclamation, in word and sacrament. Certainly the primary miracle is Jesus Christ, the one Word of God in whom "we have to hear, and who we have to trust and obey in life and in death," but might it also be possible that one dimension of the miraculous-ness of this miracle is that Jesus Christ uses and takes up particular human words in order to bear witness to Himself in the church's life together and struggle to witness?

The vision of the church in the Barmen Declaration is an ecclesial vision that has its basis in the threefold Word of God.[125] The description of the church's life and task in the world put forward by the *Barmen Declaration* offers a theology of the church that boldly and courageously calls the church back to its one and only hope and source of life. Michael Weinrich goes so far as to say that the "doctrine of God and the ecclesiology of the Barmen Declaration remained landmark decisions for Barth's theology."[126] Dirk Smit qualifies Weinrich's claim in regard to Barth's theology of the church, noting that Barth warned against too much attention being given to the church and its inner life and practices.[127] Still Smit, admits, the life and action of the church were important to Barth even if they could not replace the main thing, Jesus Christ, the one Word of God. Indeed, according to Nicolas Healy, the great threat to the church, at Barmen and in our own time, was not individualism or militant secularism or any of the threatening –isms at work in the world, but the greatest threat and danger to the church is that the church would fail to be the church.[128] To become the church again was not a rebuilding of a past edifice, but a movement, a venture of risk, a falling back upon the one Word of God, a return to the hope that in spite of the

124. Barth, *CD* II/1:176.

125. Weinrich, "God's Free Grace and the Freedom of the Church," 410.

126. Ibid., 405.

127. Smit, "'. . . The Doing of the Little Righteousness,'" 140, see n32.

128. Healy, "Karl Barth's Ecclesiology Reconsidered," 298.

church's glaring flaws and limitations, Christ is present in the life and witness of the church as it ventures into the world to proclaim the gospel and to
make its witness in complete dependence on the risen Christ.[129]

In a classroom seminar in the mid-1950s, a student in the seminar
asked Karl Barth: "Ought we not enter the pulpit with the expectation that
God will speak through us? Ought we not to hope?"[130] Barth replied by
suggesting that the student ought to underscore the word *hope*. Hope is not
a desperation last-minute human sentiment for Barth; rather it is integral
to the church's life and activity. One cannot make Christ present when the
Scriptures are read and proclaimed, one cannot ensure it or be assured of it,
but one can trust in faith and expect in hope that Christ will become God's
Word, that Christ will become present in the human words and witness of
the Christian community. In this same way, the Barmen Declaration was a
declaration of hope: it was the attempt to confess the one true God and to
trust that this God's life would be made manifest in the church's proclamation, confession, and witness in a particular time and place.[131]

The reverberations of the Barmen Declaration and the effects of the
theology and ecclesiology of the threefold Word of God did not end in 1934
or even with the failures and eventual collapse of the Confessing Church
movement in Germany. Michael Weinrich marks 75th anniversary of the
Barmen Declaration by pointing out that the confessional nature of the
Barmen Declaration has been a particular source of aid and relevance to
churches engaging the world in situations of stress and outside pressure
from the ruling powers and principalities, citing South Africa, Cuba, and
Indonesia as examples.[132] Within Germany, Weinrich argues that Barmen

129. Weinrich, "God's Free Grace and the Freedom of the Church," 413.

130. Barth, *Karl Barth's Table Talk*, 26. Reconstructed conversations between Barth
and his students were recorded by John Godsey, one of the students in the seminar.

131. Like any confession arising out of the church's broken life together in the
world, the Barmen Declaration was by no means a perfect confession. While the Barmen Declaration sought to protest the theology of the German Christians and the
totalitarian claims of National Socialism, Barmen was silent on the problem of anti-
Semitism, Jesus Christ's own Jewishness, and the church's responsibility to its Jewish
brothers and sisters. In addition, Fergusson notes that all of the scriptural references
in the Barmen Declaration are drawn from the New Testament, which along with the
former omissions, lead to a troubling silence on the part of the Barmen Declaration in
regard to the Jewish question. See Fergusson, *Church, State, & Civil Society*, 126–27.
See also, Horn, "From Barmen to Belhar and Kairos," 110–12. See also, Barth, *Letters 1961–1968*, 250. In a letter to Bonhoeffer biographer and friend Eberhard Bethge,
Barth expressed his regret for not trying to incorporate the Jewish question into the
church's confession at Barmen.

132. Weinrich, "God's Free Grace and the Freedom of the Church," 418.

held a much greater theological influence and service to the witness of the churches in what was formerly East Germany than it did in the more "free" churches of the West.[133] Similarly, Dirk Smit makes the case that Barmen and its theology of church, as well as Barth's account of the church's struggle for human righteousness, was an inspiration to churches and Reformed theologians in South Africa in their own struggles against apartheid.[134]

The Barmen Declaration served and still serves as a shorthand expression of Barth's vision of the church and the particular pattern of divine activity conceptualized in the threefold Word of God.[135] Contained in the language of the Barmen Declaration is an initial expression of the church's purpose and mission in and to the world in light of Jesus Christ. It should not be taken for granted that the theology and church that produced the Barmen Declaration was guided by the central conviction that Jesus Christ acts presently in the church's proclamation. Without that central conviction and expectation in and for the church, it is fair to ask, whether or not a church and theology less bold about the proclamation of the gospel and the proclaimed Word of God becoming the Word of God, could have ever produced the Barmen Declaration in the first place.

The theology and ecclesiology evidenced in the Barmen Declaration have also influenced the church in its ongoing life and praxis up to the present times. This theological declaration begins with the one Word of God, God's reign and dominion in all creation, but it also seeks to describe the particular way God manifests Godself in the proclamation and witness of the church. The power and possibility of the one Word of God, Jesus Christ, is that God wills to enter into the strife of human beings, perhaps especially in the remote corners of the earth, ahead of, but also in and through the life of the church. Karl Barth referred to the formation and production of the Barmen Declaration as a miracle, and a dimension of its miraculous nature was the role of the threefold Word of God.[136] The threefold Word of God is not merely an abstract theological construct. The threefold Word of God, particularly its third form, offers historical testimony to the conviction that

133. Ibid.

134. Smit, "'. . . The Doing of the Little Righteousness,'" see also 142n35. Smit writes that the Confessing Church in Germany had a major influence on the developments in apartheid South Africa and *Barmen* and Barth's theology in particular played an important role.

135. Weinrich, "God's Free Grace and the Freedom of the Church," 404–19. In this excellent essay on the Barmen Declaration, Weinrich presents the Barmen Declaration as a re-presentation and iteration of the theology and ecclesiology of the threefold Word of God. See particularly 405, 409–10.

136. Barth, *CD* II/1:176.

God wills to speak to humanity in a worldly matter, putting the Word of God on human lips and hearts through the activity of the Holy Spirit, using the witness and proclamation of the church, and confronting and challenging the church and the larger world, with the claims of the gospel.[137]

Critical Observations

The concept of the threefold Word of God is an important way in to Karl Barth's theology of the church. Perhaps more than anywhere besides the sections on the church in the doctrine of reconciliation (IV/1, §62, IV/2, §67, IV/3, §72), does Barth go quite so far in describing the church's own life and activity in relation to God's activity in the world. The threefold Word of God is not simply a theme taken up early in the prolegomena of the *Church Dogmatics* and left behind. Rather, the theological shape and methodology of the threefold Word of God continues to shape Barth's thought and descriptions of the divine and human activity and relations in the world, from divine sign-giving to secondary objectivity to God's own glorification of Godself through the humanity and human speech of the church. That God speaks in particularity and in the contemporaneous life of the Christian community is a miracle and mystery every time it occurs, perhaps not on par with the incarnation, but akin to the incarnation. It is a miracle that cannot be conjured up by human potential, yet it is an event in which God promises to make Godself manifest.

The threefold Word of God has also served the contemporary church in confessional form. It has served the church and shaped its theological identity in resistance to false theological claims and in engagement with the powers and principalities. One must at least wonder, as feeble and fragile as the church's witness was in Nazi Germany, without the stated belief that the power of the risen Christ takes form and becomes the Word of God in the life of the Christian community, whether the Barmen Declaration and the Confessing Church resistance that was mounted, would have occurred and would have continued to offer theological aid and solidarity to the church's witness behind the Iron Curtain, under apartheid, and in our own times. The presence of the Word of God in the proclamation of the church makes the church the church, equips the church to engage the world with the gospel, and sends the church into the world to ethically challenge and resist the authoritarian demands of competing lords, in the culture, society, market, and polis. How does this happen? Barth does not go into specific detail about how the gospel is transmitted and imparted and received in

137. Barth, *CD* I/1:186. See also, Jüngel, *God's Being Is in Becoming*, 66.

the specific contexts and in the lives of the Christian community. Without overly systematizing the process or offering a one-size-fits-all account of how proclamation becomes the Word of God, perhaps further development along these lines would be beneficial; not only for purposes of explanation and clarification, but also to move, however feebly, through and beyond what Barth himself is willing to say.

For instance, in the event of proclamation, there seems to be some distinction and dissonance between the word proclaimed by the preacher and the word that becomes the Word of God for the hearer. What is crucially the central message for the proclaimer may not be exactly what is received as gospel by the hearer of the Word. Among the many places the Holy Spirit lives and works and moves is in this space between what is understood and intended to be the gospel by the preacher and what becomes the gospel in the life of the hearer. Obviously in both cases it relates to how and in what way the spoken and received words correspond and conform to the living presence of Jesus Christ. Just as God may choose to speak through Russian communism, Mozart, or a dead dog,[138] just as God may enable the very stones to cry out,[139] so may God speak the same Word in an infinitely multi-form way in the life and witness of the Christian community. The word proclaimed and the word heard, though expected to become the Word of God, may not have the exact same import in the life of the proclaimer and the life of the hearer, nor may they elicit the exact same response in the life of the community in order to be the Word of God.

For Barth, trying to peel back what is and is not the Word of God in the life of the Christian community never leads to the treasure but only to the earthen vessels and cracked pots. Perhaps the very sign of the Word of God in the midst of human words can be located in the way the Christian community trusts and expects that the Holy Spirit will make clear the presence of the Word among the words, enabling each member of the Christian community to correspond in their particular lives, sometimes together and sometimes individually, to the implications of the gospel. Rather than living lives of self-assurance, continuity, and certainty, the Christian community is constantly thrown back on grace and lives by the hope and expectation that Jesus Christ presently works in Scripture and proclamation through the Holy Spirit in its life together, even amidst its warts and weaknesses.[140] Thrown back upon grace, the promise and gifts of the Spirit may not give the Christian community certainty of a continuous divine presence, but the

---

138. Barth, *CD* I/1:55.

139. Luke 19:40.

140. Weinrich, "God's Free Grace and the Freedom of the Church," 418.

Spirit does not leave the community in a vacuum either. Indeed, Barth hints that the community's prayerful, humble, confident, and persistent expectation that God will come and speak in its own space and time is the very sign of Christ's presence already at work in the community's life and work.

In addition to the oneness and plurality of the Christian community's attempt to live out the demands and implications of the gospel, there is in Barth's concept of the threefold Word of God some flexibility and plurality as to how and when the proclaimed Word, the good news of the gospel, becomes the Word of God. In reference to the efficacy of proclamation, Barth suggests that the word proclaimed may become the Word of God in the life of the community long after the one who proclaimed the gospel and word is in the community or is even alive. Not only is God able to speak through a dead dog or flute concerto, but God may use what seemed like useless and empty words at one time or in one context to become the Word of God in another context and Christian community or in the life of an individual many years later. Though human words are limited and temporal and momentary, those words becoming the Word of God have no expiration date.

The next stage of this thesis will consider and explore the modification and revision Barth makes to the threefold Word of God, and will look into the possible consequences of this revision in regard to the presence of Christ in the life of the Christian community and the work of the Spirit in the church's proclamation and life together. In view of this reformulation of the threefold Word of God in *Church Dogmatics* IV/3, it is hoped that certain themes related to the concept of the threefold Word of God will be carried forward and pursued in relation to the primary concern. One of those themes is the unity of the Word of God with the declaration of the gospel in the life of the Christian community, however fragile and provisional that unity may be. The Word of God comes through creaturely media, but does not overcome or negate them, making room within God's speech and presence to take up and include human speech and action. Proclamation of the gospel is a human act and a human witness, but one that is enclosed within an act of God.[141] Such a theme is central to the concept of the threefold Word of God and Barth's larger theological vision, especially related to the Christian community. To be truly free, to live in Christian community, is to flourish in our own activity even as it becomes enclosed by God's activity, which makes room for and determines our own. While the church's proclamation of the gospel does not have exclusive rights to be enclosed within divine activity, perhaps the threefold Word of God serves as the paradigm

141. Barth, *CD* I/1:462.

for ways the Spirit may include human activity within God's life and work in the church and the world.

A second theme, not unrelated to the first theme, is the uniqueness of God's speech through the proclamation of the church. We have already seen Barth's theological desire not to restrict God's freedom, a desire rooted in Scripture's own narrative, that God can speak through a burning bush, a still small voice, a pillar of cloud, as well as a dead dog or a flute concerto, but God elects primarily to be heard in and through proclamation, transmission of the gospel, the *kerygma* of the church. God is not limited to this form of communication, but there does seem to be a willingness on the part of God for divine speech to occur in and through the community's broken attempts to speak the gospel. United to and inseparable from this theme is the idea that God can be, at times, outside and even against the church's proclamation. God can speak, not only in the gospel proclaimed, but can enable the gospel to be heard from outside the church. Therefore the church must constantly be ready and willing to hear the gospel from the outside in ways that challenge and reform its own proclamation and life together. Jesus Christ does not subsist in the church, the church subsists in Jesus Christ, and so the church must always be humble enough to listen for the voice of Jesus Christ in all corners of the life of the world. That said, such a qualification does not prevent the church's proclamation of the gospel from becoming the Word of God.

Two final matters to carry forward are more critical ones. First, like the doctrine of double predestination for Calvin, a teaching that was intended to provide pastoral care, but instead often led to deeper anxiety about one's own eternal destiny, there is a sense in which Barth's insistence that we can never possess the Word of God, leads to a similar anxiety. For instance, might it lead one to ask if the Word of God, since it cannot be possessed or embodied, ever really meets humanity at all? Similarly, does the becoming church ever become church? Can the church ever say with certainty, there, this is church? If not, how can one really talk about life in Christian community at all in any specific or practical ways? This is a fair question addressed to the threefold Word of God and Barth's vision of the church, and one that will continue to be explored.

Second, themes such as life together in Christ, the delight and joy of Christian worship, and Christ's presence and communion with the corporate Christian community are not given extended reflection in Barth's account of *church* in the *Church Dogmatics*. Obviously the church is not an end in itself, but is it possible to develop these themes in relation to the power of the gospel in the life of the Christian community? Can there be penultimate ends? While the church and Christian worship and community may not be ends in themselves, there is a danger in reducing them to utilitarian means. Modern Christianity, Protestantism in particular, has a long history of pious attempts to love Jesus without the church. But it is precisely the troublesome community of Christians with whom this Word of God refuses to be identified without. The city of God needs no temple because its temple is the Lamb, but even there, the primary vision of the *totus Christus* is one of worship, praise, and life together.

Summary

This chapter has explored Karl Barth's concept of the threefold Word of God as an ecclesiological resource and a crucial element in Barth's vision of the Christian community. As the Christian community encounters the living God in the witness of Scripture and its own gospel proclamation, the Christian community takes on a particular shape and identity in the world. The threefold Word of God is integral to the church's worship and witness as the church has sought to confess and live out the implications of the gospel in historical contexts.

So what becomes of the threefold Word of God? And what becomes of Barth's theology of proclamation, church, and the presence and activity of God in the life of the Christian community? Before offering a detailed assessment and explanation, Barth's revision of the threefold Word of God in *Church Dogmatics* IV/3 should be engaged and explored in the following chapter. Then, a better sense may be gained of what is at stake for the threefold Word of God and these themes, and why it matters today.

4

What Happens to the threefold Word of God:
Revision or Rejection?

Our statement is simply to the effect that Jesus Christ is the one and only Word of God, that He alone is the light of God and the revelation of God. It is in this sense that it delimits all other words, lights, revelations, prophecies and apostolates, whether of the Bible, the Church or the world, by what is declared in and with the existence of Jesus Christ. The biblical prophets and apostles are his servants, ambassadors and witnesses, so that even in their humanity the words spoken by them cannot fail to be words of great seriousness, profound comfort and supreme wisdom. And if the Church follows the biblical prophets and apostles, similar words are surely to be expected of it.

—Barth, *CD* IV/3:97

THIS CHAPTER EXAMINES KARL BARTH'S LATER THEOLOGY, PARTICULARLY *Church Dogmatics* IV/3, written in the 1950s, and published in 1959 (*CD* IV/3.1) and 1960 (*CD* IV/3.2). In *Church Dogmatics* IV/3, §69 "The Glory of the Mediator, 2. The Light of Life," Barth revisits the concept of the threefold Word of God and possibly amends it. This chapter scrutinizes Barth's re-presentation of the threefold Word of God and offers a clear account of the content and consequences of this possible revision. In addition, this chapter examines additional material from CD IV/3. This includes §69 "The Glory of the Mediator, 4. The Promise of the Spirit," regarding Christ's contemporary presence in proclamation between Christ's resurrection and Second Coming,[1] and §71 "The Vocation of

---

1. *CD* IV/3:322

Man," regarding the relationship between the Word of God and human-ity in the gospel event and on-going life in the Christian community. Recurrent themes such as *parousia*, event, correspondence, union with Christ, and witness offer the full context and rich tapestry of the con-temporaneous presence of the Word of God in the life of the Christian community and the world.

From a variety of perspectives and with a variety of theological goals, earlier and more recent Barth scholarship has sought to examine and re-examine Barth's possible modification to the threefold Word of God and the larger implications in relation to the theological content and trajectory of Barth's thought. The secondary literature related to this topic will be discussed at length in order to provide a brief history of thought about this topic and to set the context for further engagement and assessment of the threefold Word of God in *Church Dogmatics* IV/3. This chapter concludes with a discussion of the significance of this revision, possible implications, and a distinct account of what this revision might mean for proclamation and the church in Barth's own theology and contemporary theological challenges.

The Threefold Word of God Revisited

In his study of Gnostic theological tendencies within contemporary Protes-tantism, Philip Lee approvingly cites Karl Barth's theology of proclamation as a helpful weapon for "degnosticizing" modern Protestantism. "Among Protestants," Lee observes, "a confidence in the proclaimed Word of God has certainly been eroded."[2] The gains of modernity, Lee cautions, especially modern psychology, led to the suspicion that no one, "no matter how well-intentioned or authentically ordained to preach, could preach an objective Word as opposed to a word of his own choice, as opposed to a device he invents."[3] This loss of confidence in the Word of God, the proclaimed form in particular, Lee maintains, is unwarranted. Lee cites *Church Dogmatics* I/1, §4.1, "The Word of God Preached," and uses Barth's claim, that in and through human proclamation God speaks about Himself, to support his argument that God is able to speak to humanity through the fallible words of Scripture and through the imperfect proclamation of human witnesses.[4] If God is not embarrassed by the imperfections of Scripture and the all-too-human inadequacies of contemporary Christian preaching, Lee believes, then neither should we be. If the community of Christians gathered by the

2. Lee, *Against the Protestant Gnostics*, 219.

3. Ibid.

4. Ibid.

Word can no longer trust or be assured that God can and does address humanity through the strange new world within in the Bible and through the contemporaneous declaration of the gospel, then Lee argues, human beings will seek their chief end elsewhere.[5] Could it be possible, however, that Karl Barth's own theological project, at least by the time *Church Dogmatics* IV/3 was composed, also exhibited a certain loss of confidence in Scripture and proclamation as forms of the Word of God? Especially in the case of the third form of the Word of God, could such words still become the Word of God? What happens to the threefold Word of God? That is the central question that this chapter seeks to explore and answer.

Karl Barth begins the third section of the doctrine of reconciliation by exploring how the reconciliation that took place and takes place in Jesus Christ also declares itself throughout history, including our own time.[6] Because Jesus lives (not lived or will live), "Jesus Christ speaks for Himself," Jesus Christ is his own "authentic Witness," and in the power of his resurrection Jesus Christ makes Himself known and introduces Himself.[7] Barth trumpets this theme throughout *CD* IV/3, and declares emphatically that no one else can make Christ present or mediate this reality. "He does not need the help of any other. He is present Himself, and being present He himself breaks through the impenetrability of His existence."[8] The Easter event, the resurrection of Jesus from the dead, is Christ's own self-declaration as the Resurrected One. The uniqueness of the resurrection event for Barth is that it is not only an event that happened in history many many years ago, but it extends throughout history, into the present and onwards, where Christ continually comes to reign, to be present, and active in the life of the world, never in need of or dependent upon any other representatives to make him known, whether they be vicars on earth, or faithful proclaimers of Christian kerygma.[9] It is in this context that Karl Barth returns to and re-presents the earlier concept of the threefold Word of God presented in detail in *Church Dogmatics* I/1 and I/2.

The Threefold Word of God in *Church Dogmatics* IV/3

As we have seen, Barth's mature concept of the threefold Word of God presented and developed extensively in *Church Dogmatics* I/1 and I/2, had

5. Ibid.
6. Barth, *CD* IV/3:4–10.
7. Ibid., 39–46.
8. Ibid., 46.
9. Ibid., 342, 350.

its origins as far back as the Romans commentary and Barth's theological writings in Göttingen in the early 1920s. Bruce McCormack categorizes the era of the threefold Word at the center of Barth's thought from 1924–1937.[10] It would be another twenty years before Barth would revisit this material in *Church Dogmatics* IV/3. While it is hard to measure or account for the impact of the massive cultural, global, and historical changes that took place over this twenty year period, not to mention Barth's own theological development, one can hardly be surprised by Barth's admission, in the midst of §69.2 "The Light of Life," that in the present context, "we cannot establish, develop, and present it (the threefold Word of God) again as is done in detail in *C.D.* I, 1, and I, 2."[11] While a good deal of interpretive ink could be spilled as to what exactly Barth means by "in the present context," it seems clear that in the context of Christology, more specifically in regard to Christ's prophecy and self-declaration in which Christ alone speaks universally in the resurrection event, Barth sets out to root the Word of God solely in the form of Jesus Christ in which Christ alone speaks, Christ alone is the one Word of God, Christ alone introduces Himself, presents Himself, and declares the good news of the gospel.[12]

In this context, Barth saw it necessary to modify the role of Scripture and Christian proclamation as forms of the Word of God. If Christ alone is the one Word of God, if Christ alone introduces Himself, presents Himself, and declares the good news of the gospel,[13] then what is the relation between the contemporaneous presence of Christ and the contemporaneous reading of Scripture and declaration of the gospel in the life of the Christian community? According to Barth's christological presentation in *CD* IV/3, Christ does not need the help of the prophets and the apostles or even the most charismatic and compelling contemporary figures to make Himself known; no one can speak for Christ in the present except for Jesus Christ.[14] As Jesus lives, not lived, so Jesus Christ and the Easter event invade the present in Christ's self-declaration as the One raised from the dead.[15] The present is not a problem or a hurdle for the resurrected Christ. As Barth pointedly illustrates about the present: Christ "Himself is fully present and active," and Christ has no need of "any representatives, any anointed or unanointed,

10. McCormack, "The Being of Holy Scripture Is in Becoming," 57–59. See also McCormack, *Karl Barth's Critically Realistic Dialectical Theology*, 337–346.

11. Barth, *CD* IV/3:114.

12. Ibid., 46–47, 86, 114–24.

13. Ibid.

14. Ibid., 340–50.

15. Ibid., 342.

great or small, sacramentally or existentially endowed vicars."[16] Roman Catholic convictions about the Eucharistic elements containing Christ are targeted here by Barth as misguided attempts to subordinate Christology under sacramentology and ecclesiology, but perhaps less obvious is his equivalent critique of the dangers within Protestantism to elevate Scripture and *kerygma* to equal status with Jesus Christ.[17]

Perhaps with even greater emphasis than in *Church Dogmatics* I/1 and I/2, Barth identifies Jesus Christ as "the one Word of God whom we must trust and obey in life and in death."[18] Full stop. Summarizing his revisitation of the threefold Word of God, Barth clearly articulates his agenda in this section to distinguish and to elevate "the Word spoken in the existence of Jesus Christ from all others as the Word of God," including "the human words spoken in the existence and witness of the men of the Bible and the Church."[19] To be fair, in the sections already explored in regard to the three-fold Word of God in *CD* I/1, I/2, and II/1, Barth is always careful to identify Jesus Christ as the primary form of the Word of God, the first sacrament, and the primary objectivity of the being and activity of God. Nevertheless, the unity and compatibility between the three forms of the Word of God that are held together in *CD* I/1 and I/2 seem strained and possibly abandoned in Barth's presentation in *CD* IV/3. For instance, in unfolding the concept of the threefold Word of God in *CD* I/1, Barth writes that the Word of God is "one and the same whether we understand it as revelation, Bible, or proclamation."[20] Proclamation that rests on the witness to revelation in Scripture is no less than the Word of God such that in each of the three forms, God speaks to humanity, and each form becomes God's speech.[21] While such claims are not completely absent in Barth's re-presentation in *CD* IV/3, Barth is more concerned about distinguishing and setting apart Jesus Christ as the one Word of God. While there are other good human words that can "directly or indirectly attest (not repeat or replace or rival)"

---

16. Barth, *CD* IV/3:350.

17. Ibid., 349–50.

18. Ibid., 4. Barth opens §69 "The Glory of the Mediator," with this direction quotation from the first article of the Barmen Declaration, and continues to develop this theme in this section which in sum declares that through the power of his resurrection, Jesus Christ speak for himself and needs the assistance of no one to make himself heard in the present life of the world.

19. Ibid., 99.

20. Barth, *CD* I/1:120.

21. Ibid., 121, 125.

the one Word of God, "there is only one Prophet who speaks the Word of God as He is Himself this Word, and this One is called and is Jesus."[22]

So what does this mean for the second and third forms of the Word of God? A good amount of the material in §69.2 "Light of Life," is spent addressing the status of the words of Scripture and the church's declaration of the gospel and the particular position of these words in light of Jesus Christ, the one Word of God. In short, Barth lays out a revised presentation of the threefold Word of God. Even as he seeks to lay out the certain possibilities for secondary forms and words to relate to the one Word of God, Barth begins again by asserting the supremacy, sufficiency, distinctiveness, and adequacy of Jesus Christ alone as the continually complete Word of God.[23] There is no equal plane of relation or equal truth and content in these secondary words of Scripture and proclamation in relation to the one Word of God Jesus Christ,[24] nor can Jesus Christ be combined and enclosed with these other words in a larger system.[25] Yet in spite of the supremacy of Jesus Christ, in spite of the once-and-for-all nature of his revelation as the Word of God, Jesus Christ finds it fitting and imperative to "bring Himself into the closest conjunction with such words."[26] In fact, Jesus Christ united Himself so intimately with such witnesses and words that, in a paraphrase of Luke 10:16, Barth maintains, to hear the witness of Scripture and Christian community is to hear the voice of Christ himself.[27] The being and activity of the church do not produce Christ or present Christ, rather the living reality of Jesus Christ, his own being and activity, includes the world, not to mention Scripture and church. They subsist in Him, so that Jesus Christ cannot be synthesized or contained within any of these constructs.[28] Instead, they are found and they have a place and a reality in Him.

In this reiteration and presentation of the threefold Word of God, Barth relativizes and qualifies the version of the earlier concept in light of his deepening christological concentration and also in light of the universal nature of Christ's life, death, and resurrection. At the risk of sounding too glib,

22. Barth, *CD* IV/3:98–99.

23. Ibid., 99.

24. Ibid., 111.

25. Ibid., 101. One is led to wonder when Barth refers to Jesus Christ not being enclosed with other words in a "system superior to both Him and them" if he is making specific reference to his earlier presentation of the threefold Word of God in *CD* I/1 and I/2.

26. Ibid., 101.

27. Ibid.

28. Ibid.

one might refer to what Barth unfolds in this section (§69.2) as a fourfold Word of God, or more accurately, the one Word of God and three secondary forms or parables of the kingdom. In this expression, Barth emphasizes the centrality and supremacy of the dynamic and contemporaneous presence of Jesus Christ in the world, who in the past has entered into a union with the prophets and the apostles and their witness, who also promises to enter into a union with the Christian community, and who is even free to enter into similar unions *extra muros ecclesiae* with those outside the scope of the Christian community or with those not directly engaged in Christian faith and practice, but whose lives in some way reflect the life of Jesus Christ as they carry out their tasks in the world and society.[29]

So do Scripture and Christian proclamation still become the Word of God? Barth does not affirm or deny this question directly. While not denying to Scripture and to the church that God's Word can be on their lips in witness to Jesus Christ, Barth is careful to maintain the distinctiveness of Jesus Christ in relation to all other words. The one Word of God comes through human words, enabling them to become true human words and to say the same thing as the one Word of God, yet the human words maintain their distinct identity, without confusion, change or alteration, and without ever purporting to claim equal truth for themselves in relation to the one Word of God.[30] Instead, the one Word of God, Jesus Christ, comes to inhabit the lives of his community, and while Barth refuses to offer a systematic explanation of exactly how this miracle occurs, he concedes that Jesus Christ must somehow encounter and come through those who speak his words, "giving Himself to be seen and heard and perceived and known by them," and enabling fallen and fallible human beings "to take his Word on their lips in the form of witness to Him."[31] While not articulating the concept of the threefold Word of God in exactly the same way, Barth does not deny the real presence of Jesus Christ in and with the witness of Scripture and the witness of the church either. Jesus Christ, the one Word of God, according to Barth, has the ability to be "in some sense reflected and reproduced in the words of these men."[32] In such places and among such people, Jesus Christ and the grace of his real presence are located where human beings are able

29. Ibid., 102, 110. There is no question that Barth believes Jesus Christ is active and at work inside and outside the life and witness of the church calling forth various signs of witness throughout the world. The threefold Word of God, especially the spheres of Scripture and church, while important and central, Barth maintains, are not the ends or limits of Christ's redemptive activity.

30. Ibid., 111.

31. Ibid.

32. Ibid.

to declare the Word of God in their own human words beyond any capacity of their own.[33]

In addition to wanting to distinguish the supremacy of Jesus Christ yesterday, today and tomorrow, Barth relativizes the secondary forms of the Word of God and also unburdens these forms from the illusion that they are somehow an "Atlas bearing the burden of the whole world on its shoulders," as they seek to speak God's Word.[34] The sphere of Christ's dominion is cosmic and while it includes the church, it is not limited to the church. At the same time, the church's declaration of the gospel and its expectation that it will speak the Word of God is not merely a human pipedream but grounded in the very ways and works of the Word of God, Jesus Christ, so that the "greater sphere of His dominion and therefore His Word enfolds the lesser sphere of their word of ministry."[35] Just as in CD I/1, human witness to Christ and words signifying Christ are both distinct from but also enclosed in the Word of God. While the second and third forms of the Word of God are relativized and qualified, Barth does not abolish or abandon the concept of the threefold Word of God, rather he expands its capacity, arguing that there are at least (my emphasis) two words (Scripture and proclamation) that correspond to Jesus Christ, attest Jesus Christ, and in and through which Jesus Christ shines.[36]

Instead of rejecting or severely limiting the divine possibilities for Scripture or Christian proclamation, Barth makes allowance for the possibility that in Jesus Christ there is a capacity to create human witnesses not "restricted to His working on and in prophets and apostles and what is thus made possible and actual in His community."[37] Barth expands the possibility for Jesus Christ to speak and act and operate beyond the domain of Scripture and ecclesial proclamation, a possibility Barth also articulated in CD I/1 and even earlier in Göttingen.[38] Jesus Christ's capacity to speak

33. Ibid.

34. Ibid, 115.

35. Ibid., 116.

36. Ibid., 114.

37. Ibid., 118.

38 Barth, GD, 34. As early as the 1920s, Barth would affirm that "God's Word might even come through voices that belong to no church, that are perhaps directed against every church, that have nothing to with what we call religion, and yet that I have to listen to if I am not to be disobedient to the heavenly voice." See also, Barth, CD I/1:55. God, Barth maintains, is free "to speak to us through Russian Communism, a flute concerto, a blossoming shrub, or a dead dog. We do well to listen to Him if He really does . . . God may speak to us through a pagan or an atheist, and thus give us to understand the boundary between the Church and the secular world can still take at

and declare Himself transcends the limits of these spheres and the living presence of Jesus Christ is always and everywhere able to "raise up of the stones children to Abraham," witnesses to share in Christ's witness by no capacity of their own.[39] In spite of this qualification or additional allowance, Barth is still quite clear about the centrality of proclamation and declaration of the gospel as the paradigmatic instruments through which Jesus Christ as the one Word of God confronts the church and the world.[40] No matter how frail or broken the church's witness is or becomes, Barth maintains, the church possesses a certain dogged sacramental confidence that Jesus Christ, the one Word of God, is able to get Himself heard "through the instrumentality of the word and preaching, the instruction and worship, the whole life of the community."[41]

While Barth resists ecclesial depictions of the church having the burden of mediating Jesus Christ with its words and worship, Barth's later presentation of the threefold Word of God does not abolish the role of the church in Christ's reconciliation and redemption of the world either. Instead, Christ's resurrected and living presence in the time of the Spirit gives the church the freedom to correspond and conform to Jesus Christ, the freedom to declare the gospel of Jesus Christ in its own flawed and fallen attempts to act freely and obediently. But Barth adds, such human words and acts of correspondence have an additional dimension beyond and within their own attestations and witness to Jesus Christ: Jesus Christ speaks through the medium of such words, and they become parables of the kingdom, indirect witnesses, secondary words, in and through which the one Word of God comes and speaks and acts in the life of the Christian community.[42] Such words and parables are true, Barth contends, in two ways: first, as they in faith and freedom, seek to correspond to and bear witness to their origin and foundation in Jesus Christ, and second, as they become true words when the living presence of Jesus Christ in the world declares himself in and through these words of witness.[43] The miracle of the church's proclamation is that Jesus Christ raises up these witnesses and declares himself in them

---

any time a different course from that which we think we can discern." The very presuppositions on which the original concept of the threefold Word of God were founded are the very same ones that lead Barth to argue that there are peripheral words and parables of the kingdom outside the sphere and domain of the church where Christ is at work and calling forth witness.

39. Barth, *CD* IV/3:118.
40. Ibid., 121.
41. Ibid.
42. Ibid., 115.
43. Ibid., 123.

so that human words can become true human words and also the Word of God, just as the ordinary Christian community can become Christ's body and the earthly-historical form of Christ's existence in the world. In a miraculous event, Christ freely declares himself in these words of witness and parables of the kingdom, and in the very same event, in faith, freedom, and obedience, humanity creatively offers an echo and response brought forth by the living Christ's activity in the midst of his community.[44]

The Christian community's witness, correspondence, and signification of Christ are free human responses, free human declarations of the gospel in service to and in conformity with Jesus Christ. Yet while not offering a closed system or mechanized process to describe the work of the Spirit, Barth also acknowledges that humanity's free and obedient responses to the life and activity of God in these signs and actions are precipitated and evoked by Jesus Christ who elects to bear witness to Himself and declare Himself in the church's speech-acts of correspondence. As Jesus Christ attests Himself through the gospel, Barth declares, "the work of the Holy Spirit is done."[45] Barth asserts that the Holy Spirit is not an independent force or spirit, but the very power of Christ's contemporaneous presence, work, and word.[46] Therefore, the Holy Spirit makes the gospel the very Word of God, Christ's own self-witness, Christ's self-declaration in the human declaration of the gospel, while always making room for and creating the condition for a human witness, the community's witness to the presence of the risen Christ. God's self-witness in and with the human witness, does not come, Barth is sure to add, "at the expense of its character as a human witness to His person and work."[47]

From Threefold Word to Threefold Parousia

As the themes of parousia, witness, and vocation from *CD* IV/3 continue to be explored in relation to the threefold Word of God, it should be made clear that the original theological language and framework of the threefold Word of God became for Barth too small a theological framework to conceptualize and account for the fullness of Jesus Christ's life, presence, and activity in the world. The threefold Word of God could not fully encapsulate the intervention and revelation and redemption of the world in the life, death, resurrection, and return of Jesus Christ, even in regard to Christ's contemporaneous presence in the life of the church and world. In Barth's

44. Ibid., 121.
45. Ibid., 501.
46. Ibid., 503.
47. Ibid., 501.

later presentation of the threefold Word of God, Christ's capacity to manifest himself in the world and to create human witnesses was not limited to the sphere of Scripture and the sphere of Christian proclamation.[48] As we have seen, it is not as though Barth rejected or abolished the threefold Word of God, but instead he seemed to concede that it could not be articulated and presented in the exact same way and framework in which it was presented in *CD* I/1 and I/2.[49] As a result, Barth did not reject the threefold Word of God, but included its framework within the larger framework of his doctrine of reconciliation, which included a qualified version of the threefold Word of God. In this way, Barth could still affirm Scripture and the church's declaration of the gospel as enclosed within the Word of God, as forms of God's Word, and as serving God's purposes in contemporaneous places and times.

One of the ways Barth locates the threefold Word of God in a broader conceptual framework is in his presentation of the threefold *parousia* in §69.4 "The Promise of the Spirit." We have already seen that Barth begins his third part of the doctrine of reconciliation by describing Christ's resurrection as Christ's self-witness, his proclamation of the gospel to all the world, and so Scripture and proclamation are located within this larger action as responses to and creations of Christ's own universal declaration of the gospel to the world in the resurrection. In §69.4 "The Promise of the Spirit," Barth seeks to describe the Easter event as *parousia*, Christ's "new coming as the One who had come before."[50] What does this have to do with the threefold Word of God? Barth's presentation of the threefold nature of Christ's *parousia* is eerily similar to the concepts and actualistic event language of the threefold Word of God. While the focus in the text is on the second form of Christ's *parousia*, the coming of Christ through the impartation of the Holy Spirit in the time of the Christian community's mission in the world, Barth carefully speaks of resurrection, outpouring of the Spirit, and Second Coming as three distinct forms of one and the same event.[51]

Christ's coming in the Easter event is the primal and basic form, according to Barth, which is replicated in a different way at Pentecost with the coming of the Holy Spirit, and again when Christ's Easter resurrection is made manifest and effective for all as it reaches its eschatological goal.[52] Trying to be faithful to the witness of Scripture, Barth seeks to describe Easter,

48. Ibid., 118.
49. Ibid., 114.
50. Ibid., 291.
51. Ibid., 293–94.
52. Ibid., 295–96.

Pentecost, and Christ's return as three forms of one event, in which each particular event "contains the other two by way of anticipation or recapitulation" so that each serve as a distinct yet unified event of Christ's *parousia*.[53] Barth even compares the unity-in-distinction of this threefold *parousia* to the unity-in-distinction of the Trinity.[54] The only other place in the *Church Dogmatics* where Barth makes an analogy to the Trinity is in his explanation of the unity of the three forms of the Word of God.[55] Indeed, Barth declares that the doctrine of the threefold Word of God is the only analogy to the doctrine of the Trinity.[56] Obviously in seeking to describe Easter, Pentecost, and Second Coming as one event in the coming of Jesus Christ, Barth found another analogy.

What is interesting about this development of a threefold *parousia* is Barth's willingness to use the same concepts and framework from the earlier doctrine of the threefold Word of God and apply it to Christ's *parousia*. Equally interesting is Barth's willingness to use the analogy to the Trinity, comparing the unity-in-differentiation of the Word of God and Christ's *parousia* to the persons of the Trinity. This new development of threefold language and concepts seems to further relativize the centrality of the threefold Word of God simply due to the fact that the threefold Word of God, especially the third form, can only occur and be located within the second form of the threefold *parousia* through the impartation of the Holy Spirit. So in a way, the threefold *parousia* of Christ serves as a broader framework, and the third form of the Word of God, the church's *kerygma* and proclamation occur within the framework of the second form of Christ's threefold *parousia*, which by the power of the Holy Spirit, the contemporaneous presence of Christ, room is made for the Christian community to offer a "repetition, representation, and multiplication of the Easter revelation" in its own life and witness to the world.[57]

Barth continues to describe the present and contemporaneous form of Jesus Christ not solely in terms of the third form of the Word of God, but in terms of the second form of Christ's *parousia*. Far from being an independent presence distinct from the Easter event and the eschatological fulfilment or a non-presence or product of the human consciousness and memory, in world occurrence and in the life and witness of the Christian community, "the glory of God is present in the personal, real, visible, audible and even

53. Ibid., 296.
54. Ibid.
55. Barth, *CD* I/1:120–21.
56. Ibid., 121.
57. Barth, *CD* IV/3:304.

tangible coming again of this man."[58] To contend otherwise, Barth cautions, is to risk docetism. And so while the reconciliation of the world and humanity's justification and sanctification have taken place in Jesus Christ and been publicly and universally declared in Christ's resurrection, Barth contends that the declaration is not yet complete. Christ's resurrection declaration continues forward in the form of Pentecost and invites and includes the Christian community's own proclamation and witness as part of the second form of Christ's *parousia*, even as the *totus Christus* looks forward to the final form of Christ's *parousia* in the Spirit's consummation of all things.

This middle form of Christ's return, what Barth refers to as the promise of the Spirit,[59] is the time and place in which the presence and *parousia* of Jesus Christ makes use of the third form of the Word of God, i.e., Christian proclamation. Barth begins to describe the contemporaneous form of Christ's presence by challenging any notions of ecclesial possession or ecclesial containment of Jesus Christ, asserting that there can be no question of Jesus Christ allowing Himself to be represented by the Church or Christianity; nor should the efficacy of the gospel hang upon the credibility and veracity of Christian witnesses.[60] Hitting closer to home for the third form of the Word of God, Barth adds that "Jesus Christ cannot be absorbed and dissolved in practice into the Christian *kerygma*, Christian faith and the Christian community."[61] Because Christ is fully present in the here and now by the promise of the Spirit, the second form of Christ's *parousia*, Christ is never dependent upon the church or priests or the church's proclamation to make Christ present and active, but comes to and confronts humanity in the present as he did at Easter and will do at his consummation.[62]

Barth's claims here lead to two questions. First, has he basically dismissed any notion of a threefold Word of God, particularly a third form, by strongly differentiating between the presence of Jesus Christ in and with the Christian community, and the community's *kerygma* and faith? And second, what is the relationship between Jesus Christ and Jesus Christ's church? Are even the most qualified and humbly obedient attempts to claim the real presence of Jesus Christ in the contours and life together of Christian community really just imperialistic efforts to possess and dissolve Jesus Christ

58. Ibid., 312.

59. In other places, Barth refers to refers to the second form of Christ's presence and *parousia* as the time of the community, the time of the church (see Barth, *Dogmatics in Outline*, 128), but he does not do so in this section.

60. Ibid., 349.

61. Ibid..

62. Ibid., 349–50.

into the *kerygma*, faith, and life together of the Christian community? Barth seems willing to concede that the sign or signs of the presence and activity of God in the life together of the Christian community cannot be easily equated with proclamation of the gospel or right administration of the sacraments, both of which too easily can claim present possession and custody of Jesus Christ. Rather, Christ's presence can mainly be identified by the Christian community's prayer and expectation of Christ's eschatological fulfilment of all things. In other words, the surest sign of Christ's contemporaneous presence, the second form of the *parousia*, is the Christian community's hopeful expectation and prayer for the third form of Christ's *parousia*. Will Christ's contemporary presence not show itself, Barth asks, by the very fact that there is community of Christians "who know an honest and basic lack, and thus hope for his conclusive appearing and revelation and their own and the whole world's redemption and consummation, looking and marching toward it in Advent in a movement from Christmas, Good Friday, and especially Easter?"[63] Might the real presence of Jesus Christ be most closely aligned, not with the event of proclamation and preaching, but with the open-ended prayer and cry to God: "Lord have mercy upon us! Even so, come Lord Jesus"?[64] Barth certainly seems to be shifting emphasis from the Word of God and gospel proclamation to the action and presence of Christ in the human prayer and cry to the Lord yet to come.

Again, rather than dismissing one in favor of the other, Barth seems to attempt to hold two concepts together, perhaps challenging the church and offering a vision of the church that confesses the not yet of Christ's coming *parousia* before it celebrates and claims the continual presence of Christ in the declaration of the gospel and in its life together. It is not as if Barth denies Christ's presence in the church's declaration of the gospel and its life together between the times; he even remarks that what took place in Christ is "noted and experienced, and still takes place continually, in the existential reaching and claiming of countless individuals both within" the sphere of the church and beyond its walls throughout the world.[65] Rather, ecclesial attempts to contain or produce the glorious presence of Jesus Christ do not seem for Barth to be representative of the biblical witness of the early Christian communities nor to be the particular calling of the contemporary church and its witness in the world. Again, Barth does not reject the presence of Christ and the activity of God enclosing the human witness and signs of the Christian

63. Ibid., 322.
64. Ibid.
65. Ibid., 321.

community, nor does he offer a safe haven that alleviates the very real risk of praying "Come, Lord Jesus," and "Thy kingdom come."

Barth sought to articulate Christ's presence and activity on the one hand, and the free human actions of bearing witness and corresponding obedience on the other, but Barth's presentation of the Word of God in *CD* IV/3 does seem to place a greater emphasis on the free human action and its distinct witness. While Barth could still say that "it must have pleased the Word of God to allow itself to be in some sense reflected and reproduced in the words of these men," giving them and their words "the grace of its real presence," to speak the Word of God with their human words,[66] Barth has no interest in proving the presence of Christ in the here and now. Instead, what becomes central is the accompanying human expectation and complete dependence on Christ's *parousia* in the here and now. Still, Barth refuses to separate the Word of God from human language: "you cannot divide the Word of God from words."[67] Not limiting God's speech to clerical assignments or roles, Barth remarks that God's Word is always accompanied by human attempts to speak to and about God. "Our praying is an attempt to speak to God, our hearing is an attempt, our preaching is an attempt"[68] and it is by means of this very attempt that God speaks.[69] And it is under these very conditions that one can expect and hope that human words can still become the Word of God in the present time and place.

Witness Yet More than Witness

Perhaps there is a danger that Barth's earlier presentation of the threefold Word of God in *CD* I/1 and I/2 could too easily be co-opted as an automated ecclesial formula, an unsurprising given in the worshipping life of the Christian community. And perhaps this earlier presentation of the threefold Word of God too strongly assumed the centrality of clerical proclamation of the gospel as *the* third form of the Word of God. In the context of *CD* IV/3, Barth rarely distinguishes between clerical Christians and lay Christians except to criticize such distinctions.[70] As we have seen, Barth resists a direct

66. Ibid., 111.

67. Barth, *Karl Barth's Table Talk*, 27.

68. Ibid., 31.

69. Ibid.

70. See for example, Barth, *CD* IV/3:350; and *CD* IV/3:604. Not only is the line thin to nonexistent between clergy and laity, but the divide between Christians and non-Christians is quite porous. See also, *CD* IV/3:121. Here Barth distinguishes the Christian from the non-Christian only by degree, contrasting the "militant godlessness" of

identification between the threefold word of God and the clerical sphere, not equating the Word of God solely with the activity of the minister and preacher. To declare and proclaim the gospel, Barth more fully clarifies, is not relegated merely to a clerical act on Sunday during worship, but is the vocation of all Christians.

While the Christian minister may be given the most obvious and regular opportunity for Christ to declare himself in the words of Christian proclamation, any act of Christian proclamation and instruction in the life of the Christian community may "manifest the one light of the one truth" and offer a particular refraction that is a faithful reflection of the one light Jesus Christ.[71] Without rejecting the clerical aspects of Christian proclamation, Barth qualifies proclamation. It is not the sole avenue or means of the Word of God. In addition, Barth retains the basic framework and instincts of the threefold Word of God without reducing it to a pat formula that easily produces the presence of Christ. Remaining faithful to many of the very same theological principles first articulated in *Church Dogmatics* I/1 and I/2 where the threefold Word of God is presented in its most comprehensive shape, Barth nevertheless elevates the one true Word, Jesus Christ, above all other words, including Scripture and the proclamation of the church. Such human words become something more by their association with the one

---

the outer sphere of humanity with the "intricate heathenism" of the inner sphere. See also, *CD* IV/3:497. In relation to Jesus Christ, Barth adds, all human beings, for all the differences between non-Christians and Christians, "are what they are, namely, men who have their calling only before them on the one side, and men who have it both behind and before them on the other." In other words non-Christians are on the way to their true calling while the Christians is on the way from their event of vocation that already happened to the next event of vocation yet to come. Perhaps one of Barth's more famous quotations that humanity may choose to be godless, but God never chooses to be humanity-less (see *CD* IV/3:119; see *KD* IV/3, 133, "Denn man vergesse nicht: es gibt zwar eine Gottlosigkeit des Menschen, es gibt aber laut des Wortes von der Versöhnung keine Menschenlosigkeit Gottes") is illustrated by Christ's reconciliation and love for all humanity, Christian and non-Christian alike. Not only does God not discriminate toward the non-Christian, but Barth adds, neither should the Christian or the Christian community. See also, *CD* IV/3:494. While there is an unavoidable and at times painful distinction between the Christian and the non-Christian, the Christian and Christian community can only exhibit an "unlimited readiness to see in the aliens of to-day the brothers of to-morrow, and to love them as such."

71. Barth, *CD* IV/3:122–23. This view was not really an entirely new development in Barth's thought. See Barth, *GD*, 16. As early as the *Göttigen Dogmatics*, Barth would declare that Christian preaching or proclamation ought not to be restricted to oratory from the pulpit or the work of pastors, but includes all Christian attempts to hear and speak the Word of God.

true Word, Jesus Christ, as they indirectly bear witness in their own attestation and as Jesus Christ declares Himself in them.[72]

In §71 "The Vocation of Man," Barth further develops the themes of the threefold Word of God in his exploration of vocation and the characteristics of witness. In this section, Barth offers a clear account of Christ's presence in and through the church's declaration of the gospel. Barth continues to advance the importance of the human witness and his or her free correspondence and conformity to Jesus Christ in the Christian life. Equally important, Barth continues to highlight and emphasize Christ's ongoing life and witness in the world and fellowship with the Christian community in and through whom Christ declares Himself, indirectly attesting Himself in his full totality.[73] Not only does the witness correspond to Christ and bear witness to Christ, but the living reality of Jesus Christ in the world includes the witnesses, shines through and declares itself in and through the community of witnesses, giving them a share of Christ's ongoing life and work and reflecting Christ's glory in the world.[74]

So can human words become the Word of God? In contrast to *CD* I/1 and I/2, Barth is much more cautious about placing Scripture or proclamation on an equal plane with the one Word of God, Jesus Christ. But while Scripture and the church's proclamation and witness are free and distinct responses in light of the one Word of God, free human declarations of the gospel in correspondence to Jesus Christ, Barth refuses to completely cut the cord between these two qualitatively distinct entities. It is not as easily explained as God's grace on the one hand and then a corresponding act of human gratitude on the other, rather the free human response to the gospel is bracketed by the activity of God on either side, or as Barth put it in an earlier articulation, enclosed in an act of God.[75] Human words are free human responses to God's presence, nothing more, nothing less, and yet because they are precipitated and evoked by the presence and ongoing life and work of Jesus Christ in which Jesus Christ elects to bear witness to Himself in and through these words and acts of correspondence, such human words and acts of correspondence can become the very way Jesus Christ declares himself in our time and space, enabling such words and witness to become enclosed, for a time, by God's own Word.

Perhaps Barth had concerns that his initial presentation of the threefold Word of God might lead the Christian community to believe it could

---

72. Barth, *CD* IV/3:123.

73. Ibid.

74. Ibid., 614.

75. Barth, *CD* I/1:462.

commandeer control of Jesus Christ and mediate Jesus Christ to others and to the world.[76] Barth clearly corrects such a misreading by making it clear that it is Jesus Christ and his actions upon the Christian community that free the community to declare the glad tidings of the gospel while remaining fallen and broken human beings.[77] But human correspondence and freedom are not the end of the story; the witness not only witnesses to the Witness, but the Witness witnesses to the witnesses, declaring Himself in their speech, shining through their small acts of correspondence, and including and incorporating their particular ministry of witness in Christ's ongoing redemption of the world.[78]

While the church's proclamation and its witness subsist in Jesus Christ and not the other way around, while the preaching of the gospel and the reading of Scripture do not automatically produce an effect called Jesus Christ, Barth does not dismiss the framework of the threefold Word of God, stating in *CD* IV/1 that "all knowledge of Jesus Christ will have not merely its basis but its limit and standard in the witness of Scripture and the proclamation of the church."[79] The sphere of the church is a wide sphere with many more possibilities for knowledge and encounter with Jesus Christ,

76. Barth, *CD* IV/3:115–16.

77. Ibid., 115.

78. Frei, *The Identity of Jesus Christ*, 194. While Frei does not cite Barth directly, he does offer an interpretation of what the mode of Christ's presence now might take. Frei includes the sacraments in his interpretation which would obviously conflict with some of Barth's later conclusions regarding the sacraments, but I think it is still possible not to discount Frei's interpretation as far as proclamation goes, and therefore it is possible to include the threefold Word of God in the mode of Christ's presence here and now. In an interpretation of the gospel of John, Frei writes that "the center of the Christian message is a mystery—the presence of God. To that center, to that message, Jesus Christ himself is a witness, so that he points away from himself to God. But the mysterious reversal is that the witness who points away from himself is the one who is witnessed to be the very God and the very Spirit to whom he witnesses. By analogy, the feeble, often naïve and simple word of written Scripture—and even its usually pathetic, clumsy interpretation in the spoken word—becomes a true witness, yet more than a witness." The primary functions and tasks of Scripture and proclamation are always to point away from themselves and bear witness to Jesus Christ; as human witnesses, in the power of the Spirit, such human freedom and human obedience are the way of faith, discipleship, and Christian discipleship. And yet equally true and part of the true human witness, Frei reminds, is the fact that God witnesses to it, "that he makes himself present to it so that the Word may become the temporal basis of the Spirit who is the presence of God in Jesus Christ." In other words, the witness becomes more than a witness as it is bracketed and enclosed and included in the activity of God, the presence of Jesus Christ, through the power of the Holy Spirit.

79. Barth, *CD* IV/1:763.

perhaps more than the church is always able to identify, but outside the sphere of the church, outside the sphere of Scripture and proclamation, Barth cautions, "Jesus Christ has no form for us."[80] Instead, Barth resists applying the threefold Word of God as a uniform and one-size-fits-all mode of Christ's presence and the Spirit's impartation of Christ in the life of the Christian community.

From Proclamation to Invocation, from Preaching to Prayer

As some Barth interpreters and commentators have noticed, there is a shift in the content of the *Church Dogmatics* that comes to emphasize the doctrine of election, and as a result, the event of vocation takes on a more central role in place of the event of proclamation.[81] Perhaps a similar framework shift occurs regarding the event of the Word of God. The hearing and response to the gospel occur in the event of vocation, which includes the event of proclamation, but in which vocation becomes the larger theological framework. Similarly, the centrality of human proclamation gives way to human invocation, a shift of emphasis from preaching to prayer, if not a complete shift, at least an equal partnership. Perhaps this is one more reason why the threefold

80. Ibid., 763. Is it possible that Barth adheres to a stricter presentation of the threefold Word of God in *CD* IV/1 than he does in IV/3? Is it possible that there is some tension between what Barth says about Jesus Christ's presence and Christ's impartation of himself through Scripture in proclamation in *CD* IV/1 and what he says about Christ's self-witness in *CD* IV/3? As we have seen, there is some sense of a qualification of the threefold Word of God in *CD* IV/3 and an attempt to set it in the larger context of Christ's own self-declaration preceding and alongside the church's declaration of the gospel, but passages such as this one from *CD* IV/1 reveal the continuing centrality of the threefold Word of God as well as its important role as a sphere and mark of Christ's contemporary presence in the life of the world.

81. McCormack, *Orthodox and Modern*, 214–15. McCormack argues that this shift in theological content or concentration is due to Barth's revision of the doctrine of election. After hearing Pierre Maury's lecture on the subject of election, Barth rethought the doctrine and disassociated election from the revelatory event, placing it on a christological foundation within the doctrine of God. The question remains whether Barth thought the witness of Scripture and the church's proclamation could become indirect media of revelation outside the flesh of Jesus Christ. Barth seeks to answer this question in *CD* IV/3, §69.2 "The Light of Life," but as we have seen, while Barth seeks to relativize and qualify Scripture and proclamation as forms of the Word of God because Jesus Christ does not need such forms in order to communicate and proclaim himself in the present, Barth does not prohibit the Word of God from electing to annex such forms to be the primary way of Christ's own self-declaration for the sake of the reconciliation and redemption of the world.

Word of God does not disappear altogether, but certainly becomes qualified and relativized by other theological concepts in Barth's theological project.

Again, in §71 "The Vocation of Man," Barth does not dismiss the threefold Word of God but frames it within the event of vocation, in which "the living Jesus Christ encounters definite men at definite times in their lives as their Contemporary, makes Himself known to them as the One He is, i.e., as the One He is for the world, for all men, and therefore for them too, and addresses and claims them as partners in His covenant and sinners justified and sanctified in Him."[82] While the event of vocation often may include preaching and sacraments and the witness of Scripture, the event of vocation is always the "direct and personal work of God, of Jesus Christ, of the Holy Spirit," and neither Scripture nor contemporary witnesses mediate God's call for it is the Lord himself who proclaims Himself and makes Himself known in the event of vocation.[83] Here again Barth both maintains the use of a modified threefold Word of God while also qualifying it, ensuring and asserting the freedom of the living Lord Jesus Christ. The living Jesus Christ is not bound to preaching and the sacraments in the encounter and call of humanity, Barth maintains, but "may very well, *extra muros ecclesiae*," independently of the church and its ministry, "know and tread the very different possibilities of most effective calling."[84]

Whereas the proclamation of the gospel through preaching and sacraments can easily be reduced to the clerical vocation, the event of vocation and the vocation of the Christian apply to all Christians equally. Though Barth does not get into specifics, church proclamation and its central role in the life of the Christian community need not be displaced or even abolished in favour of a more democratic event of vocation, rather proclamation is incorporated into and under vocation rather than the other way around. In the event of vocation, all are called to the office of the Word of God. Yet Barth does not throw out the framework or the theological spirit of the threefold Word of God.[85] Barth describes this office of vocation and witness in biblical terms:

> In the biblical narratives those called by God are men who are summoned, commanded and empowered to declare this message. They are responsible for addressing the message of God

82. Barth, *CD* IV/3:502.

83. Ibid., 515.

84. Ibid., 516.

85. Ibid., 576.

to His creatures. As witnesses they have to repeat what God Himself has first said to them.[86]

Any sense of ecclesial mediation, scriptural mediation, or even three-fold mediation is relativized and qualified. What is maintained however is that as the witness bears witness to and accompanies the action and presence of the living Jesus Christ, the witness participates in the being-in-action of Jesus Christ and Jesus Christ, in his contemporary form (second form of *parousia*), declares Himself in this witness.[87] The community of witnesses and the individual witness become, not spectators, nor dead instruments, but those whose small acts of witness and discipleship are included in the work of God, cooperating and heralding Christ's prophetic work, trusting that it will be united in and with the second form of Christ's *parousia* until it is brought to completion in the third form of *parousia*, Christ's universal redemption and revelation.[88] Barth uses a provocative illustration taken from Roman Catholic ecclesial imagery to describe the Christian's role and the church's role in the contemporary form of the Word of God:

> To use for once the imagery of Roman Catholic worship, the Christian is not the priest, nor does he read the mass, nor have anything to do with the transformation, the sacrifice and the dispensing of communion; he is only the server or altar-boy who carries the missal backward and forward and swings the incense and rings the bell at the decisive moment. Yet he is this, and assists in this way. He is called to this ministering presence. What makes him a Christian, and distinguishes him as such, is that he also acts as minister in what Christ does. In this sense we may well say that he co-operates in the work of Christ.[89]

86. Ibid.

87. Ibid., 602.

88. Ibid., 606.

89. Ibid., 602. See Hütter, *Suffering Divine Things: Theology as Church Practice*, 110. Hütter references this illustration as an admission by Barth that he would no longer speak about three forms of God's Word as he did in *CD* I/1. Hütter references Walter Kreck, who claimed that Barth used this illustration late in his life to characterize the more qualified, solely human role of proclamation, which announces and responds to the Spirit's presence in the form of Christ's own self-proclamation. There are a couple of problems with Hütter's analysis and presentation. First, Barth did not revise the threefold Word of God in some small circle of students and theologians shortly be-fore his death; he did so long before in *CD* IV/3:114–15. Second, this reference to a late in life illustration about Barth also appears in the *CD* IV/3:602. Hütter is right to show Barth's resistance to equate the human proclamation of the gospel directly with the execution of the transformation that occurs by the presence of the Spirit, but Barth uses this illustration in the *CD*, not to simply segregate the human work

Christ's contemporaneous presence not only makes room for the words and witness of the Christian and the Christian community, but gives and invites each member of the Christian community to offer an echo of Christ's revealing and proclaiming.[90] This witness and role are not to be confused with Jesus Christ and the sufficiency of his own self-witness, but are included and enclosed in the prophetic work of Jesus Christ and become an additional part of the being and life of the *totus Christus* in the life of the world.[91] It is not as if Jesus Christ needs such a witness or this extra dimension of his life. Barth even wonders if the world might be better off with only the proclamation of Jesus Christ alone, "without any

---

of proclamation from the divine work of the Spirit, but also to offer the hope and possibility that Christ's work in the Spirit takes up the human act of proclamation, distinguishing it as human action, but also taking it up, using it, and incorporating it into the work and presence of Christ. Christ does not need this missal, this altar-boy, this servant, but Christ's self-declaration does not occur without it, enabling humanity to join in the presence and work of Christ, enabling human words to be enclosed and incorporated into an act of God.

90. While Barth's illustration from Roman Catholic liturgy (*CD* IV/3:602) stresses the distinction between the human action and the coming of Jesus Christ, earlier in *CD* IV/2:112–13, Barth also offers an illustration of Christ's contemporaneous presence in the gospel proclamation in the Christian community that underscores the continuity and unity between the living Christ and contemporary Christian life together in Christ. Barth wonders whether marking Christmas, Good Friday, and Easter, "proclaiming and hearing Jesus Christ as the Word of God spoken to the world and ourselves," can only make sense as acts of "remembrance and representation" alone, or if such acts only make sense if the One who is remembered and proclaimed comes in and through these acts. Could the Christian community exist, Barth asks, without the basis of this presupposition? In a tribute to his youth minister and mentor/teacher (Abel Burckhardt), Barth offers a description of Christ's presence in and through the declaration of the gospel in the teachings of his childhood pastor who presented the events of Christmas, Good Friday, Easter, the Ascension, and Pentecost, not as history or doctrine or dogma or myth, but "as things which might take place any day in Basel or its environs like any other important happenings" (*CD* IV/2:112). In the stories and songs of Christ's life, death, and resurrection, Barth declared, "the Saviour made His entry," in the context of the biblical story, and in the life together of that particular Christian community (*CD* IV/2:112). Barth continues with another illustration and reference to Roman Catholic liturgy: "was this representation, like the unbloody repetition of the sacrifice of Christ in the Roman doctrine of the Mass? Was it the kind of faith which in that rather convulsive doctrine is supposed to consist in a re-enactment of the crucifixion of Christ in our own existence? Again, no. It was all present without needing to be made present" (*CD* IV/2:113). Christ was present, without the need to be made present by the priest or the church or anyone else, but Christ did not come apart from this gospel declaration in this little Christian community.

91. Barth, *CD* IV/3:606–7.

co-operation on the part of Peter and Paul, let alone the rest of us."[92] Christ
does not need the witnesses or their words to make the Word of God a
reality, Christ is not bound to such forms, and yet, Barth adds, Christ's own
divine grace creates this dimension that "does not exclude but includes this
human co-operation."[93]

So it is that the self-proclamation of Christ makes room for the proclamation and witness of the Christian community. And so it is that the threefold Word of God continues to have a place in Barth's theology of Christian
witness and the Christian church. Though the words of proclamation and
words of Christian witness will remain and always be fully human words,
Barth believes there is a place in Jesus Christ's own being for the words of
human beings to become God's own Word. That is not to say that Barth's
conception of the threefold Word of God does not evolve; it is not presented
in the same way as *CD* I/1 and I/2. Rather, the threefold Word of God is
absorbed into the larger framework of the three forms of Christ's resurrected presence. In addition, the third form of the Word of God becomes
a much broader category than only preaching (though preaching still has a
prominent, even paradigmatic role in this framework). Still, preaching becomes simply one form of the Word of God in the present, finding its place
in the larger framework of the declaration of the gospel, the vocation and
activity of all Christians.

Perhaps Barth's earlier presentation of the threefold Word of God unfairly saddled the concept with the full freight of Christ's presence in the
here and now. In *CD* IV/3, Barth clearly deepens the christological concentration of the one form of the Word of God, contending that the presence
of Jesus Christ in the world can include the witness of Scripture and church
proclamation and other forms of witness inside and outside the church. It
his highly questionable to conclude that because of this modification and
qualification in regards to the threefold Word of God, Barth no longer had
any use for it. In *CD* IV/3, the church's ministry and witness, elaborated
in twelve different forms of speech and action, is still conceived chiefly as
twelve variations of one form: the declaration of the gospel (i.e., the third
form of the Word of God). This third form of the Word of God takes a variety of forms in the church's life and ministry, sometimes emphasizing one
form more than others at different places, times, and contexts.[94] Barth had
already offered a presentation of Christ's inexhaustible richness and multiform presence in *CD* IV/1, asserting that Christ does not present Himself in

92. Ibid.
93. Ibid., 608.
94. Ibid., 859–901.

one form, but in many, that Christ in his own life and activity in the world is not "uniform but multiform."[95]

Rather than a setting aside of the threefold Word of God or dismissing the threefold Word of God, a case can be made that Barth is intensifying the third form of the Word of God, allowing for the variety of ways Christ is active and at work in the Christian community's declaration of the gospel. The proclamation or declaration of the gospel, Barth clearly maintains, is not relegated solely to the preaching office of the church, but is the vocation of all Christians and can take a variety of forms. As we have seen, Barth qualifies the threefold Word of God, underscoring the centrality of the one Word of God Jesus Christ, who lives and manifests himself in the world without assistance. In another sense, Barth democratizes the threefold Word of God, maintaining the centrality of the declaration of the gospel, but describing this human witness and activity in many forms. Still, Christ speaks and acts in and through the church's declaration of the gospel, including the witness of Christians in his own self-witness, and the church lives as it hears and proclaims and declares the gospel, the reconciliation and redemption of all things in Jesus Christ. There is a sense then of sacramental status related to the declaration of the gospel, which shares in the secondary objectivity or the indirect identity of the one and primary sacrament, Jesus Christ.

As we have seen, Karl Barth does not do away with the threefold Word of God, but he certainly qualifies it, relativizes it, and democratizes it. Additional forms of human speech and action may become the context and location of God's Word and the presence of Jesus Christ in the here and now of Christian life together and witness.[96] Barth's own theology of prayer and preaching might serve as a prime illustration of this slight shift in emphasis but also as an illustration of Christ's multiform presence and activity in and with the life and witness of the Christian community.[97] In a short collection

95. Barth, *Church Dogmatics* IV/1:763.

96. See §72.4 "The Service of the Community," in Barth, *CD* IV/3:830–901. A detailed engagement with this section will not be possible here, but two themes from this section have already been used to make the case of Christ's multiform, inexhaustible presence in the life and witness of the Christian community. Christ's presence is both multiform, embracing the twelve types of speech and action in the church's ministry, but the declaration of the gospel is the uniform of all the forms, the uniting paradigm of these multi-forms of speech and action (*CD* IV/3:859–66).

97. Hunsinger, "The Mediator of Communion," 161, 173–77. Hunsinger writes, in an examination of the role of the Holy Spirit in Barth's theology and ecclesiology, that "in the power of the Spirit through proclamation of the gospel, Jesus Christ is present to believers and believers to him" (161). Later Hunsinger states that "through the proclamation of God's Word, the Spirit acts to make contemporary, to reveal, and to impart the reconciliation wrought and embodied by Jesus Christ" (173). Hunsinger

of theological reflections on prayer first published in the late 1940s, Barth writes that "it is prayer that puts us in rapport with God and permits us to collaborate with him."[98] In a commentary on Barth's remarks on prayer, Daniel Migliore claims that for Barth, prayer is the most basic and proper enactment of human freedom before God.[99] For Barth, prayer reveals complete human dependence upon God. Prayer also confidently trusts that God will speak and on the other side of human prayers, cooperate in human action to fulfil and complete God's work in the world. Prayer serves as a form of gospel declaration, the third form of the Word of God, as human beings in freedom call upon God and God joins, unites, cooperates, and witnesses within this human activity. Prayer for Barth can certainly be on an equal plane with proclamation. Prayer even becomes at times the quintessential mark of human correspondence and collaboration with God as well the common pattern of God's uniting and ongoing redemptive activity in the life of human beings and the world.

While there is some shift in Barth's theological content from the Word of God and the corresponding word of humanity to perhaps the call of God and the corresponding invocation of humanity or prayer of humanity, it is a change by addition not subtraction. The importance and centrality of the declaration of the gospel for the Christian community remains, even as it happens in concert with Christ's self-declaration in a multitude of forms. Barth does not deny that God speaks through human words. However, he wants to strongly caution the Christian community from making any presumptuous claims. "If Christ deigns to be present when we are speaking,"

---

describes the distinct yet equal coming of Christ in this middle form of *parousia* as no less real and complete than the coming of Christ in the Easter event and the Second Coming (176). The wholeness of Christ's being and activity is not uniform but multiform. Hunsinger does not mention the threefold Word of God, but within this multiform mode of Christ's self-manifestation, there is certainly room for a modified expression of the threefold Word of God in the time and form between Christ's resurrection and Christ's redemption. Barth's later theology (*CD* IV/3:859–60), however, comes to emphasize the declaration of the gospel (the vocation of all Christians) rather than the proclamation of the gospel (the specific clerical activity), which is not noted by Hunsinger. While proclamation could and should be an integral part of the declaration of the gospel, the event of the declaration of the gospel is, at least in Barth's later presentation, a more broad and multiform concept that could take different forms in a variety of ecclesial contexts rather than a more one-size-fits-all, uniform proclamation and a one-size-fits-all, uniform threefold Word of God.

98. Barth, *Prayer*, 20.

99. Migliore, "Freedom to Pray," in *Prayer* by Karl Barth, 96. Migliore does not mention proclamation, and while proclamation is not dismissed or rejected, prayer becomes the primary action and responsibility of the Christian more so than proclamation and declaration of the gospel.

Barth writes in a collection of remarks on preaching, "it is precisely because that action is God's not ours."[100] The Christian community or the proclaimer of the gospel cannot manufacture the miracle, assume the miracle, or "build on the miracle in advance."[101] The preacher and all those who declare the gospel are always in danger of becoming a "sort of Pope," arrogantly claiming and confusing one's own ideas, speech, or action with the Word of God.[102]

Yet Barth still insists in *CD* IV/3, much as he did in Göttingen and throughout the earlier volumes of the *CD,* that God's Word makes itself "perceptible even in the witness of humanly conditioned and limited words," that God "puts His word on the lips" of human beings, that by grace God continues to put his Word on human lips, sanctifying the profane and giving human beings the power and freedom to proclaim the gospel and bear witness to Jesus Christ.[103] Far from relegating proclamation to an insignificant afterthought in the life of the Christian community, Barth remains clear that "God wills to use human proclamation for the proclamation of His Word," though such declarations of the gospel may occur in a number of forms of ministry and service.[104] From the perspective of the Christian community, however, human beings can never and should never aspire to do anything more than point to, herald, and create respect for the self-witness of God, letting the Word of God speak for itself.[105] Barth holds these twin concepts together, stressing at times the qualitatively distinct chasm between the Word of God and human words, but also at other times stressing the ability of Jesus Christ to overcome the chasm and to place the Word of God on human lips and human hearts.

In remarks with an English-speaking seminar held in the late 1950s, Barth's conversation with students serve as a summary of Barth's attempt to uphold a modified threefold Word of God while enriching it and expanding it. First, Barth insists that one can never be absolutely certain that God will speak through human beings; one can only hope.[106] Second, Barth insists that there is no magic formula or place of ecclesial certainty, but in spite of the secularity and humanity of such activity and language, God speaks in and through such human words. Third, Barth does not relegate the Word of God solely to proclamation and the preaching office, but stresses the many

---

100. Barth, *Prayer and Preaching,* 69.

101. Ibid.

102. Ibid., 70.

103. Barth, *CD* IV/3:737.

104. Ibid., 738.

105. Ibid., 738–39.

106. Barth, *Karl Barth's Table Talk,* 26.

forms in which God addresses humanity through His Word. Humanity seeks to speak about God and to God in praying, preaching, and hearing the gospel, all of which are only attempts, but by means of these attempts, "God speaks!"[107] Fourth, no permanent fusion or confusion of the divine Word and human words takes place in the proclamation event. Ultimately preaching has no effect on the coming of the Word: "it may be that our preaching is bad; nevertheless, it is possible that through our ineffectively preached words and bad language, the Holy Spirit may speak."[108] What is impossible for human beings is made possible and real in and through Jesus Christ.[109]

Thus the case for the threefold Word of God remains strong even as Barth revises and enlarges it. In spite of Barth's revisions and qualifications, it remains the case that through the declaration of the gospel, the Word of God comes and speaks, manifesting itself in the Christian community in a multitude of forms. It also remains the case, however, that one can never stop and dissect the presence of the Word of God or empirically verify the moment of the gospel's becoming God's Word in the life together of the Christian community. To do so is to reverse the divine and human sovereignty and freedom, turning Jesus Christ into a human possession and the activity of the Holy Spirit into a predictable human phenomenon. Instead, the Christian and the Christian community prays for Christ to come, trusting in God's grace and mercy that has come many times before and that promises to come again; and the Christian and the Christian community live with humble confidence that the Word of God has, does, and will continually make use of human words and humanity's declaration of the gospel, for God's glory and as part of Christ's mission and redemption of the world.

Contemporary Scholarship and the Threefold Word of God

The changes and modifications made by Barth in regard to the threefold Word of God have not gone unnoticed by more recent scholars and theologians. In a number of theological and scholarly contexts, Barth's revision and modification to the threefold Word of God has been addressed, both directly and indirectly.[110] Eberhard Jüngel believes Barth's earlier presenta-

107. Ibid., 31.

108. Barth, *Karl Barth's Table Talk*, 38.

109. Ibid., 38–39.

110. Thus far this study has considered the relationship primarily between the Word of God, Jesus Christ, and the church's proclamation, the third form of the Word of God, from Barth's early theology and the early volumes of the *Church Dogmatics*

tion of the threefold Word of God (*CD* I/1 and I/2) and his presentation of church proclamation as a form of the Word of God are both problematized by Barth's later doctrine of baptism in *Church Dogmatics* IV/4.[111] In addition to the baptismal fragment, Jüngel also engages material from *CD* IV/3, and believes Barth corrects his earlier presentation of the threefold Word of

---

up to *CD* IV/3. The content of Barth's baptism fragment, or *CD* IV/4, is beyond the survey and scope of this study, as are the lecture fragments compiled posthumously in *The Christian Life*. Some of the conclusions, however, drawn by scholars in regard to the threefold Word of God, come as result of theological engagement with the content of *CD* IV/4 and *The Christian Life*. Neither the subject matter of the threefold Word of God nor proclamation is addressed directly in the content of these volumes; however, when engaging with the various explanations of Barth's shift in relation to the threefold Word of God, an attempt will be made to refer to the relevant content from *CD* IV/4 and *The Christian Life* when necessary.

111. Jüngel, "Karl Barths Lehre von Der Taufe," 274–75. See also, Barth, *Church Dogmatics* IV/4:32–34. In this section, Barth presents baptism with the Holy Spirit as something that precedes baptism with water and something that creates the possibility for baptism with water in the life of the Christian and Christian community. Barth maintains that baptism with the Holy Spirit and baptism with water are one event, but that the divine aspect and the human aspect of this one event are qualitatively distinct, without confusion, each with its own function, role, and identity. "Whatever one may have to say about the other aspect of the event, namely, about the human decision which acknowledges, confirms, attests and indicates it, and no matter how seriously one has to consider the profound inadequacy of this compared with the fulness of the divine change which primarily establishes the Christian life, even in face of the worst of human failure there can be no diminution of the fulness of that which is addressed to man in it. As the self-attestation of the living Jesus Christ in the work of the Holy Ghost it is, in distinction from even the fullest and strongest human attestation of Jesus Christ, His own self-impartation to man, His own almighty and perfect work on him and in him. To belittle what is done to man in Him is to belittle Him. The baptism of the Spirit is more than a reference and indication through image and symbol. It is more than an offer and opportunity" (*CD* IV/4:34). Barth writes that, "[I]n other words, the baptism of the Spirit certainly calls for the baptism with water which is requested of the community and administered by it, which is received by the man who accepts the Word of Jesus Christ. But it is not identical with this, nor is water baptism identical with it. Baptism with the Spirit does not take place in a man either with or through the fact that he receives water baptism. He also becomes a Christian in his human decision, in the fact that he requests and receives baptism with water. But he does not become a Christian through his human decision or his water baptism" (*CD* IV/4:32). Though Barth maintains the unity of the baptism of the Spirit and the baptism with water in one totality, one baptismal event, stressing that both elements "will be misunderstood if it is either separated from or, instead of being distinguished, mixed together or confused with the other" (CD IV/4:41). Baptism with the Holy Spirit does not exclude baptism with water, Barth contends, but Barth does not offer a conceptual or concrete description of how these distinct actions and movements are brought together and united in one event.

God in the third part of the doctrine of reconciliation. Because Jesus Christ is the sole occupant of the prophetic office, Jüngel argues, Jesus Christ himself proclaims his own story in the Word of God, and the congregation's service of witness to Jesus Christ "is now pointedly juxtaposed as a human act which truly witnesses to the witness of Jesus Christ."[112] Jüngel interprets Barth as making a clear separation between proclamation and Jesus Christ in which the sole action of proclamation is to point and signify as the reality of the Word of God is withdrawn.[113]

Arguing that there is clear separation between the living presence of Jesus Christ and all forms of human action in Barth's mature theology, Jüngel concludes that there is no reason why proclamation could not also be included in the ethics of the doctrine of reconciliation alongside baptism and the Lord's supper.[114] The being-in-action of God is a movement in history to which the Christian community and individual Christians seek to correspond, asymmetrically, in their own being-in-action. Jüngel believes Barth's earlier presentation of the threefold Word of God goes too far and fails to adequately acknowledge the absolute qualitative distinction in the life of God and the life of humanity, especially in regard to Scripture and proclamation.[115] Only in Jesus Christ do the qualitatively distinct divine and human realities and movements have a basis for unity.

Jüngel also believes that the ecclesiology presented in *CD* IV/4 is an earlier revision of *CD* I/1 and I/2, specifically in regard to the threefold Word of God and the sacraments, and that Barth reserves the concept of sacrament only for Christ.[116] What is not clear is whether Jüngel believes Barth ultimately rejects all forms of secondary objectivity in the life of the

---

112. My translation of: "Aber der 'Zeugendienst' der Gemeinde ist jetzt pointiert als menschliche Tat dem zu bezeugenden wahren Zeugen Jesus Christus gegenübergestellt." Jüngel, "Karl Barths Lehre von Der Taufe," 276.

113. Ibid.

114. Ibid., 276–77.

115. Ibid., 277.

116. Jüngel, *Karl Barth: A Theological Legacy*, 47. Jüngel does not mention this, but the theology of the church presented in *CD* IV/4, which explores the qualitative distinctiveness of the divine action and the human action while assuming their unity but never discussing its specifics, could also be contrasted not only with the theology of church and gospel presented in *CD* I/1 and I/2, but also with the material that has been explored in this chapter from *CD* IV/1, IV/2, and IV/3. How are tensions and possible contradictions, within the doctrine of reconciliation itself as far as the relationship between divine and human action in the gospel proclamation and in the life of the Christian community, to be reconciled? That is a more difficult question. I would argue that maintaining some sense of the threefold Word of God, even in an altered and qualified form, would help toward resolving those tensions and contradictions.

Christian community or any form of divine mediation in the life and activity of the church. While we have already explored Barth's own relativizing of the threefold Word of God, Jüngel's interpretation of Barth seems to go farther than Barth himself did, relegating all ecclesial activity to the ethical realm and reading the hyper distinctions between divinity and humanity set out in *CD* IV/4 backwards through the entire *Church Dogmatics*. Such a reading of Barth is certainly possible and indeed a helpful way to see the consistency of Barth's adherence to the qualitative distinction throughout his work. But such a reading also problematizes significant portions of Barth's work, not only in *CD* I/1 and I/2, but elsewhere within the doctrine of reconciliation, and such a reading makes the ontological distinction the chief interpretative framework for interpreting the entirety of the *Church Dogmatics*. Shifting proclamation into the ethics of reconciliation also risks collapsing Christian faith and life together into the ethical realm, which Jüngel believes is precisely what Barth achieves, noting that Barth desacramentalized the sacraments, but also proclamation, and all forms of ecclesial activity, so that Jesus Christ is the only sacrament.[117]

Is this Barth's intention? Is this the direction of Barth's most recent thought? Jüngel certainly believes this to be the case, but Jüngel's own writings on church proclamation, which perhaps sought to build on Barth's theological foundations, offer a more nuanced view. In his essay, "The Church as Sacrament," Jüngel continues to maintain the ontological distinction between divine and human action, yet he proposes a Reformation theology of church proclamation which seeks to offer precisely what he believes Barth's baptismal fragment does not, a description of the asymmetrical unity between Jesus Christ and the event of gospel proclamation. While the work of salvation and reconciliation are complete in Christ's death on the cross, Jüngel argues along the lines of Barth that church proclamation does not need to complete (how could it?) the divine work of reconciliation, it brings to speech what has taken place in Christ, and it also presents this event of cross

117. Jüngel, "Karl Barths Lehre von Der Taufe," 277. One of the reasons Jüngel commends Barth for doing this is due to Barth's insistence that the sacraments are not means of grace and thus unnecessary soteriological components of God's saving activity. Still, the threefold Word of God was never put forward by Barth as a soteriological necessity. Rather, the church's proclamation is a secondary form or an annexed component or the particular pattern of Christ's ongoing presence in the life of the Christian community and the life of the world. It is not clear whether Jüngel believes Barth maintained this role of secondary objectivity or indirect identity with Jesus Christ for Scripture and the church's gospel ministry. While Jüngel believes proclamation could easily have a place in *CD* IV/4 in the ethics of reconciliation, he does not account for Barth's revised presentation in *CD* IV/3 of the declaration of the gospel as the central form of the church's witness that happens in a plurality of actions.

and resurrection so that it can be received in faith in the present. Jüngel then adds that the proclamation of the gospel is a "representation of Christ's work" and also a presentation of Christ's work, and *"as such a manifestation of the presence of Christ in the power of the Holy Spirit"* (my emphasis).[118]

Qualifications aside, it seems Jüngel seeks to maintain some sense of the third form of the Word of God in the event of the gospel proclamation where "the action of the church generates on the human side that creative receptivity and passivity which allows God alone to be the benefactor and to work his work in us."[119] Jüngel believes the church paradoxically represents Christ, precisely in its renunciation of self-representation, as it points to Jesus Christ alone as the "declaration and impartation of God's gracious presence," and makes room for the self-representation of Jesus Christ to occur in its life together and its actions.[120] The question remains whether Jüngel's own presentation of the relationship between Word-event and Jesus Christ is in accord with Barth. Like Barth, Jüngel seeks to maintain the clear distinction between divine being-in-action and human being-in-action while at the same time offering a vision of the gospel proclamation, that not only responds to what has happened, but in its presentation of that work, trusts, hopes, and expects that Christ is present in the power of the Holy Spirit, and that somehow God speaks in this act of human speaking.[121]

While much of Jüngel's interpretation of Barth suggests that Barth ultimately rejects any identity and uniting of divine and human actions together (i.e., threefold Word of God), Jüngel's own thought offers a vision of how Christ is made manifest in the speech-event of the gospel, even as the distinction between divinity and humanity is maintained. Whether Barth would wholeheartedly endorse Jüngel's presentation *in toto* is hard to say, but such a presentation certainly seems in accord with Barth's insistence that the one Word of God "allows itself to be in some sense reflected and reproduced in the words" of human beings.[122] Barth may have sought to emphasize more greatly the ontological distinction in relation to the church's life and activity in *CD* IV/4, but not at the expense of Jesus Christ's proclivity to manifest himself in and through the words of the gospel declaration.

At the end of the baptismal fragment, Barth depicts cheap grace as the real enemy and resists Christian attempts to claim Christ's free grace as if it was one's due, as if one could handle Jesus Christ "with the same assurance

118. Jüngel, "The Church as Sacrament?" in *Theological Essays*, 204.

119. Ibid.

120. Ibid., 206.

121. Ibid., 205.

122. Barth, *CD* IV/3:111.

and familiarity as we do a bank account."[123] Grace, the coming presence of Jesus Christ, can never be counted upon in advance, but can only be prayed for and hoped for in radical dependence on Christ's return. Once again, Barth identifies prayer as the central and most faithful Christian activity. Hope in Jesus Christ and his coming is most faithfully embodied by the Christian community in the prayer of hope, "which is confident of being heard" (but not automatically), which does not seek to control or take or have, but hopes in Jesus Christ.[124] Barth rejects sacramental notions of means of grace (divine mediation) in favor of means of gratitude (human response), but might it be possible to refer to the gospel proclamation (and even baptism and the Lord's Supper) as sacraments of hope? These would be human words and actions, in and through which the Christian community prays that Christ will come and incorporate and use these actions in his own being-in-action in the life of the world. Such a theological framework then, could also make room for the concept of the threefold Word of God.

In addition to Eberhard Jüngel's extensive work related to Barth's theology, another German scholar, Harmut Genest, has offered an extensive study of Barth's theology of preaching, *Karl Barth und die Predigt*. In this study, Genest focuses extensively on Barth's own sermons, homiletical instruction, and the theological and practical implications of Barth's sermons and theology of proclamation. Genest follows a direction of thought similar to Jüngel, arguing that in *CD* IV/3 Barth marginalizes proclamation, first in relation to the Word of God, which is announced and proclaimed and made manifest wholly in Christ, and second as it is reduced from one form to a plurality of forms of witness.[125] Genest covers the already well trod ground of §69.2 "The Light of Life," and argues that Barth modifies and carries forward the teaching of the threefold Word of God only as the living Word of God, Jesus Christ, confronts the word of Scripture and the word of proclamation in the life of the Christian community.[126]

Genest believes Barth makes this shift and relativizes the church's preaching as a soteriological consequence of Barth's engagement with the existential theology of Rudolf Bultmann.[127] The sermon is not a saving event, but only a proclamation or announcement of the saving event of Christ's life, death, and resurrection that occurred in the event of election

---

123. Barth, *CD* IV/4:208–9.

124. Barth, *CD* IV/4:209.

125. Genest, *Karl Barth und die Predigt*, 218.

126. Ibid.

127. Ibid., 219.

and that was actualized in history two millennia ago.[128] As a result, the proclaimer is liberated to bear witness to the event of the cross and resurrection rather than being debilitated by the impossible task of producing a saving existential event in one's own ecclesial milieu.[129] Again, one is left to wonder whether Barth *ever* attached soteriological significance to the second and third forms of the threefold Word of God at any point in his dogmatics. Certainly Barth wanted to distinguish the once and for all nature of Christ's life, death, and resurrection, from the early and contemporary *kerygma* of the church (perhaps in contrast to Bultmann), but Genest gives scant attention to Barth's continuous insistence upon a reproduction and representation of the once and for all event occurring in the word-event of the Christian community through Christ's contemporaneous presence in the Spirit.

In addition to German scholars such as Jüngel and Genest, but in a similar vein, Bruce McCormack's emphasis on Barth's theological ontology or actualistic ontology has led him to highlight Barth's preservation of the ontological distinction between God and humanity in Jesus Christ as a central interpretative tool and characteristic of Barth's Christology and broader theology. Apart from an essay on Scripture and the threefold Word of God,[130] most of McCormack's work is focused on the doctrine of election and Barth's Christology. Along the lines of Jüngel, McCormack uses what he calls a "theological ontology" to serve as the chief hermeneutical framework for interpreting Barth's theology.[131] In terms of present realization and activity of the Word in the world and in the life of the Christian community, Barth's actualistic ontology emphasizes divine action and human correspondence as an ongoing movement and shared history, rather than a static completed action.[132] Jesus Christ's life, death, and resurrection, are a shared history, a uniting between a divine act of self-determination and "a historical human act of self-determination."[133] McCormack believes Barth focuses primarily on the two distinct and differentiated actions that occur in the one event. The two distinct movements can only be discussed in analogy and correspondence: the divine act of self-determination and

128. Ibid.

129. Ibid.

130. McCormack, "The Being of Holy Scripture Is in Becoming," 55–75.

131. McCormack, "Participation in God, Yes; Deification, No," in *Orthodox and Modern*, 246.

132. McCormack, "Grace and Being," in *Orthodox and Modern*, 199–200; "Karl Barth's Historicized Christology," in *Orthodox and Modern*, 231; and "Participation in God, Yes; Deification, No," in *Orthodox and Modern*, 243.

133. McCormack, "Grace and Being," in *Orthodox and Modern*, 200.

self-giving, and the corresponding human response of self-determination in faith and obedience. McCormack observes that the basis of continuity and union in the divine-human relationship never belong to the creature but to the Creator in relation to the creature.[134]

Applying this reading of Barth to the concepts and terms of the three-fold Word of God, it is clear that Scripture and proclamation cannot be presented by Barth as realities in themselves that contain the reality of God or that possess the possibility of becoming God's Word. Rather, it is the Word of God that becomes the word of humanity, but the word of humanity always remains the word of humanity. This is true in Jesus Christ, McCormack maintains, so how could it not apply all the more to the divine relation to all humanity?[135] The continuity and union between divinity and humanity happen as the Creator, the Word of God, acts on the creature and the creature's word. When Barth confesses, in *CD* IV/3 that he can no longer "establish, develop, and present" the threefold Word of God as revealed, written, and proclaimed, as he did in *CD* I/1 and I/2, might it be precisely this qualification that requires him to do so?[136] Barth has consistently maintained throughout the *Church Dogmatics* that God speaks and makes Godself manifest in and through human lips and hearts. Any elements in the threefold Word of God that might suggest that the creature's word and speech in itself could become the Word of God or contain the Word of God needed to be revised. Rather, it is the Word of God that becomes the word of humanity.[137] The word of humanity can only correspond to the Word of God.

McCormack's scholarship on Barth leads one to conclude that the Word of God can become the word of human beings, the Word of God can become the preached word, but the preached word cannot become the Word of God, but is, remains, and can become a witness to the Word of God, but nothing more. The question remains in Barth's later work, however, as to the extent and nature of the relationship, union, and identity of the Word of God with the church's witness and words. To put it another way, can the inseparability and unity of the Word of God with corresponding human speech-acts only be assumed by their correspondence, or is it possible to offer a theological and ecclesiological description of their unity and inseparability? McCormack does not answer this question directly, but by

---

134. Ibid., 200n36.

135. McCormack, "Participation in God, Yes; Deification, No," 247.

136. Barth, *CD* IV/3:114.

137. Barth, *CD* I/1:266. See McCormack, "Karl Barth's Historicized Christology," 233.

the direction of his own work and his interpretation of Barth's later work, McCormack is clear that the witness "is not the thing itself."[138]

While McCormack's work focuses primarily on election and Christology, the recent work of Paul Nimmo has engaged Barth's actualistic ontology from the perspective of Barth's ethics. Like McCormack, Nimmo stresses the ontological distinction throughout Barth's thought and offers an actualistic concept of witness in which neither the church's declaration of the gospel, the human words of Scripture, nor the humanity of Jesus Christ are divinized. Instead, what happens when the Spirit enables the Word of God to create in Scripture and the church's life a refection and witness is more accurately described by Nimmo as humanization, allowing humanity to flourish in freedom and obedience.[139] While Nimmo stresses the ontological distinction and the fully human witness and ethical dimension of the Christian community's action, he does leave room, secondarily, for God's glorification of the creature where God's glory shines in and through the witness and word of the creature.[140]

Again, it is not as if the Word of God, Jesus Christ, and the word of the creature, proclamation, operate in two separate and unrelated planes indefinitely. From the side of humanity, such a prospect is indeed reality, but from the other side, from Jesus Christ, there is no God without humanity. Therefore, from below, from humanity, all actions can only be ethical, human speech and actions that seek to correspond to the reality of Jesus Christ. From the other side, the side of God, however, there is no disjunction between the divine and human elements; thus the Word of God includes the word of the creature.[141] Still, Nimmo, in his reading of Barth, seems resis-

---

138. McCormack, "Karl Barth's Historicized Christology," 233.

139. Nimmo, *Being in Action*, 177.

140. Ibid., 184.

141. Ibid. Nimmo and McCormack, in contrast to other readers of Barth, emphasize or prioritize correspondence over union in terms of the divine-human relation in Jesus Christ and secondarily between God and humanity. Indeed, Barth's revision of the threefold Word of God in CD IV/3 further prioritizes the there and then of Christ's life, death, and resurrection, making it difficult to equate the presence of Jesus Christ in the present, in Scripture, and in church proclamation on equal terms with Christ's life and ministry in time. However, the problem is that these interpretations of Barth, while acknowledging the presence of Christ in the event of witness and correspondence, do not seek to describe or explore the relationship between the presence of Christ in the event and the corresponding human witness in the event. Because the ontological distinction and the ethical activity are prioritized, it is more difficult to sense how it is, other than a possibility that the declaration of the gospel might serve as the basis for the indirect presence and/or secondary objectivity of Jesus Christ in the present. It is not that such possibilities are ruled out, but neither are they explored.

tant to claim too quickly that the witness of humanity is incorporated and enclosed in the ongoing life and work of Jesus Christ in the world. While this may be true, Nimmo emphasizes that God also makes room for a truly free human response, not an automatic formula or a perfunctory word, but a genuine free human response.

Most of the scholarship engaged with thus far has either been culled from German theological scholarship on Barth or from recent interpretations of Barth's theological ontology. In addition to these areas of interpretation related to the threefold Word of God, a fair amount of Anglo-American scholarship has also engaged with the implications of Barth's revision to the teaching of the threefold Word of God. In some ways, Robert Jenson represents both the German and the Anglo-American appropriation of Barth's work. As early as the late 1950s, Barth himself acknowledged Robert Jenson's University of Heidelberg dissertation as a "penetrating analysis and interesting evaluation" of the *Church Dogmatics*.[142] Yet much of Jenson's engagement with Barth and Jenson's own scholarship has taken place in a North American context. In addition, while Jenson is certainly appreciative and indebted to Barth's theological work, his attempts to clarify Barth represent a more critical form of theological engagement than the scholarship that has been explored thus far.

In an essay on Barth's doctrine of reconciliation, specifically Barth's christological claims presented in *CD* IV/3, Jenson addresses Barth's revision to the teaching of the threefold Word of God and the problematic implications for the church's proclamation and witness in the present. Though Jenson does not take up the concept of theological ontology, Jenson explains Barth's revision to the threefold Word of God in relation to the ontic priority of Christ. Because the resurrection is *the* proclamation event, the universal proclamation of the gospel in which "all persons had the gospel preached to them when Christ rose," then the present time is simply an outworking of the ongoing self-revelation of Jesus Christ.[143] Jenson believes Barth maintains the ontic priority of Christ and the doctrine of justification, at the expense of the church, "allowing the church's witness only the status of a reflection of Christ's Word, not the status of Christ's Word itself."[144] As

---

142. Barth, *How I Changed My Mind*, 69.

143. Jenson, "Religious Pluralism, Christology, and Barth," 33.

144. Ibid., 36. While Jenson's reading of Barth is accurate here, Barth does not always clearly distinguish between the reflection of Christ's word and Christ's Word itself. One of the reasons for maintaining the spirit of the threefold Word of God if not the letter of it is precisely because Barth speaks at times of the church's witness and words as becoming more than reflections or mirrors but united with, incorporated in, and inseparable from Christ's own voice in the gospel event. Though Barth attempts

we have seen in Barth, the status of Christ's Word remains Christ's alone in his threefold *parousia*: resurrection, Pentecost, and second coming. For Jenson, the human utterance of the gospel, "'Jesus is risen,' is God speaking."[145] Barth might not reject such a claim, but would certainly want to qualify it. Barth does not deny God's speech causing and becoming present in the human declaration that "Jesus is risen," but such events can only be prayed for and hoped for, never presumed, empirically verified or identified directly.[146]

In contrast to Jenson, whose Lutheran instincts lead first to the unity of the human word with the speech and presence of God, Barth is not just revealing an unwillingness to pin down Jesus Christ in the contemporary life and witness of the Christian community only for the sake of an ontological principle, but also a conviction to orient the church's witness and Christian proclamation eschatologically rather than existentially.[147] For

---

to maintain some sense of the church's witness and proclamation as God speaking, Jenson does not believe he accomplishes it, and when push comes to shove, will favor making the ontological distinction between Jesus Christ and the church's witness (e.g., McCormack).

145. Ibid., 37.

146. Jenson, *Systematic Theology*, 271. Perhaps this is a case of where the accents are laid. While Barth can acknowledge the continuity and asymmetrical relationship between the Word of God and the word of humanity, his Reformed instincts lead him equally to emphasize the distinction in the speech event between the Word of God and act of gospel proclamation. Jenson, on the other hand, from a Lutheran perspective, is much more eager to present the union of the gospel declaration and the Word of God with less anxiety about maintaining their distinction and differentiation. In his own *Systematic Theology,* Jenson writes that Christ "is the Speech of the Father; as the Father's speech to us he is embodied in the church and therefore does not, whatever might have been, speak except by this body. When the church pronounces absolution, this is Christ's absolution. When two or three gather as the church to petition the Father, there he is, praying with and indeed through them." Barth does locate the presence and voice of Jesus Christ with the actions and speech of humanity in the gospel event, but Barth also does not want to confuse these two actions or mix them together into one. On the other hand, Jenson seeks to locate the presence and voice of Jesus Christ with the actions and speech of humanity in the one gospel event, but does not want to separate or divide these actions.

147. Jenson, "Recovery of the Word," in *America's Theologian: A Recommendation of Jonathan Edwards*, 187. In the concluding chapters of his survey of Jonathan Edwards's theology, Jenson offers a critique of Calvinism's separation (which includes Barth) of the Word of God from the human communication thereby always separating the transforming act of the Spirit ontologically from the word of the gospel. Does the gospel event only point to or does it in some sense contain the grace it signifies? Barth does not ignore these questions and seeks to offer the possibility of the grace of Jesus Christ assuming the gospel declaration, while at the same time maintaining the distinction between divinity and humanity in the event.

Barth, especially in his later work, the mark of Christ's presence is as much identified with the community's prayer and hope for Christ's return as it is with the actualization of the proclaimed word, and certainly more so than sacramental fulfilment or consummation. In addition to Robert Jenson, John Webster's own work has sought to engage with both German and English speaking interpretations of Barth's theology. Webster has particularly stressed the centrality of humanity in Barth's theology, and the moral and ethical responses to the being-in-action of God that accompany the life of faith. Webster has also explored in detail Barth's doctrine of reconciliation and has engaged with Barth's revision to the threefold Word of God.

Webster believes that Jesus' prophetic self-declaration and its triumphant manifestation in history "shifts the primary locus of activity away from the community of believers onto Jesus himself, who is the agent of his own realization."[148] Webster covers much of the same material that has been covered in §69 and §71 and concludes that the church's proclamation and prophecy "is in no sense a bearer of Jesus' own prophetic self-utterance, but an indicator of a perfect and communicative divine activity."[149] Webster properly conveys Barth's intent that the resurrection of Jesus Christ includes Christ's contemporary presence and activity in the church and world and that the church is not the contemporaneous agent through which a passive Christ is activated.[150] In an essay entitled, "The Visible Attests the Invisible," Webster puts forward his own theological interpretation of the Word of God, which seeks to go beyond Barth while remaining faithful to Barth's own christological commitments.

Webster's own theology of the Word of God could loosely be termed a two-fold Word of God. The living contemporaneous Jesus Christ presents himself and communicates himself "to the communion of saints in the canon of Holy Scripture," and Scripture becomes the "consecrated auxiliary through which the living One walks among the church and makes known his presence."[151] The church's own words of declaration and attestation respond in gratitude and witness to the presence of Christ, but do not seem to be "consecrated auxiliaries" in and through which Christ makes himself known.[152] Like Barth, the church's witness is subordinate and dependent upon Scripture's witness, but Webster seems to suggest a twofold form of the Word of God. Whereas Scripture can in some sense become the way Christ

148. Webster, "'Eloquent and Radiant,'" 142.

149. Ibid., 146.

150. Ibid., 149.

151. Webster, "The Visible Attests the Invisible," 109–10.

152. Ibid.

speaks presently, contemporary acts of witness and declarations of the gospel can only attest and point to Christ's presence, but are not the means or way Jesus Christ speaks and makes himself known and heard to the world through the words and life of the Christian community.[153] The life of the Christian community is restricted in a sense from speaking or offering the larger the world the Word of God.

In addition to framing the threefold Word of God within larger studies of central themes in Barth's theology, other scholars have engaged the theological implications of the threefold Word of God to get at broader philosophical and theological questions beyond Barth. In his philosophical engagement with the theological claim that God speaks, Nicholas Wolterstorff engages with Barth's doctrine of the threefold Word of God and questions whether or not divine action and revelatory activity are to be equated with divine speech.[154] While most of his study focuses on *CD* I/1 and I/2, Wolterstorff explores the theological claims Barth makes about the threefold Word of God. Wolterstorff questions whether Scripture and proclamation can become the speech of God, not so much out of actualistic ontological hesitations, but for more practical reasons. Wolterstorff does not dispute Barth's claim that God speaks in Jesus Christ and in the present, and God is able to present Himself and bring about a response in Scripture and in contemporary human speech and witness. However, Wolterstorff wonders, if this "'bringing about' is something different from speaking."[155] Wolterstorff acknowledges that the being and presence of Jesus Christ act on humanity through the witness of Scripture and proclamation but what Wolterstorff wants to know is whether such action can be called speaking, specifically, God's speaking.[156] Wolterstorff does not think so and presents his own modified version of the threefold Word of God: "God speaks in Jesus Christ, and only there; then on multiple occasions, God activates, ratifies, and fulfils in us what God says in Jesus Christ."[157] Wolterstorff's points are well taken and one wonders if the modifications to the threefold Word of God that Barth made in *CD* IV/3 might reflect them. Perhaps a more accurate description of Barth's revision could be described as the threefold presence of God, where Barth keeps more to the spirit than the letter of the threefold Word of God.

153. Ibid., 109–12.
154. Wolterstorff, *Divine Discourse*, 63–74.
155. Ibid., 73.
156. Ibid.
157. Ibid.

In his exploration of Barth's theology and its relationship to post-modernity, William Stacy Johnson addresses the charge that Barth's rejection of the sacraments in *CD* IV/4 signalled a decisive shift away from his earlier teaching.[158] Specifically, Johnson asks whether or not Barth's rejection of baptism and the Lord's Supper also means that there is no longer room for proclamation (I/1) or sign-bearing (I/2) or secondary objectivity (II/1) or indirect identity and sacramental continuity (II/1) to have a place in God's being in the world. While Johnson acknowledges that Barth never answers this question directly, he concludes that Barth eliminates sacramental continuity but retains symbolic continuity in which the Christian community attests, answers, and proclaims the good news of the gospel alongside Christ's declaration of Himself through the Holy Spirit.[159] Again, the relationship or possible unity between Christ's presentation and declaration of Himself and humanity's proclamation of Christ is not explored. "Whatever character we may attribute to these signs bearing witness to Jesus Christ," Johnson concludes, "they are not 'of the same rank'" as the humanity of Jesus Christ.[160] If the glory of Christ shines in and through these signs and if their witness is also enclosed by grace and exalted by the presence of Christ, might one also speak of a sacramental continuity, or a proximity to the grace of Christ's real presence that accompanies and embraces these signs and witnesses?

Gabriel Fackre asks this very question of Barth in his study of the doctrine of revelation.[161] Fackre identifies Barth's Reformed theological emphasis on the divine sovereignty and notes that Barth presents Christ's continuity of presence only in his ongoing *parousia* in the world. While the promise of Christ's address and presence is there for Scripture, the church, and the world, "the actual address happens only when and where He wills it to be so—by the act of divine freedom working through the internal testimony of the Holy Spirit."[162] Following Barth's presentation of this material in *CD* IV/3, Fackre believes Barth protects the divine freedom and the sovereignty of the risen Christ in the world by offering no assurance that "media—Bible, Church, World—are in their respective ways always and everywhere bearers of the knowledge of God."[163] Fackre goes on to argue that while Barth places the needed Reformed accents on the divine sovereignty in the once and for all event of Christ's life, death, and resurrection, rather than

158. Johnson, *The Mystery of God*, 168.

159. Ibid., 169.

160. Ibid. See also Karl Barth, *Church Dogmatics* IV/1:296.

161. Fackre, *The Doctrine of Revelation*, 138–40.

162. Ibid., 137.

163. Ibid., 138.

an unbroken and ongoing continuation in the *ecclesia*, Barth goes too far in "requiring the denial of the 'present possession of the glorious presence' of Jesus Christ."[164] Fackre believes Barth is persisting with the Reformed *non capax* ontological distinction between humanity and divinity, but he does not acknowledge Barth's more primary christological conviction, which is that the living Christ is able to proclaim and declare himself in the present time apart from and in spite of the church and even Scripture.[165] Fackre believes that because Barth places the emphasis on divine sovereignty and the lack of continuity between Word, Scripture, and church, Barth renders any conception of "divine haveability" of the Word in the church as problematic and a Reformed overreach.[166]

To be fair, Barth does not deny the uninterrupted presence of Christ to the Christian community, but places the accents on the divine sovereignty of the risen Christ rather than the fusion of Christ with a sacramental form, be it proclamation or baptism or the Lord's Supper. Perhaps more accurately, Fackre can accuse Barth of placing the greater emphasis on the supremacy of Christ and his ongoing self-proclamation and its differentiation from the church's proclamation, rather than depicting their unity and inseparability. Rather than treating those accents equally, Barth presents the sovereignty and centrality of the living Christ in the major key, and places the corresponding proclamation and life of the Christian community in the minor key or secondary role. Again, Barth does not reject or refute Christ's presence and solidarity with the church's proclamation, but places greater emphasis on Christ's resurrection, self-declaration of the gospel, and *parousia* before, above, beyond, and addition to Christ's presence in and with the church. But Fackre leads us to a very important question: just because Jesus Christ is larger, more complex, vast, mysterious and inexhaustible than perhaps the concept of the threefold Word of God allows, is it still possible that such a concept is an adequate pattern or paradigm for Christ's life in and with the Christian community? I believe it remains an important concept and way of describing the shape of the church's life and witness and that such a concept offers some uniformity to the plurality of the church's witness, a form of continuity within the discontinuity of the Spirit's movement.

In his study of Barth's soteriology, Donald Bloesch sees within Barth's theology two converging and opposing paradigms: "a theology of universal reconciliation in which the pre-existent and incarnate Christ seems to figure more prominently than the indwelling Christ and in which the triumph

164. Ibid., 139.
165. Ibid.
166. Ibid.

of grace effected in the past tends to overshadow the crisis of faith."[167] This convergence of paradigms plays out in Barth's emphasis of the ethical over and against the mystical, it plays out in Barth's concept of the communion of saints as "the cherished memory of the departed in the presence conscious-ness of the church," over and against a mystical communion between the departed and those on earth, and it plays out in Barth's conception of the church as a sign and witness over and against a unique means of grace and instrument of salvation.[168] Referring specifically to the threefold Word of God and its third form, Barth, according to Bloesch, affirms that the "Spirit is presumably at work as the pastor preaches, but he works not so much in and through the words of the sermon as with, over, and against these words."[169] Bloesch contrasts Barth's vision of proclamation and preaching as bearing witness to the one great miracle over and against proclamation and preaching that seeks to create a miracle.[170]

Bloesch assumes that these two converging paradigms cannot coexist or co-inhere as Barth shifts to a more christologically concentrated empha-sis. Still, one wonders, if Barth does not leave room for elements of both paradigms even if he places a greater emphasis on one over the other. For example with preaching, certainly it bears witness to the one great miracle, but there is also the hope and the prayer that Christ will be present in and with that proclamation creating smaller miracles of faith and obedience in correspondence to the one great miracle. Cannot the present memory of the departed in the contemporary life together of the Christian community also be a grace and communion with the church triumphant? Might the church's witness and signifying also be incorporated into Christ's presence, work, and ministry in, to, and for the sake of the world? Bloesch seems to believe Barth rejects one paradigm in favor of the other, but in my view Barth places emphasis on one paradigm or vision while also incorporating elements of the other one in his larger vision of the Christian community. There is a shift in emphasis but there is no abandonment.

Donald Dayton offers a similar reading of Barth, even recounting a conversation he had with Bloesch about some of the directions of Barth's later theology, particularly *CD* IV/3 and *CD* IV/4. In an unpublished pa-per given at a meeting of the Karl Barth Society, Dayton presents some of the implications of Barth's "radicalization of his 'Christological concentra-tion'" which suggested that Jesus Christ was the one true intersection of

167. Bloesch, *Jesus Is Victor!*, 16.

168. Ibid., 84–85, 87.

169. Ibid., 130.

170. Ibid.

divinity and humanity in human history.[171] Dayton points out that Bloesch was concerned about how Barth's elevation of Jesus Christ as the one true sacrament and the sole means of grace might undercut Scripture and the sacraments, and notes ironically that "that perhaps the most quoted text in the Dogmatics (in I/1 on the threefold word of God as the 'living word' [Christ], the 'written word' [Scripture], and the 'spoken word' [the sermon] may not be representative of the 'mature' Barth."[172] Dayton suggests, similarly to Jüngel, that Barth de-sacramentalizes the sacraments but also the church and the Christian life and takes "a radically 'restorationist' position in which he claims that the church had begun to go astray by the end of the first century."[173]

While Bloesch was concerned about this development in Barth's theology, Dayton sees it as a more positive one. What both assume however is that Barth has completely implemented one paradigm and rejected or eliminated the other, setting out henceforth and moving in a fixed direction. Perhaps proclamation and even the sacraments "merely" seek to correspond ethically to the one true sacrament Jesus Christ from a christological vantage point, but the emphasis may also shift again from a pneumatological perspective. In relation to Jesus Christ, perhaps humanity can only seek to correspond and conform, but is it possible that in the distinct action of the Holy Spirit, there is the eschatological goal of union and communion in Christ, but also a penultimate and provisional union between Christ and the Christian community through word and witness?[174] Though Barth was

171. Dayton, "Response to George Hunsinger, *The Eucharist and Ecumenism,*" 19.

172. Ibid.

173. Ibid., 20.

174. Hunsinger, "The Mediator of Communion," 161n13. In this essay Hunsinger writes that in *CD* IV (Christology), Barth preferred to speak primarily in terms of Christ (the agent) making himself present through the Spirit, whereas one would expect if Barth had gotten to a doctrine of redemption, the agential language for the Spirit, where the Spirit makes Christ present, would figure more prominently. Barth, *CD* IV/3:761. When Barth use agential language of the Spirit in *CD* IV/3, he does speak of the Spirit uniting ontologically distinct and qualitatively differentiated elements: "The work of the Holy Spirit, however, is to bring and to hold together that which is different and therefore, as it would seem, necessarily and irresistibly disruptive in the relationship of Jesus Christ to His community, namely, the divine working, being and action on the one side and the human on the other, the creative freedom and act on the one side and the creaturely on the other, the eternal reality and possibility on the one side and the temporal on the other. His work is to bring and to hold them together, not to identify, intermingle nor confound them, not to change the one into the other nor to merge the one into the other, but to co-ordinate them, to make them parallel, to bring them into harmony and therefore to bind them into a true unity."

never able to complete a systematic pneumatology, perhaps in such a context, the three forms of the Word of God could be described in greater unity.

In Barth's revision of the teaching of the threefold Word of God, proclamation and the community of proclamation are unburdened from the task of making Christ present or speaking the Word of God, but the question remains about the relationship between the Word and the words and the particular role of the Holy Spirit in relation to the threefold Word of God. Barth's early presentation of the threefold Word of God did not seek to assert that human proclamation sought to make Christ present; in *CD* I/1 and I/2, it is very much Christ who proclaims himself in and through Scripture and proclamation. The question is to what extent the divine action, Christ's sufficient self-declaration, includes and manifests itself in creaturely speech and Christian proclamation. Does Christ's self-declaration include and manifest itself through the Christian community's flawed declarations of the gospel? Is there a union, or to put it more actualistically, a uniting, a becoming of the *totus Christus*, a joining together of the voice and presence of Jesus Christ with the speech and life together of the Christian community?[175] As the Christian community exists and lives between election and eschaton, might the present reality of Jesus Christ come and locate itself in "the speaking from one to another of the concrete tale of hope," and might Christ be called upon and trusted to inhabit and make use of such human utterances and witnesses?[176] The threefold Word of God offers such a vision and vision of Christian community, seeking to describe Christ's way of life in and through the Christian community in the time between the times.

All of the commentators agree that Barth's christological concentration underscores the distinction and differentiation between Jesus Christ, Scripture and proclamation. Some think this movement leads to a greater emphasis on the separation of agency and rejection of any sense of continuity

175. Barth, *CD* IV/3:760–61. See also McDowell, *Hope in Barth's Eschatology*, 232–34. In his study of Barth's the concept of hope in Barth's eschatology, McDowell notes that Barth uses the concept of witness in *CD* IV/3, where God chooses people to be his witnesses, "through whom he freely works and speaks [see, e.g., *CD* IV/3:607–10]." McDowell notes that this aspect of witness is dropped and replaced in favor of correspondence, which depicts human agency responding to and following after prior divine action. The question remains how this deeper distinction between divine and human activity presented in *CD* IV/4 relates to other sections in *CD* IV that speak of God's activity including and working in and through human activity. My own view is that Barth can talk about mediation and union and God working in and through human activity when divine action is at the center of his dogmatic focus (*CD* IV/1, IV/2, IV/3), but when human agency and activity are on center-stage (*CD* IV/4), correspondence, obedient following after, and responsive gratitude become primary.

176. Jenson, *God After God*, 193.

of divine presence or secondary objectivity or indirect identity in Scripture, proclamation, and the church's life. Eberhard Jüngel and Donald Dayton suggest as much, as does John Yocum, who thinks this revision problematizes much of Barth's earlier work. Yocum begins with Barth's sacramental revision and believes that this revision leads to contradictions elsewhere: "if the sacraments are denied to be instances of divine-human communion of action and a reliable means of grace, on a principle of the disjunction of the divine and human acts, as Barth often asserts in *Church Dogmatics* IV/4, the consequences for the integrity of the *Church Dogmatics* are profound."[177] Like Bloesch, Yocum believes this principle of disjunction calls into question the reliability and authority of the written form of the Word of God as well as the proclamation of the gospel.[178] Yocum suggests that whole of the church's life together and activity is swallowed up into the ethical realm.

Paul Nimmo suggests, a bit more prudently, that at the very least Barth's actualistic ontology should be prioritized over readings of Barth that present divine-human relation and *unio cum Christo* as continuous union and communion in Scripture, proclamation, sacraments, and church.[179] There is no question where Barth places the greater emphasis in these later volumes of the doctrine of reconciliation, the question is whether this means that Barth rejects the other paradigm or whether he simply moves it to the background in light of the centrality of Jesus Christ and Barth's singular emphasis of the once and for all nature of Christ's person and work. Again, in my view, I wonder if this this separation between human agency and divine agency continues to be as uniform and stark from a pneumatological vantage point.

Last but not least, Barth himself leaves us a few bits of his own engagement with the threefold Word of God late in his life. Eberhard Busch, in his biography of Barth, offers a summary of Barth's last seminar in his last semester of teaching in the spring of 1962, lectures which would become published as *Evangelical Theology*. In what Barth referred to as his "swan song," rather than plodding on with the *CD,* Barth sought to give a summary account of "what I had looked for, learnt, and represented from among all the ways and detours I had so far followed in the field of evangelical theology during my five years as a student, twelve as a pastor, and forty as a professor."[180] In these lectures Barth distinguished "The Word" on the one hand from its witnesses, Scripture (primary witness) and the

---

177. Yocum, *Ecclesial Mediation in Karl Barth*, 30.

178. Ibid., 30.

179. Nimmo, *Being in Action*, 179.

180. Busch, *Karl Barth: His Life from Letters*, 455.

secondary witnesses, the community the Word confronts, creates, and gathers.[181] Eberhard Busch describes this revision as a "new feature" that distinguished between the Word of God and the word of the Bible and the church as "the mere *testimony*—primary and secondary—to the word of God." This distinction, Busch believes, "was evidently a correction to his earlier doctrine of the threefold form of the Word of God (in revelation, Bible and preaching)."[182]

In addition, one other insight from Barth himself reveals that Barth was at least aware of the tension and divergence between his presentation of the threefold Word of God and the theological implications of his baptism fragment and later work. In a letter to a Professor Heinrich Stirnimann, a Dominican in Freiburg, Switzerland, who reviewed Barth's baptism fragment and offered a critique in the *Freiburger Zeitschrift*, Barth refers Professor Stirnimann to an article published by a Dutch theologian, J.M. Hasselaar, that questions whether Barth's doctrine of baptism calls into question the doctrine of the threefold Word of God (I/1, §4) and Barth's ecclesiological section in CD IV/2, §67.[183] At the end of his letter to Stirnimann, Barth chides him for missing an argument against his doctrine of baptism which comes from within the *Church Dogmatics* itself, but Barth does not seek to resolve this tension nor correct either doctrine with the other. Perhaps Barth's unwillingness to offer a resolution speaks volumes in and of itself.

From Threefold Word to Threefold Presence

While Barth revised the concept of the threefold Word of God in *CD* IV/3, it is important to stress that Barth did not abolish the threefold Word of God nor reject Scripture and proclamation as primary contexts and patterns of Christ's contemporaneous presence in the life of the world. The threefold Word of God does not become an empty concept nor is it simply relinquished; it is modified, but not rejected and allowed to fade away into an earlier period of Barth's thought. Instead, the threefold Word of God becomes qualified, de-formulized, democratized, and made pluriform so as to better reflect the contemporaneous presence of Jesus Christ in the world and in the particular life and witness of the Christian community. To reject the threefold Word of God completely is not just an inaccurate reading of

---

181. Barth, *Evangelical Theology*, 37–38.

182. Busch, *Karl Barth: His Life from Letters*, 455.

183. Barth, "An Prof. Dr. Heinrich Stirnimann O. P., Freiburg (Schweiz), 1968." See also Barth, *Letters, 1961–1968*, 300. I am indebted to Dr. Paul Nimmo for directing me to this piece of correspondence.

Barth's re-presentation of the material in *CD* IV/3, but also risks misinterpreting Barth's theology of Scripture and the church.

Surveying the broad theological themes and content of *CD* IV/3 and *CD* IV/4, Barth places an emphasis on a number of themes and concepts. There is a more concentrated eschatological emphasis on the not-yet over and against the already of Christ's kingdom; there is a prioritization of the discontinuity between Christ and the Christian community over and against any continuity between Christ and the Christian community. As far as the sacraments and the church's interior life and worship are addressed, Barth places a greater emphasis on the ethical dimensions of the church's life and witness, over and against the mystical or sacramental basis for divine and human communion. In a similar vein, Barth stresses the discontinuity between church's life and the divine activity, and prioritizes this distinction over any continuity of divine presence. As others have observed, correspondence becomes more central, while other concepts like union, fellowship, and divine and human unity are subdued.[184] The sign of the Spirit is not so much possession of Christ, as possession of Christ's promise of presence in the form of human hope and prayer. As a result, while the contemporary presence of Jesus Christ remains at the center of the church's life, the center of the Christian community's life shifts from a focus on the means of grace itself (i.e., Scripture, proclamation, sacraments), to a focus on the human prayer and hope that such instruments may by God's grace become a means of God's ongoing presence, activity, and speech. As Barth places the emphasis on one particular theological concept or theme, others seem to be marginalized. One must discern, however, whether Barth is narrowing his theological focus upon one correct account or whether he is offering a multi-form and multi-layered account of divine action, human action, and their convergence and divergence in the life of Christian community, using a variety of concepts, sometimes in contradictory ways, to offer the fullest and richest depiction of the divine life, human life, and the fruitful possibilities for Christian life.

What happens to the threefold Word of God? Rather than seeing it dismissed in favor of new theological concepts or more strict theological depictions of divine and human activity, Barth presents the activity of God through a number of converging paradigms. Barth prioritizes one paradigm over another, i.e., ontological distinction and correspondence, but he still weaves in the other paradigms, perhaps playing them in a minor key. In this way,

---

184. McCormack, "Karl Barth's Historicized Christology," in *Orthodox and Modern*, 229–33; McDowell, *Hope in Barth's Eschatology*, 233; Yocum, *Ecclesial Mediation in Karl Barth*, 170–75.

the unity of the threefold Word of God is not simply rejected and rendered incompatible with the other parts of Barth's theological account. Rather, as Christ's life becomes the justification, sanctification, and vocation of humanity in the doctrine of reconciliation, concepts of divine and human conjunction, union, and fellowship recede into the background but are not left behind; they continue to be played in the minor key rather than the major key.

From the perspective of the doctrine of redemption, where the divine Spirit meets and unites with the human spirit, might the paradigms switch? Might the life of the Spirit and God's promise to be wherever two or three are gathered emphasize themes of union and continuity?[185] Might God's promise to be with the Christian community until the end of the age strike a different chord?[186] In the redemption of the world, the contemporaneous power of the Holy Spirit, the contemporaneous presence of Jesus Christ, is manifest in words of the gospel proclamation and the ongoing life of the Christian community. While humanity can only seek to follow after and correspond to Jesus Christ, it is also possible, within the trajectory of Barth's thought, to talk about the Holy Spirit as the source of union with Christ, and Christ's uniting with those who hear, are transformed by, and proclaim his gospel in and through the Christian community. In such a context it is also possible to discuss the unity of the three forms of the one Word of God, of the contemporary presence of Jesus Christ in the gospel event, in and with the Christian community. Such a depiction of the threefold Word of God does not claim too much for Scripture and for Christian proclamation, but seeks to maintain their distinction from the one Word of God while also seeking to illustrate their unity with Jesus Christ in the gospel event and in the Christian community's witness and life together.

It is certainly possible that Barth was indeed embarking in *CD* IV/4 on a more radical ecclesiology and a more radical movement away from any theological attempts to locate divine identity and presence in the life and particular actions of the Christian community.[187] Barth's revision of the threefold Word of God, however, is not evidence of such a move. Rather it reveals a limitation and qualification that Barth sought to emphasize in the role of Scripture and the church's life within Christ's on-going redemption of the world. Christ's universal proclamation of the gospel in the resurrection may have freed ongoing human proclamations of the gospel from the burden

185. Matt 18:20.

186. Matt 28:20.

187. Mangina, *Karl Barth on the Christian Life*, 196n53. Mangina is but one example of someone who concludes that by the time *CD* IV/4 written, Barth had abandoned the "quasi-sacramental conception" of Scripture and church proclamation as forms of the Word of God.

of making Christ present. Barth's doctrine of reconciliation certainly stresses that Christ does not need the flawed and sinful proclaimer to present Christ to others. Nevertheless the ways and works of the Holy Spirit seem to suggest that the risen Christ chooses to become present in and through just such acts and utterances of gospel proclamation. This is why maintaining the threefold Word of God is not only faithful to Barth's doctrine of reconciliation and redemption, but also Barth's theology of the church.

Summary

This chapter has examined Karl Barth's revision to the threefold Word of God in *Church Dogmatics* IV/3. Through a detailed engagement with Barth's own writings and a thorough attempt to address the views of Barth's constructive and more critical commentators, this chapter argues that while there was a shift in Barth's position in regard to the threefold Word of God, the concept was accommodated and reframed rather than abandoned altogether. In addition, the concept of the threefold Word of God offers Barth's theological vision of the church a sense of the coherence between Jesus Christ and His body, the Christian community, alongside Barth's attempts to distinguish and set apart the contemporary presence of Jesus Christ from the witness of Scripture and the living community of witnesses. Why such a role for the threefold Word of God continues to matter for Barth's theology of the church and for contemporary ecclesiology today will be explored more deeply in the chapter to come.

5
The Threefold Word of God Today: Why It Matters

... the man Jesus is a beginning of which there are continuations.

—Karl Barth, *CD* II/1:54

We believe the Church as the place where the crown of humanity, namely, man's fellow-humanity, may become visible in Christocratic brotherhood. Moreover, we believe it as the place where God's glory wills to dwell upon earth, that is, where humanity—the humanity of God—wills to assume tangible form in time and here upon earth.

—Karl Barth, *The Humanity of God*, 65

In the work of the Holy Spirit it takes place that Jesus Christ is present and received in the life of His community of this or that century, land or place; that He issues recognisable commands and with some degree of perfection or imperfection is also obeyed; that He himself actively precedes this people; that in its action or refraining from action there is more or less genuine and clear reflection, illustration and attestation of His action, more or less faithful discipleship in the life of this people, and therefore a fulfilment of its commission.

—Karl Barth, *CD* IV/3:761

THUS FAR THE ORIGINS OF THE THREEFOLD WORD OF GOD IN KARL BARTH'S dogmatic work and the place and importance of that teaching for his theology have been examined and assessed. In addition, the relationship between the Word of God and the church's proclamation and witness in the world have been examined and explored, especially the implications of the threefold Word of God for Barth's ecclesiology and vision of the church. Finally, Barth's later revision to the concept of the threefold Word of God in his doctrine of reconciliation has been explained and a case made for the persistence of the threefold Word of God in the trajectory of Barth's thought and ecclesiology. Our remaining questions, while continuing to engage with Barth's past work, also seek to engage present and future concerns in relation to the threefold Word of God. [1]

Therefore, while this chapter will continue to stress the significant place of the threefold Word of God in relation to Karl Barth's theology of the church and the distinctive importance of the gospel declaration (third form), this chapter will build upon Barth's vision of the church in which the content of the church's life is not a set of practices, nor is it a static divine and human union actualized in the sacraments or any particular act of worship, but the presence of the Word of God, Jesus Christ, in the gospel proclamation, and in the life together and witness made possible as the frequency of this event occurs in the life of the Christian community. Karl Barth's concept of the threefold Word of God is crucial to Barth's theology of the church. In addition to the particularities of the threefold Word of God, this chapter seeks to draw Barth's theological commentators and contemporary ecclesiologists into closer engagement by discussing Barth's ecclesiology in light of its shortcomings and deficiencies, but also by using Barth's own theology of the church as a corrective to the trajectory of much contemporary ecclesiology. Ultimately, this chapter argues that the threefold Word of God is crucial to Karl Barth's ecclesiology and contemporary Reformed and ecumenical ecclesiological expressions.

Does Barth's ecclesiology preserve the important qualitative distinction between humanity and divinity, but offer a robust theology of the church that seeks to offer more than theological protection of this distinction? Does Barth's theology of the church capture the momentary event of divine-human joining together that occur in the life and witness of the Christian community? While certainly taking into account modern criticisms of Barth's ecclesiology, this chapter will affirm Barth's Reformed

---

1. Guder, "Gathering, Upbuilding, Sending: Barth's Formation of the Missional Community," 1. "The fact that Barth renamed his project '*Church Dogmatics*' needs to be pondered."

emphasis in maintaining the distinction between divinity and humanity in the concept of the church, while also providing some illustrations from the *Church Dogmatics* that offer some account of divine and human unity in the life of the Christian community, in the gospel declaration, in the particular ecclesial role of the Holy Spirit, and in the existence and reality of the *totus Christus*. This chapter concludes with a reflection on the threefold Word of God and the church today, seeking to move forward with Karl Barth, but suggesting some ways of moving beyond his teaching or at least offering concrete parables of the threefold Word in practice. While certainly sympathetic to Barth's concerns, these parables of the threefold Word of God in practice seek to offer a fragmentary but concrete vision of the church. They seek to offer some colorful illustrations of a theology of Christian community in which divine activity and human activity operate in careful distinction, and a Christian community where the divine activity seeks to be joined together with human words, actions, witness, and fellowship in the life of the Christian community, for the sake of the world.

The Threefold Word of God and the Church

One of the signs of ecclesial crisis in the late twentieth and early twenty-first centuries is a renewed interest in the field of ecclesiology. If Christendom is indeed crumbling in the West, then the existence and identity of the church cannot simply be assumed as a facet and function of the larger Christendom culture, nor can it be assumed in dogmatic endeavors. Ironically, declining and aging church membership, rising secularism, and the impending collapse of Christendom, may have led simultaneously to a renewed interest in the interior life and identity of the church, its place and role in the life and activity of God, and its identifiable markers and concrete features in its worldly existence. In many ways, the quest for ecclesiology has also led to renewed interest in and engagement with Barth's own theology of the church.[2] This engagement has occurred by constructive analysis of Barth's ecclesiology as a positive conversation partner, but this engagement has also led many to challenge and critique Barth's theology of the church as part of the problem, concluding

---

2. Obviously I am painting with a broad brush here, but I am thinking loosely of theologians like Stanley Hauerwas, Reinhard Hütter, Robert Jenson, Joseph Mangina, and Nicholas Healy, as well as contemporary theological movements such as Radical Orthodoxy and Emergent Christianity. In engagement and reaction to Barth's own ecclesiology, these new ecclesiologies seek to conduct theological reflection and locate the divine life in the concrete life of the Christian community. See Hawksley, "The freedom of the Spirit: the pneumatological point of Barth's ecclesiological minimalism," 180.

Barth's ecclesiology to be an incomplete and unsuccessful presentation of the church for the contemporary context and age.[3]

While Barth's own theology of the church is often interpreted as lacking in concreteness, visibility, and mediatorial function, a retrieval of and a renewed development of the threefold Word of God as central to Barth's theology of the church would go a long way to assuage such criticisms by offering an ecclesial framework that presents the dynamic and local movement of Christ in the life of the Christian community, while also maintaining the actualistic nature of the divine life in the church's life. In addition, the threefold Word of God applied to the life and activity of the church offers one of the few ecclesial examples from within Barth's own theological *corpus* as to how the distinct activity of God and humanity can at times be depicted together in their differentiated unity and shared life together.[4] Maintaining and applying the threefold Word of God to the life of the Christian community offers the concrete possibility for an account of the church in which the church becomes the means of God's self-proclamation, the sphere of God's presence and activity, and a community whose life together bears the marks of Christ's presence.

Karl Barth's theology of the church is often criticized by modern theological interpreters for its "lack of concreteness," "ecclesial Docetism," and "aversion to ecclesial mediation."[5] While these descriptions may fairly

3. See in particular the publication of Hauerwas's Gifford Lectures, *With the Grain of the Universe*; Hütter, *Suffering Divine Things*; Mangina, *Karl Barth on the Christian Life*; Healy, "The Logic of Karl Barth's Ecclesiology," 253–70; Mangina, "Bearing the Marks of Jesus," 269–305. Healy also wrote a very important revision and rejoinder to his first essay in response to Hauerwas's criticisms of Barth's ecclesiology in *With the Grain of the Universe*. See Healy, "Karl Barth's ecclesiology reconsidered," 287–99. Healy's second article lays out the strengths and aspects of Barth's ecclesiology worth carrying forward into late modernity. In addition Bender offers a detailed exploration of the content and foundations of Barth's ecclesiology and seeks to engage some of Barth's contemporary critics in this area of his theological corpus. See Bender, *Karl Barth's Christological Ecclesiology*, 270–87.

4. Bender, *Karl Barth's Christological Ecclesiology*, 281. Bender argues that Barth is very careful to protect and clarify the distinction between the activity of God and the activity of the church, but is weak in his attempts to "articulate how they are united and conjoined." He continues: "[W]hat is largely missing is a satisfactory account of how the activity of the church is not only a response to the Gospel, but a means taken up by God for its proclamation and a community shaped by the Gospel itself." Maintaining the concept and a proper application of the threefold Word of God to the life of the Christian community, offers some coherence and concrete direction for the life of the Christian community without rendering God static and seeking to manipulate and control the divine life and activity.

5. See for example Hauerwas, *With the Grain of the Universe*, 191–93; Hütter,

or unfairly characterize Barth's concept of the church, it is my contention that their frustrations and criticisms are all symptoms of a lone root cause grounded in Barth's Reformed commitment to protect, delineate, and distinguish the presence of Christ on the one hand and the life and activity of the Christian community on the other. It is this distinction and qualification, this refusal to identify the presence of the risen Christ directly with the proclamation of his gospel or any one feature of the community shaped by Christ's life, it is this *extra Calvinistic* attempt to always carefully distinguish the reality of Jesus Christ from contemporary ecclesial activities and the visible life together of the Christian community, that causes modern theological interpreters to have problems with Karl Barth's theology of the church.[6]

Since, according to Barth, the essence of the church is found and only made manifest in the living reality of Jesus Christ, since in no way does the church make Christ present through any action of its own, since in no way is the church complete and self-evidently fully itself in its visible form alone, Barth's interpreters and critics are led to wonder whether the true church ever touches down or becomes a visible reality in Barth's understanding of the day to day life of Christian community. Barth's commentators and critics are led to wonder whether the presence of Christ can ever be said to be identical in and with the contextual particularities of the church's proclamation of the gospel and the Christian community's life together. They question Barth as to whether Christ's present reality ever really manifests itself in the celebration of the gospel in sacrament or with any of the church's activities and ethical witness in the world.

For many contemporary ecclesiologists, Barth's distrust of ecclesial attempts to manipulate grace and direct the movement of the Holy Spirit, leads Barth to produce a defective and incomplete theology of the Christian community. The church has no mediatory function in the economy of salvation and the church is not a necessary prerequisite for Christ's presence, ministry, and transformation of the present world until the eschaton. As a result, to those interested in identifying specific activities, sacramental acts, or ecclesial marks that establish the church's identity and locate the divine presence, Barth's theology of the church, derivative as it is from Christology and pneumatology, has proven to be an unhelpful option and resource for modern ecclesiology. For other reasons, Barth's theology of the church has not proven to be a central topic of study for contemporary Barth scholars and commentators. Barth's theological innovations and relevance are seen to be

---

Suffering Divine Things, 109–10; Yocum, *Ecclesial Mediation in Karl Barth*, 131–34; Webster, *Barth's Ethics of Reconciliation*, 171–72.

6. Bender, *Karl Barth's Christological Ecclesiology*, 272–76.

concentrated in his doctrine of God, election, and Christology,[7] and there is also a renewed interest in Barth's theological ethics and moral ontology.[8] While the church is the pivot point, the community, the sphere of life where theology and ethics overlap, engage, and interact, many scholars of Barth's theology do not see Barth's theological presentation of the church as the place where Barth is at his most profound, innovative, or relevant. Barth's presentation of the church's theological identity and the church's role in his larger theological project do not seem to be of great concern to contemporary ecclesiologists, and Barth's theology of the church is rarely of central importance to those interested in the ongoing relevance of Barth's theology.[9]

Word Makes Church

In the third part of the doctrine of reconciliation (*CD* IV/3, §72.1 *The People of God in World-Occurrence*), Karl Barth presents his theology of Christian community as a people in the world who are gathered and oriented as a community in response to the present reality of Jesus Christ. For Barth,

7. McCormack, *Orthodox and Modern*, 109–277. McCormack believes Barth is his most revolutionary in his doctrine of election, his Christology, and what McCormack refers to as his comprehensive theological ontology.

8. See most recently, Nimmo, *Being in Action*; Migliore, *Commanding Grace*. In addition, studies by Webster and Biggar helped initiate a rediscovery and re-engagement with Barth's theological ethics. See Biggar, *The Hastening that Waits*; and Webster, *Barth's Ethics of Reconciliation*.

9. Perhaps because of Barth's own misgivings of misplaced theological weight being placed on the role of the church between resurrection and return, i.e., "Atlas bearing the burdens of the world on its shoulders," he believed that the church could only be an indirect subject matter for theological inquiry, never a direct one. See Barth, *CD* IV/3:115. The significance and centrality of the church in Barth's theology is not completely overlooked by scholarship related to the *Church Dogmatics* and Barth's larger theological corpus. See Bender, *Karl Barth's Christological Ecclesiology*; Flett, *The Witness of God*; Webster, "'Assured and Patient and Cheerful Expectation,'" in *Barth's Moral Ontology*, 77–97; Webster, "'Eloquent and Radiant,'" 125–50; Guder, "Gathering, Upbuilding, Sending," 1–11; Healy, "Karl Barth's Ecclesiology Reconsidered," 187–299; and most recently Holmes, "The Church and the Presence of Christ," 268–80. In addition, Hunsinger and Nimmo, in different ways, seek to relate Barth's theology and ethics to reality of the Christian community. See Nimmo, *Being in Action*, 136–85; and Hunsinger, "Barth, Barmen, and the Confessing Church Today," in *Disruptive Grace*, 60–88; Hunsinger, "Where the Battle Rages," in *Disruptive Grace*, 89–113; and Hunsinger, "The Mediator of Communion," 148–85. In spite of these efforts to relate Barth and the church in the work of modern ecclesiology among modern Barth scholars and commentators, more work needs to be done to illustrate the distinct features of Barth's theology of the church and its ongoing relevance to contemporary ecclesiological expressions and constructive attempts related to Reformed and ecumenical ecclesiology.

the church is a community that seeks to live and act in the world in correspondence to the living presence of Jesus Christ. According to Barth, the Holy Spirit is the present power of Jesus Christ that evokes a "counterpart here and now in human faith and love and hope and knowledge, its echo in human confession at this specific time and place; that its creative freedom finds an equivalent in real creaturely freedom."[10] God's accomplished act of reconciliation in Jesus Christ causes and evokes a creaturely echo in creaturely contexts all over the world.

Though the qualitative distinction between God and humanity remains, Christ's presence also has a uniting function in the life of the Christian community.[11] The risen Christ's presence and universal reality shines objectively throughout all the earth, but Barth also speaks of the church and Christian community as a second dimension of the being of Jesus Christ, where Jesus Christ is also present as the community's present life—its content and essence.[12] Indeed, according to Barth, the basis and secret of the church's existence is the "unity of its being with that of Jesus Christ, the existence of Jesus Christ in His singularity but also His totality."[13] That is what makes the church the church: the risen Christ's unfolding life taking up space in the Christian community, uniting with and continually becoming present in the community's particular witness and attestation to Christ.

The contemporaneous presence of Jesus Christ, the power and work of the Holy Spirit in space and time and history, is at once distinct from the concrete life of the Christian community, but encloses, includes, and is made manifest in the Christian community.[14] Barth believes the Holy Spirit is Christ's presence in contemporary space and time, he believes the Holy Spirit evokes acts of faith and obedience through its life in and with the Christian community, and he believes that the Holy Spirit is the bond, the guarantor, and the source of unity enabling the Christian community to become a part and a dimension of the *totus Christus*. The contemporaneous presence of the risen Christ makes it possible for a shared life of two

10. Karl Barth, *CD* IV/3:761.

11. Barth, *CD* IV/2:106. In the possibilities of the present, the life together in Christ of the Christian community being no exception, Barth maintains the ontological distinction between Creator and creature, and does not believe the ontological distinction is abolished or confused in the union and fellowship with Christ made possible by the Spirit's presence in the Christian community through the gospel declaration. Barth modifies the Athanasian formula by answering that "God became man in order that man may—not become God, but come to God."

12. Barth, *CD* IV/3:757.

13. Ibid.

14. Ibid., 760.

infinitely qualitatively distinct realities to occur and to be held together and united in the power of the Holy Spirit.[15] It is in this ecclesial context that the threefold Word of God remains a useful concept for presenting the concrete aspects of Barth's ecclesiology, offering an account of this unity in the event of the Word of God.

Through the Holy Spirit, Barth declares, the being of Jesus Christ causes the Christian community "to become what it is," to become a "second dimension and form of Christ's own being," enabling this fully human community to become simultaneously "the people of His possession, the Christ community."[16] What does this look like and how does this happen in the encounter between the Holy Spirit and the concrete life of the Christian community? Barth offers a general blueprint of the relationship between the Holy Spirit and the Christian community, but is not willing to wed the Holy Spirit to any particular model, example, or ecclesial action. Still, Barth affirms the Spirit's role in uniting and holding together the primary form of Jesus Christ and his secondary form and dimension as Christ manifests Himself in the life of the Christian community. The church is, as Christ's secondary form and dimension unfolds within the life of the Christian community, and the church is as Christ's secondary form and dimension evokes and shapes the life and witness of the Christian community uniquely in its particular context in the life of the world.

The threefold Word of God does not serve as a one-size-fits-all uniform concept of all Christ's ways and works in the contemporary life of the world. By the time of *Church Dogmatics* IV/3 was written in the late 1950s, amidst the heady days of the ecumenical movement and the post-war church expansion in the West, Barth had grown suspicious of any sure-fire formulas of God's presence or triumphalistic identifications of the presence of God with contemporary ecclesial expressions and movements. In coming to emphasize the "humanity of God," Barth would also lay a greater stress on the "humanity of the church," where human words, even in the case of Scripture and church proclamation, were meant to attest and point in all their humanity to the one Word of God, Jesus Christ,[17] where the people of God in the world see "no more than others,"[18] where God never makes a member of the Christian community "a mere spectator, let alone a

---

15. Ibid., 761.
16. Ibid., 759.
17. Ibid., 97–100.
18. Ibid., 716.

puppet,"[19] and where Christians in the world are in as much need of Christ's redemption as non-Christians, and indeed the totality of humanity.[20]

Yet in Barth's second presentation of the threefold Word of God, the presence of Christ in the words and action of the Christian community was not toned down, removed, or abolished. What Barth rejected more severely in his revision of the threefold Word of God were attempts to clutch, possess, or lay claim to the contemporary presence of Christ. The church is not a crutch, it possesses no inside track nor does it exist as a sphere of superiority in relation to others. The Christian community cannot live in self-assured certainty nor can the community presume that God's Word will automatically make itself perceptible in the witness of the church's humanly conditioned words.[21] The Christian community, more so than any community and people, must pray for the coming of Christ and his kingdom.[22] The Christian community's life, existence, and history in the world depend entirely on the constant coming of the Holy Spirit and the self-witness of God in its speech and action.[23] Its witness is "not divine or semi-divine," but is human speech of people like everyone else, always standing in need of assurance and never having any reason for self-assurance in advance.[24]

In this context, through the Christian community's engagement with Scripture and in its own words and witness, the miracle of grace happens and Christ is present and at work, enabling Himself to be recognized and acknowledged.[25] Far from a lack of concreteness, Barth argues that this communication and report of what took place in Jesus Christ always has a visible and concrete form, not as "an ideal commune or universum," but in time and space as the members of the Christian community are "fused together by the common action of the Word which they have heard into a definite fellowship."[26] While "threefold Word of God" may not be the only suitable description of what happens in the event of grace, there is no ques-

19. Ibid., 529.

20. Ibid., 494–97. Barth illustrates the totality of Christ's reconciliation and work beyond the life of the Christian community: "For all the seriousness with which we distinguish between Christians and non-Christians, we can never think in terms of rigid separation. All that is possible is a genuinely unlimited openness of the called in relation to the uncalled, an unlimited readiness to see in the aliens of to-day the brothers of to-morrow, and to love them as such" (494).

21. Ibid., 737.

22. Ibid., 715.

23. Ibid., 738.

24. Ibid., 839.

25. Barth, *CD* IV/1:17.

26. Barth, *CD* IV/1:653.

tion Barth continues to maintain that in the on-going life of the Christian community, God puts his Word on humanity's lips, "that He sanctifies their profane language, that he gives them the power and freedom to speak of Him in their humanly secular words and expressions and sentences, and therefore to become and to be His witnesses to other men."[27] Thus, one of the central, distinctive, and concrete marks of this Christian community is that in and through this gathering, "God wills to use human speech for the proclamation of His Word."[28]

The gospel of Jesus Christ makes the church, shapes the church, and demands the Christian community's obedience in its life together and in the living of its days. Again, the threefold Word of God is not the only description of this kerygmatic ecclesiology, but the declaration of the gospel of Jesus Christ is crucial for Barth as it constitutes the church and as it becomes the church's central day to day task, commission, and identity in the world. Whatever else the Christian community may be, do, undertake, plan, and claim about itself, the declaration of the gospel of Jesus Christ is its chief end.[29] Though the Christian community never produces or reproduces the divine historical fact of Jesus Christ's life, death, and resurrection, the Christian community lives "by the fact that God has created and reveals it, (and) that He is actively and eloquently present in it," empowering the community to offer the world a corresponding echo and witness of this gospel as it witnesses to others.[30]

No contemporary dissection of the threefold Word of God is ever going to unearth the divine kernel in some concrete form. The church's ministry and inner life together do not possess the Word of God at all times nor does the Christian community have the Word of God at its disposal for distribution to all. The risen Christ always comes in the form of a promise and gift. While Jesus Christ creates a secondary dimension of his existence in the life of the Christian community, the Christian community cannot claim this presence as its sole possession, but can only "reach out for it with empty hands" by carrying out its life and work with the confident expectation that Christ will speak in and through the community's declaration of the gospel

27. Barth, *CD* IV/3:737.

28. Ibid., 738. Barth will maintain that the risen Christ's presence extends well beyond the bounds, speech, and actions of the church, addressing the church and speaking to the church, at times quite harshly, from outside its walls and its comfortable state of affairs. Yet Barth also maintains that God wills to use the church's human words for the proclamation of the Word and that such activity is central to the church's mission, life together, and identity in the world.

29. Ibid., 844.

30. Ibid.

and that Christ will manifest himself in and through the community's life together and its attempts to live out the implications of its gospel declaration in the day to day of world occurrence.[31] The act of hearing and imparting the gospel to others is and remains a distinctive mark of Barth's theology of the church, so that the presence of Christ places a claim upon the gathered community and causes an event to occur, whether it be in the words and actions of the preacher, teacher, parent, or factory worker, to use all his or her creative powers, gifts, and inspiration to illustrate and re-present Christ's life, death, and resurrection in contemporary words and actions. Such a vision of the church continues to rely upon the concept of threefold Word of God as the basic pattern Christ's life takes in and with the Christian community, and the conceptual language of the threefold Word of God helps contribute to a general framework and a concrete characterization of the Christian community without reducing the church's life to a formula or to a set of practices or to a static definition.

What makes the church the church is the presence of Jesus Christ as Christ continues to manifest himself in Scripture and in the Christian community's speech, life together, and action. Christ's presence creates a predicate in space and time, a second dimension, of the one Word of God, Jesus Christ's *parousia* (in its second form) in the life of the Christian community. Theological reflection on the life, death, and resurrection of Jesus Christ, makes use of the secondary concepts of the Word of God in the life and witness of the Christian community as they serve as the common ways in which Christ chooses to become present in the life of the Christian community and in its witness to the world. In this context, theological reflection on Jesus Christ, i.e., Christology, not only makes use of the concept of the threefold Word of God, but leads to a robust and concrete account of the Christian community. What can only be distorted and incoherent, in Barth's view, is a theological account of the Christian community whose central subject is the church, where Jesus Christ plays a secondary role and the church becomes the primary instrument and vehicle of God's saving purposes in the world in the present.

In a sense, the fullest account of the church exists from the side of God and the life of the risen Christ at work in and through the life of the Christian community. From the divine perspective, the church is the human community in and through which the light of Christ reflects and shines throughout the world. From the side of humanity, from the perspective within the human Christian community, the church can only be a fully human community with no elevated status or no distinct ontological identity

---

31. Ibid., 840.

that is different from any other human beings. The Christian community cannot produce Christ or make Christ present, but can only call for Christ's presence and trust that Christ will come has he has promised, until the end of the age.[32] Trying to dissect the church of the present, the contemporary human community made up of particular activities and practices, can never lead to a whole account of the church because the church can never be seen as a whole or complete community apart from the reality of Jesus Christ. Only through Christology, only through theological reflection upon and worship of the risen Lord, only by the Christian community's own poverty and its hope for Christ's coming, can a whole vision and full expression of the church come into focus.

Though static union with or present possession of Christ is not possible in the church, Barth does not rule out any sense of union between Christ and the Christian community. In one sense, all are united to Christ through God's primal decision not to be God without humanity; all our united to Christ by election. In the contemporary life of the Christian community, as the Spirit works in and through the life of the Christian community, there is also the possibility of a dynamic and actualistic union of the Spirit in which the Spirit manifests the presence of Christ locally in the Christian community's engagement with the gospel. The Holy Spirit holds together the living Word Jesus Christ with the corresponding speech and actions of the Christian community as Christ is re-presented and attested by human speech and action (correspondence), but also as Christ testifies to himself in and through these actions (union).[33] Again, from the side of humanity, the human community can only seek to correspond to the life

---

32. Matt 28:16–20.

33. Barth, *CD* IV/3:761. "The work of the Holy Spirit, however, is to bring and hold together that which is different and therefore, as it would seem, necessarily and irresistibly disruptive in the relationship of Jesus Christ to His community, namely, the divine working, being and action on the one side and the human on the other, the creative freedom and act on the one side and the creaturely on the other, the eternal reality and possibility on the one side and the temporal on the other. His work is to bring and to hold them together, not to identify, intermingle nor confound them, not to change the one into the other not to merge the one into the other, but to co-ordinate them, to make them parallel, to bring them into harmony and therefore to bind them into a true unity" (537). In regard to union with Christ, Barth writes that "Christ does not merge into the Christian nor the Christian with Christ. There is no disappearance nor destruction of one in favor of the other. Christ remains the One who speaks, commands, and gives as Lord. And the Christian remains the one who hears and answers and receives as the slave of the Lord." Their roles are not confused or lost, even in their fellowship and unity. But there is a real unity as the Holy Spirit coordinates "the being of Jesus Christ and that of His community as distinct from and yet enclosed within it" (760).

of the risen Christ (vs. pursuing or claiming union), but it is in such efforts to correspond, that the risen Christ chooses to unite and declare himself in and through the speech and actions of the Christian community. From above, union precedes and brackets correspondence, but from below, a greater emphasis is placed on correspondence than union.

This is another reason for maintaining the concept of the threefold Word of God in the life of the Christian community. The threefold Word of God helps identify and define the church as the place and people, no more special or superior than others, except that in the will and purpose of God's history in the world, the resurrected Christ wills to manifest himself in and through their words and actions, for the sake of the world, until he comes again. Though Eberhard Jüngel claims that Barth eventually treats Christian proclamation as an ethical action like baptism and the Lord's supper, Barth does not place the declaration of the gospel in the ethical section of CD IV/4, but presents it as the essence of the church's ministry in CD IV/3,[34] as the church shares in the ongoing life and action of the risen Christ.[35] Kimlyn Bender rightly notes that Barth rejects "strong notions of ecclesial mediation," or any requirements that the church mediate the presence of Christ in the present.[36] In relation to the proclamation and declaration of the Word of God, however, Bender wonders if the risen Christ in his own self-proclamation "invites others to share in his Self-proclamation, not as equal partners, but as those through whom he graciously calls the world to faith and obedience."[37]

The second form of Christ's *parousia*, the secondary dimension of Christ's being, the union the Holy Spirit makes possible between Christ and church, and Barth's references to Christ's own taking up human actions in the declaration of the gospel, all seek to offer an ecclesiology that distinguishes divine and human activity, but also an ecclesiology that anticipates Christ's coming and uniting in the life of the Christian community. Barth

---

34. Ibid., 831. "He, or the Gospel which He proclaims and which proclaims Him, is the content of the witness which is alone at issue in its ministry."

35. Jüngel, "Karl Barths Lehre von Der Taufe," 276–77.

36. Bender, *Karl Barth's Christological Ecclesiology*, 279–80.

37. Ibid., 280. Bender believes Barth's concept of witness requires some form of creaturely mediation; otherwise, if Barth cannot allow for any form of creaturely mediation outside of the humanity of Jesus Christ, "Barth's notions of correspondence seem to some to be strained and inadequate" (281). Such a position would seem to remove any sense of the secondary forms of the Word of God as forms of mediation, even weak mediation, and would further problematize the church's life in terms of the secondary dimension of Christ's historical existence on earth in the time between the times. See also Yocum, *Ecclesial Mediation in Karl Barth*, 126–29.

offers an ecclesiology that highlights the freedom and importance of the human response to the gospel and the gospel's implications in the lived life of the witnesses. At the same time, Barth also presents an ecclesiology that provides an account of the way God speaks in and through the community through the gospel, the way God shapes the community's life together by God's presence in and with the gospel, and the way God frees the church from the burden of making Christ present so that Christ may declare himself in and through such creaturely freedom.

What gives Barth's ecclesiology a different dimension and thrust can be described in two ways: a) around the notion of union with Christ and b) around the goal (*telos*) of Christ's presence in the life of the Christian community. While Barth's vision of the church includes an account of divinity uniting with humanity as the church declares the gospel and points to the reality of Christ in the world, for Barth, union with Christ is not the only goal or *telos* of the Christian life. At least in the present age, as the church seeks to live her life as a sign and witness in and for all humanity, the church has no static state. Rather than statically completing the church, Christ's union with the church in and through the gospel declaration, actually propels the church out into the world so that she may become Christ's true witness and correspond in her own space and time to the crucified and risen Lord, thus reaching her vocational fulfilment in communion with the world. The church does not simply long for the coming of the gospel event for the sake of eternal fulfilment and union with Christ. Rather, in and through the gospel event the church is not only united to Christ through the Spirit, but is also sent by the Spirit. Sent, the church follows after the risen Christ into the world in order to become a human sign of God's love for the world, to exist for others and for the world, and to become a living witness to the glory of God.[38] Union with Christ and Christ's union with the church cannot by itself serve as the ultimate goal of the Christian life, because such

---

38. Flett, *The Witness of God*, 293. In emphasizing the church's ontological solidarity with all humanity and the dynamic and actualistic being of the church, Flett's reading of Barth offers an actualistic and missional ecclesiology in which the church can never claim static completion but is always on the way, moving from "the origins in which she is already complete to the visibility in which her completion will be manifest" (295). In regards to the threefold Word of God, I believe it continues to be possible and important in Barth's ecclesiology, without claiming "static completion," for Scripture and the church's declaration of the gospel to serve as sacramental instruments in the life of the Christian community, where Christ wills to bear witness to himself in the life of the Christian community so that the community may be his witnesses in the world.

union happens dynamically in Christ's self-proclamation "for the *purpose of proclaiming*" the gospel and bearing witness to it in and for the world.[39]

Instead of finding its fulfilment in one act or in one episode of its life, the church is a community in movement, entering the world to risk the gospel on others, to minister to the world in speech and action, and in such self-forgetful endeavors, finding and becoming its true self. The church's primary mission cannot be focused on ecclesial descriptions and iron-clad theological descriptions of what the church is, rather the church is called to look outside of itself, to call upon God, trusting in the living Christ's coming again and declaring himself through the community's life together of human speech and action.[40] That is what gives the church its true form and shape. Only the fresh coming of Christ makes the church the church. Jesus Christ is not only proclaimed by the Christian community but Christ proclaims Himself through the Christian community's proclamation and witness.[41] Christ's continuous movement shapes the Christian community into a people differentiated from others but not separated from them,[42] and the living Christ chooses to exist and to be spatially present where Christians are, so they may join in his prophetic work and glorify their risen Lord in their speech and action.[43]

39. Flett, *The Witness of God*, 279. Flett argues that the Christian community ceases to be the Christian community when it abandons the task of announcing the kingdom of God: "[I]t is a word that goes forth, and the community is swept up in this torrent."

40. Barth, *CD* IV/3:542. Barth describes Christ's life in the Christian community analogously to the incarnation: "He does not go alone but wills to be what He is and do what He does in company with others whom He calls for the purpose, namely, the despicable folk called Christians. He attests to the world the reconciliation to God effected in Him, the covenant of God with man fulfilled in Him, as He associates with Christians making common cause and conjoining Himself with them." He does not do this from afar, Barth adds, "but as He calls them to Himself in the divine power of the His Spirit, He refreshes them by offering and giving Himself to them and making them His own." See also ibid., 544. In this movement of union, Christ attaches himself to the Christian in the gift of faith and obedience, and the Christian attaches and unites himself in glorifying and giving himself to the One who gave himself to him.

41. Holmes, "What Jesus Is Doing," 27.

42. Barth, *CD* IV/3:533.

43. Ibid., 547. In his reflection on what it means to be in Christ and for Christ to be in the Christian, Barth is clear that in fellowship and union with Christ, that the spatial distance disappears between Christ and the Christian and between the Christian and Christ, so that Christians are not "merely alongside" Christ, "but exactly in the same spot." Barth continues with an extra-Calvinistic qualification that the word "in," as being in Christ, "transcends even though it also includes its local signification." In terms of the declaration of the Word of God, this suggests that Christ's transcendent presence, by the power of the Holy Spirit, is also able to manifest itself in the witness of Scripture and acts of proclamation in local space and time.

That is why it is so hard to pin Barth down on the visible church's identity and visibility apart from Jesus Christ. It is almost as if theological reflection on the Christian community alone or any kind of formal ecclesiology is a perverse and distorted theological task from the start. Instead, by devoting its attention to humanity's justification, sanctification, and vocation in Jesus Christ, Barth believes the church becomes most visible and concrete. In contrast, theological attempts at ecclesiology will always be incomplete accounts, not only because of Barth's actualism, but also because theological descriptions of the church are one step removed from the reality and presence of Jesus Christ who alone can make the true church come to life and visibility, whose presence alone empowers the Christian community to proclaim the gospel until Christ comes again. There is a sense in which Barth might caution that focus on ecclesiology proper is actually destructive to the church because it distorts the church, focusing too much on what the community is in itself or what it is in its own visible practice and activities.[44] Additionally, if ecclesiology focuses solely on capturing where Christ is or is not in this or that action in the life of the Christian community, making such endeavors the central act of its theological reflection, theology is in danger of losing sight of Jesus Christ all together. In his recent defense of Barth's actualistic ecclesiology, Christopher J. Holmes writes that Barth's ecclesiology gives the church no firm ground to stand on, no crutch to lean on, rather "to be the church is to always face the threat that it may not be the true church" and precisely "when the church thinks itself the church it is probably least the church."[45]

Instead, a theology of the church has to be, in a certain sense, self-forgetful and incomplete, not trusting solely in its own resources or believing it possesses the kingdom *in toto*. Such an ecclesiology devotes its resources and attention to God's existence in Jesus Christ's life, death, resurrection,

44. Healy, "Karl Barth's Ecclesiology Reconsidered," 296–97.

45. Holmes, "The Church and the Presence of Christ: Defending Actualist Ecclesiology," 277. See also, Healy, "Karl Barth's Ecclesiology Reconsidered," 297–99. In Healy's reevaluation of Barth's ecclesiology, he contrasts Barth's theology of the church with the danger of ecclesial self-preservation seen in contemporary ecclesiologists like Stanley Hauerwas, but also in Reinhard Hütter, Radical Orthodoxy, and in forms of communion ecclesiology as well. Healy particularly notes one of Barth's central marks of the Christian community is its willingness not to take itself and its existence too seriously, but to trust that one way or another, Christ will make himself heard in the church's life in spite of the church's weakness and cultural accommodation. Instead of ecclesial attempts to preserve a strong sense of the church, the church can only really be strong, robust, and truly the church as it calls upon God and "trusts God to act to preserve the body of Christ in its historical and Spirit-filled form until the eschaton" (299).

and the gospel's ongoing implications in the present context, offering and including a robust theology of the Christian community within the larger theological loci. As soon as the Christian community thinks its primary task is to identify itself and its identity by its own visible existence and practices, as soon as the Christian community becomes preoccupied with attempts to identify Christ's exact location within its own life and action, it risks ceasing to be the Christian community. The church cannot become the church by trying to be the church, the church becomes the church by calling on Jesus Christ and seeking to live as his disciples and witnesses in the world. The church becomes the church by not trying to "be the church," but as it seeks, praises, and follows Jesus Christ in its contemporary life. Barth explains his theological vision of the church this way: "I would never say that any church ceases to be Church . . . Looking at us, I say the Church must cease; looking at Him, I say the church will always be preserved."[46] Or to paraphrase Charles Wesley's hymn, the church becomes the church as it loses itself in "wonder, love, and praise," and in service of Jesus Christ.[47]

The Threefold Word of God and Ecclesiology Today

It has been argued here that the threefold Word of God offers Karl Barth's ecclesiology a paradigm and ecclesial pattern, a particular form and concrete shape that Christ's life frequently takes as it joins with and moves in and through the Christian community. To dismiss the threefold Word of God as a concept no longer essential to Barth's theology of the church is to risk offering an incoherent conception of the church's common life together. To do so is also to risk limiting the Christian community's being and action solely to a human response to the gospel of Jesus Christ. Certainly the church seeks to live as a response and correspondence to the gospel, but might the church also serve as a means and a community in the world through whose life together God speaks? Might the church become, through the work of the Spirit, a community through whom God chooses to speak and bear witness in his own loving activity for all creation, until Christ comes again in fullness?

As Reformed theology in particular seeks to move forward with Barth and beyond Barth in the challenges and context of the present, there is no need to do so without the threefold Word of God. Neither Barth's actualistic theology nor his theological ontology require the elimination or qualified

---

46. Barth, *Karl Barth's Table Talk*, 99.

47. See also, Phil 2:1–11.

dilution of the threefold Word of God in Barth's larger theological *corpus*.[48] Instead Barth's revisitation and revision of the threefold Word of God suggest two complementary ecclesiological claims. First, that Jesus Christ can and does speak outside and over and against the proclamation of the church, but second and most often, by the power of the Holy Spirit, Christ comes in and with the church's proclamation of the gospel. It is not that Jesus Christ needs the church, but Christ does not seek to manifest himself in the present time without the Christian community. To dismiss the threefold Word of God risks doing damage to a more comprehensive account of Barth's theology of the church and it risks limiting his description of the Christian community to a community of human response.

Barth offers some important lessons about attempts to form a theology of the Christian community, even as he subjects himself to some criticisms. For Barth, the central act and task of the Christian community is the declaration of the gospel in speech and action, and Barth's later presentation of the declaration of the gospel in the life of the Christian community emphasizes its pluriformity and its democratic vocation for all in the Christian community. Barth suggests that making the gospel proclamation just a clerical exercise is a reduction of the gospel's implications and Christ's demands on all Christians in the Christian community. However, because Barth wants the declaration of the gospel to be the task of all Christians, he risks diminishing and over-relativizing the centrality of the preaching event in the life of the worshipping community. In his *Introduction to the Reformed Tradition*, John H. Leith argues that the church's preaching is a "unique act, *sui generis*" in the life of the Christian community, and that the Reformed Christian community has always placed great confidence in the power of preaching, "when blessed by the Holy Spirit," to transform human beings and their surrounding context and larger community.[49] In addition, Leith reminds us that the Reformers, specifically Calvin and Bullinger used language that sought to establish the act of preaching as the usual means of God's grace and power in the life of the Christian community.[50] In this unique event in the life of the Christian community, Leith declares that "an ordinary human being, called, trained, and certified by the church, stands over against the people of God in the name of God and proclaims the word of God."[51]

---

48. Mangina, "Bearing the Marks of Jesus," 281. Mangina notes that Barth's concerns about ecclesial triumphalism led him to reject any theological claims that elevated the church above the rest of humanity and the world in any way.

49. Leith, *Introduction to the Reformed Tradition*, 218, 81.

50. Ibid., 80.

51. Ibid., 218.

To relativize or minimize the significance of this act of proclamation in the Christian community, Leith argues, is for the Christian community to forfeit its greatest missionary opportunity to engage the large communal gathering with the good news of the gospel.[52] Is it possible to recognize the pluriformity of Christ's manifestation in and through the Christian community while also identifying and maintaining the primary patterns and forms through which Christ comes? The threefold Word of God seems to offer such a paradigm and to make such a case. In a time of anxiety about future of the church, particularly in the West, the threefold Word of God offers an ecclesiological vision that acknowledges the reality of gospel pluriformity while also maintaining a sense of the historical and common ways the church has understood Jesus Christ to come in the life of the community, to be present in, and to order the Christian community's life and action. In addition, such a reading of the threefold Word of God offers a theology of Christian worship that sees the church's worship as more than human praise and human response to the gospel, but as the regular and faithful coming of God into the midst of the Christian community on the Lord's Day. In such an event, the Word of God, Jesus Christ, elicits and enables a grateful and obedient response, but this self-same Word of God, speaks and dwells with and encloses the community's regular and repeatable acts of gratitude in God's own regular and repeatable acts of grace.

While it would be hard to make the case that a relativizing of the preaching event was Barth's intention, his multiform presentation of the gospel declaration in the twelve ministries of speech and action within the Christian community risks diminishing the role of the preaching event in the life of the Christian community and risks diminishing the central nature of this event.[53] Does one have to come at the expense of the other? Can the risen Christ speak through Scripture, through the declaration of the gospel in the life of the Christian community, and can the risen Christ be heard and obeyed in particular acts of witness and correspondence, all in different aspects of one event or in one movement of actualization? While the threefold Word of God cannot presume to possess and contain the risen Christ and the Word of God in contemporaneity, the life of God in the world is never without form, and thus Christ does not choose to be without his witnesses, the Christian community, "by whose proclamation he lives."[54] As a result, the threefold Word of God gives form and shape to the Christian community's identity, task, and marks in the world. While Christ tran-

52. Ibid.

53. Barth, *CD* IV/3:865–901.

54. Holmes, "The Church and the Presence of Christ," 280, 279.

scends and precedes the Christian community, he nevertheless comes in and through the church's proclamation, creating acts of correspondence and gospel declaration as the Christian community lives out its life in solidarity with all humanity and in service to the larger world. While Christ does not present himself as Scripture and as the proclaimer's words, Christ elects to come and speak through these witnesses. While Christ is not present as the church in Barth's actualistic ecclesiology, Christ's form in the present age is never without the church.[55]

Some critics of Barth's presentation of the Christian community believe that Barth offers, along similar lines to Calvin, only qualifications about whether the proclamation of the gospel ever contains the grace it signifies, leaving him unable to identify God's grace in the words of the gospel and the sacraments, leaving it up to the Holy Spirit to make Christ present or withdraw that presence in the church's life, therefore leaving an incomplete or bifurcated presentation of the gospel's visibility and tangibility in the life of the Christian community.[56] Barth himself once remarked that, "the Word of God can only be believed, not perceived" as it is "an object that is different from all other objects," something we can "have," only "because it gives itself."[57] The point, Barth emphasizes, is not the human action producing the Word of God, "but the Word of God in the human action."[58] It is the Word of God, Jesus Christ, through the power of the Holy Spirit, who contains, embraces, and exalts the human words of the Christian community and makes them a dimension of his life in the world. The Christian community, though it does not contain the grace it signifies, trusts, believes, and prays that the grace it signifies embraces and contains its own life and witness.

It is in this way that the threefold Word of God offers a helpful paradigm of divine and human unity in the life of the Christian community. It is in this way that the church becomes something more than a human response to the gospel as it shares in Christ's own life and self-proclamation to the world. It is not the church's humanity that determines whether the church can proclaim or contain the Word of God, but it is Jesus Christ, the union of divinity and humanity, who determines what the Christian community is capable of bearing and containing through the work of the Spirit, who brings and holds together that which is different.[59]

---

55. Ibid., 280.

56. Jenson, "Recovery of the Word," in *America's Theologian*, 187.

57. Barth, *Karl Barth's Table Talk*, 25.

58. Ibid.

59. Barth, *CD* IV/3:761.

To strive for a robust theology of the church along the lines laid out by Barth in the present age requires some additional lines of exploration and evaluation. At times, Barth is able to depict the aesthetic dimension of the life of hearing the gospel and living out the gospel, particularly as he finds a gospel analogue in creation in the music of Wolfgang Amadeus Mozart, a true word *extra muros ecclesiae*.[60] At other times, the dimensions of beauty and fellowship found in Christian community are presented minimally. As Kimlyn Bender notes, Barth's account of the church is primarily an account of how the activity of the church is a response to the gospel, but Barth offers very little about the particular ways the community itself, in its life together, and in its particular patterns of living, embody the gospel of Jesus Christ.[61] Perhaps because the risen Christ's life in the world extends beyond the church and the church's life, even contradicting and chastening the Christian community at times, Barth does not seek to offer an account of the ways the gospel shapes the Christian community, as such an account would risk exalting the church as a superior or triumphalist people over and against the rest of humanity.[62]

Rather than depicting the declaration of the gospel solely in terms of speech and action however, there is also an aesthetic dimension to the glory of God in the world that calls out of the Christian community a corresponding life of beauty and glorification. The Word of God is not only true, dynamic, and transformative, but it is also beautiful, a beautiful way of life, whose grace attracts disciples by the beauty of the life it creates in and through Christian community. It is not the church that is beautiful in itself, but the life made possible by Christ in the Christian community, as Christ preserves, forms and re-forms the church and its life together. Christ's ministry in and through the church's gospel declaration leads to corresponding speech and actions that conform to the living reality of Christ. The living reality of Christ also calls forth and creates in the gospel event itself a dimension of beautiful living in Christian life together, enabling Christians not only to develop a love and solidarity with other human beings, but also enabling Christians to develop a proper love for life in the Christian community and a love for the community's purpose as a dimension of Christ's own being in the world.

As we have seen, Barth's later emphasis in relation to the Christian community underscores the infinite ontological distinction between Christ

---

60. Ibid., 117–33.

61. Bender, *Karl Barth's Christological Ecclesiology*, 280.

62. Holmes, "The Church and the Presence of Christ," 280. See also Mangina, "Bearing the Marks of Jesus," 281.

and the Christian community, prioritizing it over the unity and continuity between the church and Jesus Christ. While Barth's Reformed instincts led him to such an emphasis, there is a danger of a talking about a Word of God that remains separated from its human counterpart. There is a danger in bypassing all possibilities for divine and human unity in the church's life together.[63] The threefold Word of God serves as one such possibility of divine and human (momentary) union and fellowship, but can Barth's ontological and actualistic commitments allow for any others? If Reformed theological accounts of the church are not to collapse under the weight of this ontological distinction, might they also include accounts of the provisional and momentary uniting activity of Christ's life in and through the Christian community? This is why it is important to maintain some notion of mediation or indirect identity between the risen Christ and the life and witness of the Christian community, not in order to privilege or preserve the church, but to offer a full account of the particular shape that life in Christ takes, an account of the ways and patterns in which the church is a dimension of Christ's life in the present time between the times. Barth is certainly justified in arguing that the church cannot be the church by focusing on what the church is, but it seems equally dangerous for ecclesiology to be consumed with delineations of what the church is not.

While the church must always refrain from attempts to assert itself as an extension of the incarnation, there is also a danger that the distinction between Christ and the Christian community becomes of greater significance than the reality of Jesus Christ in all his unity with the sinful and ontologically distinct Christian community (*totus Christus*). Moving forward and striving to avoid the dangers of complete separation and complete confusion, a vision of the church must acknowledge the church's penchant for sinful distortion and fixation on its inward life, but that cannot be all. As the church is captivated by the living reality of Christ's presence, discussions over unity or distinction give way to the church's own self-deferential pointing to the miraculous reality in its midst. In other words, when the church proclaims and seeks to live with the demands of the gospel of Jesus Christ, the church is freed from ever trying to preserve, contain, possess or establish the presence of Christ on the one hand, and on the other hand the church is freed from having to protect or search for the distinction between where Christ ends and the church begins. The church becomes the church, the church proclaims God's Word, and the church lives out the gospel, not

---

63. Bender, *Karl Barth's Christological Ecclesiology*, 274. Bender identifies Barth's emphasis on "distinction" and "irreversibility" in his account of the church and its relationship to Jesus Christ, but observes that Barth is less masterful at describing their "unity" and "relation."

by trying to be the church, not by trying to produce Christ in the present, not just by delineating Christ from the church, but the church becomes the church as it is overcome by the reality, glory, and power of the risen Christ. In devotion to the risen Lord, the Christian community becomes free to point, to signify, to rejoice, and in so doing, trusts that Christ will come and speak and manifest Himself in the life of this particular community until he comes again.

Parables of the Threefold Word of God

Karl Barth's concept of the threefold Word of God continues to be relevant to contemporary theology as a Reformed ecclesial vision of Christ's distinction from the church but also Christ's unity in and through the life of the Christian community. At the same time, the threefold Word of God does not seek to offer a static church completely fulfilled by the proclaimed Word of God in the life of the church, but maintains that by itself the Christian community can never be more than a provisional community, an incomplete community in the world moving with the rest of humanity from Easter to the Second Coming. One of Barth's best descriptions of the life of the Christian community came from his early essay and lecture where he describes the church as "God's shanty among men until the world's end."[64] The Word of God does not statically reside in Scripture or in the church's preaching, but comes to the church's hearing of Scripture, manifesting itself, not in magisterial splendour or sophisticated preaching, but in simplicity, creating a humble shanty in the world as the Scriptures are read and the gospel is heard and lived out among ordinary people. A shanty church is less likely to confuse itself with the distinction, power, and beauty of Christ's gospel even as it finds itself included in Christ's life and movement in the world, even as it offers the world a provisional place in time and space to be transformed by such grace.

In spite of the existing distinction between Christ and the church, theology and church at times must risk claiming that Jesus Christ speaks and comes in and through its gospel proclamation. In the liturgy of the church it is often a common practice after the reading of the Scriptures, particularly the gospel reading, to declare, "This is the Word of the Lord." Might such a practice also extend to the proclamation of the gospel? Must the church venture to make that claim, daring to tell the world, that in and through this community the risen Christ is not only proclaimed, but proclaims himself in the gospel proclamation? While Christ's fulfilment of the world and the

64. Barth, "The Concept of the Church," in *Theology and Church*, 285.

perfection of all things are still to come, in the interim time, the church is called upon to trust that Christ also comes through its own careful and faithful attempts to offer the world his gospel. Never to risk identifying the risen Christ's voice and life with its own words and action, especially its own proclamation, the church risks slaying the gospel by the death of a thousand qualifications. While the church's proclamation does not produce Christ, it cannot shirk offering responsible illustrations of Christ's uniting in and with the church's gospel proclamation. It is fitting then to conclude this study of the threefold Word of God in the theology of Karl Barth with some illustrations of Christ's distinct and unifying presence in the Christian community's attempts to proclaim and live out the implications of the gospel. While certainly not exhaustive, illustrations from Scripture, from Barth's own theological corpus, and from the life of a rather obscure African-American preacher will be offered as parables that seek to illustrate, responsibly and colorfully, God's voice coming and speaking in and through humanity's voice, in Scripture, in theology, and in the life of the church.

The word of the Lord comes to the prophet Jeremiah and in the opening chapter of the book of Jeremiah, in Jeremiah's own call to the prophetic vocation, a glimpse of the intersection and union of the divine voice and the human voice is also disclosed.[65] The divine action and human actions are distinguished and differentiated as God's time and action precede and initiate Jeremiah's own call to the prophetic word. First comes the word of the Lord: "Before I formed you in the womb I knew you, and before you were born I consecrated you, I appointed you; I appointed you a prophet to the nations."[66] Far from a desire to possess or control or master the word of the Lord, the prophet does not believe such a role is humanly possible for him, confessing, "Ah, Lord God! Truly I do not know how to speak, for I am only a boy."[67] The ontological distinction remains in place, but Jeremiah's mortality and the God of Israel's eternal divinity do not simply go their separate ways. The divine voice commands Jeremiah to go where the Lord sends him and to speak to whomever he sends him.[68] The Lord God promises to give Jeremiah the words to say but not only that, the Lord God vows to put his words in Jeremiah's mouth so that in Jeremiah's own words, Israel may hear

---

65. See Jer 1:1–9.
66. Jer 1:5.
67. Jer 1:6.
68. Jer 1:8.

and obey the God of Israel.[69] The prophet is sent by the word of the Lord to "proclaim in the hearing of Jerusalem, thus says the Lord."[70]

Jeremiah's mortality and humanity and frailty as the Lord's messenger are not ignored and yet in the life of Israel, in a time of crisis in Israel's life, the word of the Lord comes to the prophet and the prophet proclaims "in the hearing of Jerusalem," a word from the Lord. Like the prophet Jeremiah, the church is an all too human community in the world sent by the Word of the Lord, to proclaim a word from the Lord, as the Lord God "puts his Word on their lips," willing to use human speech for the proclamation of the Word.[71] Where the Word of the Lord ends and Jeremiah's own words begin cannot easily be dissected. The Word of the Lord does not remain with Jeremiah, becoming his own possession, but it comes, again and again, not triumphantly, but steadfastly, from a mortal prophet to a broken people on the verge of captivity and exile.

Jesus' reading of Scripture and proclamation in the synagogue in Luke 4 offers another parable of the threefold Word of God. Filled with the power of the Holy Spirit, Jesus goes back to his hometown synagogue in Nazareth on the Sabbath day.[72] According to Luke, Jesus stood up to read from the prophet Isaiah, proclaimed the year of the Lord's favor, deliverance to the captives, and good news to the poor.[73] After reading from the Scriptures, Jesus declares that "the Scripture has been fulfilled in your hearing," and the gathered congregation become amazed at the "gracious words that came from his mouth," even as they have to come to terms with the fact that such grace comes in the form of Joseph's son.[74] The community's reception of Jesus' own proclamation of good news not only leads to amazement and admiration, but also to anger and rage, nearly costing him his own life prematurely.[75]

Even in the humanity of Jesus Christ, the word of the Lord is not self-evident but must transform the lives of its hearers through the power of the Holy Spirit. The Christian community is not an extension of the Incarnation. The church certainly cannot claim to possess the word of the Lord nor can it be assured that those in its midst will all and always hear and obey the gospel as it becomes unveiled in its life together. However, the Christian community does pray for and expect the risen Christ to proclaim Himself

69. Jer 1:9.

70. Jer 2:1–2.

71. Barth, *CD* IV/3:737–38.

72. Luke 4:16.

73. Luke 4:18–19; Isa 61:1–2.

74. Luke 4:20–22.

75. Luke 4:28.

through the community's own reading and hearing of the Scriptures and the church offers the world a proclamation and illustration of the gospel in their own life together in response to the life and voice of God in the midst of the community. The Christian community follows what Christ does in this passage from Luke, but expects the risen Christ Himself to be and to bring the good news, to release the captives, to bind up the broken-hearted, and to proclaim the year of the Lord's favor. Yet amidst Christ's presence, the Christian community seeks to proclaim his kingdom and live out the implications of such proclamation.

In *CD* IV/2, Barth offers a description and vision of the unity of the Word of God with the Christian community through a tribute to his child-hood assistant pastor in his home church in Basel. The context of this illustra-tion is Barth's point that the Christian community's keeping of feasts such as Christmas and Easter becomes more than merely "acts of remembrance and representation," as Jesus Christ precedes the community's remembrances by coming "before us when we proclaim and hear Him as the Word of God" in acts of remembrance, response, and commemoration.[76] To illustrate the unity of the living Jesus Christ with the community's proclamation of him, overcoming "the barrier of His own time and therefore historical distance," Barth cites the example of his childhood pastor Abel Burckhardt.[77] Burck-hardt made an impression on the young Barth through a collection of songs and illustrations of Christ's life, death, and resurrection, presented in the local Swiss dialect through the ministry of his childhood church. "What made an indelible impression on me," Barth recalled, "was the homely natu-ralness with which these very modest compositions spoke of the events of Christmas, Palm Sunday, Good Friday, Easter, the Ascension, and Pentecost as things which might take place any day in Basel or its environs like any other important happenings."[78]

As the Word was proclaimed in the everyday language in the informal setting and routine of worship with children, "we took our mother's hand, as it were, and went to the stall at Bethlehem, and to the streets of Jerusalem where, greeted by children of a similar age, the Savior made His entry, and to the dark hill of Golgotha, and as the run rose to the garden of Joseph."[79] Barth then asks pointedly whether such events and moments in the life of the Christian community can be equated with a more Roman Catholic

76. Barth, *CD* IV/2:112.
77. Ibid.
78. Ibid.
79. Ibid., 112–13.

"re-enactment of Christ's crucifixion in our own existence?"[80] Christ was made present, Barth counters, without needing to be made present, instead coming freely to testify to Himself through Abel Burckhardt's proclamation in illustrations and children's songs.[81] Not just limited to a formal act on Sunday morning or a formal proclamation in the strict genre of sermon, the Word of God comes in the simple illustrations of an assistant pastor and in the songs sung by young children in the Christian community. Dissecting the event to identify where the Word of God ends and the word of proclamation begins, would risk damaging the miraculous nature of such occurrences all together.

Before Martin Luther King, Jr., served as the pastor at Dexter Avenue Baptist Church, in Montgomery, Alabama, there was Vernon Johns. Vernon Johns is a largely forgotten figure in history, except for an occasional mention in accounts of the early civil rights movement in the American South. In his own time, he was "merely another invisible man to nearly all whites, but to the invisible people themselves he was the stuff of legend."[82] Born in the last decade of the nineteenth century, Vernon Johns grew up on a farm in Farmville, Virginia, and even as a youth exhibited amazing feats of intellect, including memorizing extensive biblical passages, even the entirety of Paul's letter to the Romans.[83] Johns' self-education and courage led him to Virginia Theological Seminary, Oberlin Seminary in Ohio, and to graduate school of theology at the University of Chicago.[84] One of the only sermons Vernon Johns wrote down was published in 1926 and was the first work by an African-American published in the liberal journal *Best Sermons*.[85] Though widely considered as one of the vanguard of leading black church intellectuals of his time (along with Mordecai Johnson and Howard Thurman), "Johns was a maverick who seldom wrote anything down and who thought nothing of walking into distinguished assemblies wearing mismatched socks, with farm mud on his shoes."[86] Johns preferred to live the life of the vagabond prophet, leaving his family for months at a time, preaching in different communities, venues, and gatherings, and then returning home to Virginia to farm for a time.[87]

80. Ibid., 113.

81. Ibid.

82. Branch, *Parting the Waters*, 7.

83. Ibid., 8.

84. Ibid., 8–9.

85. Ibid., 10.

86. Ibid.

87. Ibid.

Called to the prominent pulpit of Montgomery, Alabama's Dexter Avenue Baptist Church in 1948, Vernon Johns' iconoclastic ways grated against the dignified congregation of Montgomery's black elite. When an African-American member of the community was stopped by the police for speeding and nearly beaten to death, Johns prepared the large bulletin board outside the Dexter church for the coming Sunday's sermon: "It's Safe to Murder Negroes in Montgomery."[88] Such actions led to the Ku Klux Klan burning a cross on the Dexter Church lawn and led to significant threats and hostility to Johns and his family in Montgomery. Having most of the Scriptures memorized, Johns never opened or used the pulpit Bibles in worship except to pound them, and his style led him to be both revered and disdained by the Christian community he served.[89] Beyond the pulpit, Johns saw not only a need to proclaim the equality of Christ's gospel in the inequality of the Jim Crow South, but he also sought to encourage his own congregation and the larger black community to sustain themselves economically without having to rely on leftovers from the white economy. Johns' antics of growing and selling his own home-grown produce on the church steps and in the church basement eventually led to his demise and dismissal as pastor of Dexter Avenue Baptist Church in 1952 only to pave the way for the ministry of Martin Luther King, Jr., beginning in 1954.[90]

By 1960 Vernon Johns had entered a permanent vagabond stage tending a vegetable stand in an empty lot near Petersburg, Virginia. Martin Luther King, Jr., had heard the legend of Vernon Johns and of his powerful oratory and sermons, and wanted to get the notebooks, notes, outlines, and contents of Vernon Johns preaching to aid him in his own work and preaching. The task was so important to King that he sent his personal lawyer, Chauncey Eskridge, to track Johns down, even to compensate him for all of his old sermon notebooks.[91] Upon finding Johns selling vegetables at an empty corner lot, Eskridge could scarcely believe the man before him was the distinguished and legendary Vernon Johns. Surprised himself to be found, Johns expressed his own disbelief at the request, but then slowly "began ticking off sermon titles, then reciting snatches of sermons, and finally he began preaching in full animation on the dangers of drinking Pharaoh's wine."[92] The old man without socks or shoelaces, captivated the well-tailored Chicago lawyer with gospel proclamation committed to memory. After acquiring a commitment

88. Ibid., 22.
89. Ibid., 19.
90. Ibid., 24, 114.
91. Ibid., 902.
92. Ibid.

from Johns that he would send the notebooks of sermons, Eskridge "recovered enough legal scepticism to suspect correctly that the notebooks Johns promised to send did not exist—always his sermons returned to the air from which they had come."[93] John's own life illustrated all too well the power of the risen Christ to transform the world through preaching and the life of the Christian community, but also the risen Christ's dynamic movement, returning to the air from which he came.

Just so does Christ come in the life of the Christian community, speaking through the biblical witness, creating witnesses of his own and speaking through those human declarations of the gospel. The threefold Word of God is not a solution to a problem, but an illustration of the presence of Christ, the power of the Holy Spirit, and the identity and shape of the Christian community and its life together in the world. It is through the threefold Word of God that Christ comes into the incompleteness of the Christian community, enabling it to become an echo and witness as Christ's speaks and shapes its life in the world, in the time between the times. While this Word of God dynamically returns to the air from which it came, it unites for a time with the words and lives of the Christian community, making them, at least provisionally, in their own words, life together, and engagement with the world, part of Christ's being in the world, part of the Word of God, and part of God's Word to all creation, until his kingdom comes.

93. Ibid. Branch writes that King had a hard time accepting that no notes or notebooks of Johns's sermons existed: "Even after Johns died months later, he asked Eskridge whether any had arrived in the mail."

6

Conclusion

But finally, while they cannot be equated, the voice of Christ and the voice of his Church cannot be separated. Such is the promise that our Lord has made to those who follow him. Somewhere within the Body of Christ the will of Christ is articulated.

—Richard John Neuhaus, *Freedom for Ministry*, 166

But while real, communion in Christ is still provisional. To speak of Christian communion as provisional is to say that the church must not claim to be already the reign of God.

—Daniel L. Migliore,
"The Communion of the Triune God," 150

THIS STUDY HAS ARGUED THAT THE THREEFOLD WORD OF GOD IS A CEN-tral and indispensable element of Karl Barth's theology. Though the concept of the threefold Word of God was revised, becoming less central of a theme in the later volumes of the *Church Dogmatics*, it was not abolished or re-moved from Barth's thought all together, nor were its particular ecclesial emphases abandoned. Rather in its revised form, it continues to contribute to Barth's theological vision of the church and provides a vision of Christ's unity-in-differentiation in the life together of the Christian community. In particular, the threefold Word of God offers an ecclesiological vision that claims the Christian community's worship, prayer, and life together as acts of creaturely response and obedience but also as acts of the risen Christ, the living Word of God who chooses to become embedded in the life of the ecclesial community. While presumptuousness is risked in claiming human proclamation to be the Word of God in all acts of church proclamation, it is no less presumptuous to deny Christ's presence and voice in such actions. Just as with the living God more is always possible, so more is also possible for the church's human proclamation. As the gospel is heard and proclaimed and obeyed in the life of the Christian community, such words and witnesses become the principal and common way that the risen Christ comes and proclaims himself for the sake of the world. The Christian community is neither overburdened by the impossible task of making Christ present in word or sacrament nor is the Christian community left to question whether God has much to say to and through the worship and life together of the contemporary Christian community. Instead, the church is freed to worship and proclaim and pray together, trusting that the Christ who came to the particularities of Nazareth and Capernaum and Golgotha will come again to the particularities and ordinary lives of the Christian community, proclaiming Himself through their words and witness, to all the world.

There is a danger in making bold theological claims for the church. This was Karl Barth's major criticism of Roman Catholicism, that the life and activity of the risen Christ had been supplanted by the church, that the church was imprisoned by the impossible task of Atlas bearing everything on its own, seeking to dispense Christ according to the church's own caprice. There is also a danger in claiming too little for the church, believing that God would not possibly dare to encounter human beings through the often flawed and compromised witness of the Christian community, instead extracting Christ's resurrected presence from the church's flawed involvement. At its best, the concept of the threefold Word of God seeks to claim and trace the particular shape and movement of the Spirit in the witness of Scripture and in the life of the Christian community. The threefold Word of God helps to provide certain *notae ecclesiae* and marks, giving a more concrete shape to Barth's often unrealized ecclesiology. Like his own unfinished *Church Dogmatics,* Karl Barth's theology of the threefold Word of God and church is an incomplete creation. The church only becomes anything more as Christ proclaims Himself through the church's proclamation of the gospel, and as the Holy Spirit gathers, unites, and sends forth the community into the world to follow and correspond to her risen Lord. Only in such a context, can the church find concreteness and realization, becoming something more than the sum of her parts. Only in such a context, does the threefold Word of God lead to a realized ecclesiology.

Nearly fifty years after his death, nearly eighty years after the Barmen Declaration was composed, Karl Barth's theology of proclamation and theology of the church have much to offer to theology and to the challenges posed to Christianity in the twenty-first century. To ecclesiologists and critics of Barth's ecclesiology, Barth's work serves to warn against idealizing the mundane life and inconsistent practices of the Christian community even as his own work seeks to offer, alternatively, a bold and robust ecclesiology grounded in Christ and the work of the Spirit. To theologians concentrated in the field of Barth studies, Barth's theology of the church affords the theological opportunity to enter into a larger theological discussion about the future of the church and the contribution and concerns of Reformed theology to the field of ecclesiology. This study seeks to join the concerns of Barth studies with those of modern ecclesiology, and it is hoped that the contemporary ecclesiological discussion will continue to have a place for the contributions and concerns of Karl Barth and the commitments of the threefold Word of God in particular. Though the field of Barth studies continues to be creative, prolific, and constructive in its ongoing discoveries and scholarship, it too often either assumes or overlooks the Christian community and its own distinct life and identity in the world. To take little theological notice of the contours and shape of the Christian community in light of the gospel proclamation, to avoid theological engagement with the ways Christ's life becomes manifest in the life together of the Christian community, risks missing out on the central purpose and aims of Barth's entire theological vision. The ecclesial community shaped and identified by the threefold Word of God has a distinct theological and ethical shape that should be of greater interest to the field of Barth studies, and Barth's ecclesiology offers those engaged in Barth studies the opportunity to engage with the broader ecclesiological concerns of theology and church today.

This work has sought to modestly reorient Barth studies in such a direction, by examining a seemingly well-known, well-trod concept, the threefold Word of God, exploring its origins and importance, especially in relation to the life of the Christian community and its later revision in the *Church Dogmatics*. No contemporary study has examined the threefold Word of God with this kind of depth and dimension, nor has any study sought to offer a comprehensive account and explanation of Barth's later revision of the threefold Word of God in *Church Dogmatics* IV/3. Far from being a relic that was later left behind in the early formations of Barth's theology in *Church Dogmatics* I/1 and I/2, the threefold Word of God is crucial to a comprehensive understanding of Barth's theology of the church and Christ's contemporary presence and activity in the life of the Christian community. No study has made the case in quite this way. Without the concept of the threefold Word of God, Barth's theology of the church does not cohere. The threefold Word of God gives a particular concrete theological identity and ethical shape to Barth's vision of the church, and Barth's concept of the threefold Word of God has played an important role in shaping the historical life and witness of Christian communities from Barmen and beyond. This study also strives to reorient ecclesiological engagement with Karl Barth's theology of the church. Rather than being dismissed as an inadequate ecclesiology lacking in concreteness, the threefold Word of God offers an account of a lively and bold Christian community in unity and differentiation with the divine activity on the loose in the world. This thesis argues that Barth's concept of the threefold Word of God offers contemporary ecclesiology a constructive alternative to models of church that start solely with sacramental models or models chiefly defined by concrete practices and virtuous habits. In contrast, the concept of the threefold Word of God begins with the event of the Word of God in the life of the Christian community, offering an account of the church's life together and activity in the world from, to, and in light of the gospel event.

Since the Reformation, questions about the church's identity, form, and visibility have haunted the various forms of Protestantism. Karl Barth's concept of the threefold Word seeks to answer such questions through a vision of Christ's differentiated inseparability from the Christian community's proclamation of his gospel. While such an ecclesial vision is still only fragmentary and partial, while such a theology of the church does not allow our own ecclesiological constructions the final word, Barth believes that this incompleteness and longing for the coming and completion of Christ's kingdom is also central to the church's life and can only be actualized and fulfilled by God alone. While the concept of the threefold Word of God offers a unique account of the unity of divine and human action in the gospel event, Barth's vision trusts that whatever may come out of our ecclesiological explanations, they will not be complete or fulfilled unless and until the risen Christ has the final word and incorporates them into His own life and forms of self-communication. Whatever the anxieties and challenges facing contemporary Christianity, the crucified and risen Lord is never found apart from the proclamation and life together of his disciples and witnesses, the church. Rather than starting with sacramentology or a set of practices to identify the church and to reach a sense of ecclesial and ecumenical continuity, perhaps the discussion of where and what the church is should begin with the recognition and confession of the risen Lord who continues to come through Scripture and the church's proclamation of the gospel. Then may the christological and ecclesiological questions find their inseparability and may the church again discover its only concrete hope, concrete purpose, and concrete identity on the way to Christ's kingdom.

Bibliography

Achtemeier, Elizabeth. "Relevant Remembering." In *How Karl Barth Changed My Mind*, edited by Donald McKim, 108–112. Grand Rapids: Eerdmans, 1986.

Bacote, Vincent, Laura C. Miguélez, and Dennis L. Okholm, eds. *Evangelicals and Scripture: Tradition, Authority, and Hermeneutics*. Downers Grove, IL: InterVarsity, 2004.

Balthasar, Hans Urs von. *The Theology of Karl Barth: Exposition and Interpretation*. Translated by Edward T. Oakes. San Francisco: Communio, 1992.

Barth, Karl. "An Prof. Dr. Heinrich Stirnimann O. P., Freiburg (Schweiz), 1968." In *Briefe, 1961–1968*, edited by Jürgen Fangmeier und Hinrich Stoevesandt, 482–83. Zurich: TVZ, 1979.

———. *Call for God: New Sermons from Basel Prison*. Translated by A. T. Mackay. London: SCM, 1965.

———. *The Church and the Churches*. Grand Rapids: Eerdmans, 2005.

———. *Church Dogmatics*. 4 vols. in 14 parts. Edited by Geoffrey W. Bromiley and Thomas F. Torrance. Translated by G. T. Thomson et al. Edinburgh: T. & T. Clark, 1956–69.

———. *Church Dogmatics*. Vol. I/1: *The Doctrine of the Word of God*. Edited by G. W. Bromiley and T. F. Torrance. Translated by G. W. Bromiley. 2nd ed. Edinburgh: T. & T. Clark, 1975.

———. *Deliverance to the Captives*. New York: Harper, 1961.

———. *Dogmatics in Outline*. Translated by G. T. Thomson. New York: Harper & Row, 1959.

———. *Evangelical Theology: An Introduction*. Translated by Grover Foley. Grand Rapids: Eerdmans, 1963.

———. *The Faith of the Church: A Commentary on the Apostles' Creed*. London: Fontana, 1958.

———. Foreword to *Reformed Dogmatics*, by Heinrich Heppe. Rev. and ed. Ernst Bizer. Translated by G. T. Thomson. London: Allen & Unwin, 1950.

———. *God: Here and Now*. Translated by Paul Van Buren. London: Routledge Classics, 1964, 2004.

———. *God in Action*. Translated by E. G. Homrighausen and Karl J. Ernst. Manhasset, NY: Roundtable, 1963.

———. *The Göttingen Dogmatics: Instruction in the Christian Religion*. Vol. 1. Edited by Hannelote Reiffen. Translated by Geoffrey W. Bromiley. Grand Rapids: Eerdmans, 1991.

———. *Homiletics.* Translated by Geoffrey Bromiley and Donald Daniels. Louisville: Westminster John Knox, 1991.

———. *How I Changed My Mind.* Edinburgh: St. Andrew, 1966.

———. *The Humanity of God.* Richmond: John Knox, 1966.

———. *Karl Barth Gesamtausgabe: Die Christliche Dogmatik im Entwurf 1927* (GA II.14). Edited by Gerhard Sauter. Zurich: TVZ, 1982.

———. *Karl Barth-Rudolf Bultmann Letters, 1922–1968.* Edited by Bernd Jaspert. Translated and edited by Geoffrey Bromiley. Edinburgh: T. & T. Clark, 1982.

———. *Karl Barth's Table Talk.* Edited and recorded by John D. Godsey. Edinburgh: Oliver & Boyd, 1963.

———. *Die Kirchliche Dogmatik.* 4 vols. Munich: Kaiser, 1932; Zurich: TVZ, 1938–65.

———. *Knowledge of God and Service of God according to the Teaching of the Reformation.* Translated by J. L. M. Haire and Ian Henderson. London: Hodder & Stoughton, 1938.

———. *The Knowledge of God and the Service of God according to the Teaching of the Reformation: Recalling the Scottish Confession of 1560.* The Gifford Lectures delivered in the University of Aberdeen in 1937 and 1938. London: Hodder and Stoughton, 1938.

———. *Letters, 1961–1968.* Edited by Jürgen Fangmeier and Hinrich Stoevesandt. Translated by Geoffrey W. Bromiley. Grand Rapids: Eerdmans, 1981.

———. "On Systematic Theology." *Scottish Journal of Theology* 14 (1961) 225–28.

———. *Prayer.* Louisville: Westminster John Knox, 2002.

———. *Prayer and Preaching.* London: SCM, 1964.

———. "Protestantism and Architecture." *Theology Today* 19 (1962) 272.

———. *The Teaching of the Church Regarding Baptism.* 1948. Reprint, Eugene, OR: Wipf and Stock, 2006.

———. *Theology and Church.* Translated by Louise Pettibone Smith. New York: Harper & Row, 1962.

———. *The Theology of Calvin.* Translated by Geoffrey W. Bromiley. Grand Rapids: Eerdmans, 1995.

———. *The Theology of the Reformed Confessions, 1923.* Translated by Darrell L. Guder and Judith J. Guder. Louisville: Westminster John Knox, 2002.

———. *The Word of God and the Word of Man.* Translated by Douglas Horton. New York: Harper & Row, 1957.

Barth, Karl, and Eduard Thurneysen. *Revolutionary Theology in the Making: Barth-Thurneysen Correspondence, 1914–1925.* Translated by James D. Smart. Richmond: John Knox, 1964.

Bender, Kimlyn J. *Karl Barth's Christological Ecclesiology.* Aldershot, UK: Ashgate, 2005.

Berkouwer, G. C. *The Triumph of Grace in the Theology of Karl Barth.* London: Paternoster, 1956.

Biggar, Nigel. *The Hastening That Waits: Karl Barth's Ethics.* Oxford: Clarendon, 1993.

Biggar, Nigel, ed. *Reckoning with Barth: Essays in Commemoration of the Centenary of Karl Barth's Birth.* Oxford: Mowbray, 1988.

Bloesch, Donald G. *Jesus Is Victor! Karl Barth's Doctrine of Salvation.* 1976. Reprint, Eugene, OR: Wipf & Stock, 2001.

Bolt, John. "Exploring Karl Barth's Eschatology: A Salutary Exercise for Evangelicals." In *Karl Barth and Evangelical Theology,* edited by Sung Wook Chung, 221–35.

Bonhoeffer, Dietrich. *Act and Being.* Translated by Bernard Noble. London: Collins, 1962.

Branch, Taylor. *Parting the Waters: America in the King Years, 1954–1963.* New York: Simon & Schuster, 1988.

Buckley, James J. "Christian Community, Baptism, and Lord's Supper." In *The Cambridge Companion to Karl Barth,* edited by John Webster, 195–211. Cambridge: Cambridge University Press, 2000.

———. "A Field of Living Fire: Karl Barth on the Spirit and the Church." *Modern Theology* 10 (1994) 81–102.

Bullinger, Heinrich. "The Second Helvetic Confession (1566)." Article I, *The Constitution of the Presbyterian Church (USA), Part I, Book of Confessions,* 53. Louisville: Geneva, 2004.

Busch, Eberhard. *The Barmen Theses Then and Now.* Translated by Darrell Guder and Judith Guder. Grand Rapids: Eerdmans, 2010.

———. *Karl Barth: His Life from Letters and Autobiographical Texts.* Translated by John Bowden. Philadelphia: Fortress, 1994.

Cairns, David. "Christ, the Church His Body, and Its Members." In *Essays in Christology for Karl Barth,* edited by T. H. L. Parker, 209–26. London: Lutterworth, 1956.

Casalis, Georges. *Portrait of Karl Barth.* Translated by Robert McAfee Brown. Garden City, NY: Doubleday, 1963.

Chung, Sung Wook, ed. *Karl Barth and Evangelical Theology.* Grand Rapids: Baker Academic, 2006.

Dayton, Donald. "A Response to George Hunsinger, *The Eucharist and Ecumenism.*" Paper presented at the annual meeting of the Karl Barth Society of North America, American Academy of Religion, Atlanta, Georgia, October 30, 2010.

Dorrien, Gary. *Theology without Weapons: The Barthian Revolt in Modern Theology.* Louisville: Westminster John Knox, 2000.

Fackre, Gabriel. *The Church: Signs of the Spirit and Signs of the Times.* Grand Rapids: Eerdmans, 2007.

———. *The Doctrine of Revelation: A Narrative Interpretation.* Edinburgh: Edinburgh University Press, 1997.

———. "Revelation." In *Karl Barth and Evangelical Theology,* edited by Sung Wook Chung, 1–25. Grand Rapids: Baker Academic, 2006.

Fergusson, David. *Church, State, and Civil Society.* Cambridge: Cambridge University Press, 2004.

Flett, John G. *The Witness of God: The Trinity, Missio Dei, Karl Barth, and the Nature of the Christian Community.* Grand Rapids: Eerdmans, 2010.

Frei, Hans. *The Identity of Jesus Christ: The Hemeneutical Bases of Dogmatic Theology.* 1975. Reprint, Eugene, OR: Wipf & Stock, 1997.

Genest, Helmut. *Karl Barth und die Predigt: Darstellung und Deutung von Predigtwerk und Predigtlehre Karl Barths.* Neukirchen-Vluyn: Neukirchener, 1995.

George, Timothy. "Running Like a Herald to Deliver the Message: Barth on the Church and Sacraments." In *Karl Barth and Evangelical Theology,* edited by Sung Wook Chung, 191–208. Grand Rapids: Baker Academic, 2006.

Guder, Darrell. "Gathering, Upbuilding, Sending: Barth's Formation of the Missional Community." Conference paper, Center for Barth Studies Annual Conference, Princeton Theological Seminary, Princeton, New Jersey, July 20–23, 2010.

Gunton, Colin. *The Barth Lectures.* Edited by P. H. Brazier. London: T. & T. Clark, 2007.

Guretzki, David. *Karl Barth on the Filioque*. Surrey, UK: Ashgate, 2009.

Hall, Douglas John. "Cross and Context." *The Christian Century* 127, no. 18 (2010) 34–40.

Hamer, Jerome. *Karl Barth*. Glasgow: Sands, 1962.

Hauerwas, Stanley. *With the Grain of the Universe*. London: SCM, 2002.

Hawksley, Theodora. "The Freedom of the Spirit: The Pneumatological Ppoint of Barth's Ecclesiological Minimalism." *Scottish Journal of Theology* 64 (2011) 180–94.

Hart, Trevor. *Regarding Karl Barth: Toward a Reading of His Theology*. Carlisle, UK: Paternoster, 1999.

———. "The Word, the Words, and the Witness: Proclamation as Divine and Human Reality." In *Regarding Karl Barth: Toward a Reading of His Theology*, 28–47. Carlisle: Paternoster, 1999.

Healy, Nicholas M. *Church, World, and the Christian Life: Practical-Prophetic Ecclesiology*. Cambridge: Cambridge University Press, 2000.

———. "Karl Barth's Ecclesiology Reconsidered." *Scottish Journal of Theology* 57 (2004) 287–99.

———. "The Logic of Karl Barth's Ecclesiology: Analysis, Assessment and Proposed Modifications." *Modern Theology* 10 (1994) 253–70.

Holmes, Christopher. "The Church and the Presence of Christ: Defending Actualist Ecclesiology." *Pro Ecclesia* 21 (2012) 268–80.

———. "What Jesus Is Doing." *The Christian Century* 129, no. 19 (2012) 26–29.

Horn, Nico. "From Barmen to Belhar to Kairos." In *On Reading Karl Barth in South Africa*, edited by Charles Villa-Vicencio, 105–20. Grand Rapids: Eerdmans, 1988.

Hunsinger, George. *Disruptive Grace: Studies in the Theology of Karl Barth*. Grand Rapids: Eerdmans, 2000.

———. *How to Read Karl Barth: The Shape of His Theology*. Oxford: Oxford University Press, 1991.

———. "The Mediator of Communion: Karl Barth's Doctrine of the Holy Spirit." In *Disruptive Grace: Studies in the Theology of Karl Barth*, 148–85. Grand Rapids: Eerdmans, 2000.

Husbands, Mark, and Daniel J. Treier, eds. *The Community of the Word: Toward an Evangelical Ecclesiology*. Leicester: Apollos, 2005.

Hütter, Reinhard. "Barth Between McCormack and Von Balthasar: A Dialetic." *Pro Ecclesia* 8 (1999) 105–9.

———. "The Church as Public: Dogma, Practice, and the Holy Spirit." *Pro Ecclesia* 3 (1994) 334–61.

———. "The Church's Public Ministry in Her Babylonian Captivity." *Pro Ecclesia* 2 (1993) 18–20.

———. "Ecclesial Ethics, The Church's Vocation, and Paraclesis." *Pro Ecclesia* 2 (1993) 433–50.

———. "Karl Barth's Dialectical Catholicity: Sic et Non." *Modern Theology* 16 (2000) 137–57.

———. *Suffering Divine Things: Theology as Church Practice*. Translated by Doug Stott. Grand Rapids: Eerdmans, 2000.

Jenson, Robert W. *America's Theologian: A Recommendation of Jonathan Edwards*. New York: Oxford University Press, 1988.

———. *God after God: The God of the Past and the God of the Future, Seen in the Work of Karl Barth*. New York: Bobbs-Merrill, 1969.

————. "Religious Pluralism, Christology, and Barth." *Dialog* 20 (1981) 31–38.

————. *Systematic Theology.* Vol. 2, *The Works of God.* Oxford: Oxford University Press, 1999.

————. "You Wonder Where the Spirit Went." *Pro Ecclesia* 2 (1993) 296–304.

Johnson, Keith. *Karl Barth and the Analogia Entis.* London: T. & T. Clark, 2010.

Johnson, William Stacy. *The Mystery of God: Karl Barth and the Postmodern Foundations of Theology.* Louisville: Westminster John Knox, 1997.

Jüngel, Eberhard. *God's Being Is in Becoming.* London: T. & T. Clark, 2001.

————. *Karl Barth: A Theological Legacy.* Philadelphia: Westminster, 1986.

————. "Karl Barths Lehre von der Taufe. Ein Hinweis auf ihre Probleme." In *Barth-Studien*, 246–90. Zürich-Köln: Benziger, 1982.

————. *Theological Essays.* Translated by John B. Webster. Edinburgh: T. & T. Clark, 1989.

Kay, James. *Preaching and Theology.* St. Louis: Chalice, 2007.

Lee, Philip J. *Against the Protestant Gnostics.* Oxford: Oxford University Press, 1987.

Leith, John H. *Introduction to the Reformed Tradition: A Way of Being the Christian Community.* Atlanta: John Knox, 1977.

Macchia, Frank D. "The Spirit of God and the Spirit of Life: An Evangelical Response to Karl Barth's Pneumatology." In *Karl Barth and Evangelical Theology*, edited by Sung Wook Chung, 149–71. Grand Rapids: Baker Academic, 2006.

Macken, John. *The Autonomy Theme in Tthe Church Dogmatics: Karl Barth and His Critics.* Cambridge: Cambridge University Press, 1990.

Macleod, Donald. "'Church' Dogmatics: Karl Barth as Ecclesial Theologian." In *Engaging with Barth: Contemporary Evangelical Critiques*, edited by David Gibson and Daniel Strange, 323–45. Nottingham: Apollos, 2008.

Mangina, Joseph. "Bearing the Marks of Jesus: The Church in the Economy of Salvation in Barth and Hauerwas." *Scottish Journal of Theology* 52 (1999) 269–305.

————. *Karl Barth on the Christian Life.* Oxford: Lang, 2001.

————. *Karl Barth: Theologian of Christian Witness.* Louisville: Westminster John Knox, 2004.

McCormack, Bruce L. "The Being of Holy Scripture Is in Becoming." In *Evangelicals & Scripture: Tradition, Authority, and Hermeneutics*, edited by Vincent Bacote, Laura C. Miguélez and Dennis L. Okholm, 55–75.

————. *Karl Barth's Critically Realistic Dialectical Theology: Its Genesis and Development, 1909–1936.* Oxford: Oxford University Press, 1995.

————. *Orthodox and Modern: Studies in the Theology of Karl Barth.* Grand Rapids: Baker, 2008.

————. "A Scholastic of a Higher Order: The Development of Karl Barth's Theology, 1921–31." PhD diss., Princeton Theological Seminary, 1989.

McDowell, John C. *Hope in Barth's Eschatalogy.* Aldershot, UK: Ashgate, 2000.

McKim, Donald, ed. *How Karl Barth Changed My Mind.* Grand Rapids: Eerdmans, 1986.

Migliore, Daniel L. "The Communion of the Triune God: Towards a Trinitarian Ecclesiology in Reformed Perspective." In *Reformed Theology: Identity and Ecumenicity*, edited by Wallace M. Alston Jr. and Michael Welker, 140–54. Grand Rapids: Eerdmans, 2003.

————. "Freedom to Pray." In *Karl Barth, Prayer*, 95–113. Louisville: Westminster John Knox, 2002.

Migliore, Daniel L., ed. *Commanding Grace: Studies in Karl Barth's Ethics*. Grand Rapids: Eerdmans, 2010.

Neder, Adam. *Participation in Christ: An Entry into Karl Barth's Church Dogmatics*. Louisville: Westminster John Knox, 2009.

Neuhaus, Richard John. *Freedom for Ministry*. Rev. ed. Grand Rapids: Eerdmans, 1991.

Nimmo, Paul. *Being in Action: The Theological Shape of Barth's Ethical Vision*. London: T. & T. Clark, 2007.

———. "Karl Barth and the *concursus Dei*—A Chalcedonianism Too Far?" *International Journal of Systematic Theology* 9 (2007) 58–72.

O'Grady, Colm. *The Church in Catholic Theology: Dialogue with Karl Barth*. Washington, DC: Corpus, 1969.

———. *The Church in the Theology of Karl Barth*. Washington, DC: Corpus, 1968.

Parker, T. H. L.. "Word and Gospel." In *Essays in Christology for Karl Barth*, edited by T. H. L. Parker, 177–90. London: Lutterworth, 1956.

Parker, T. H. L., ed. *Essays in Christology for Karl Barth*. London: Lutterworth, 1956.

Placher, William. "Eating Gracefully: A Reformed Perspective on How to Be a Church." *Pro Ecclesia* 2 (1993) 21–36.

Rendtorrff, Trutz. *Church and Theology: The Systematic Function of the Church Concept in Modern Theology*. Translated by Reginald H. Fuller. Philadelphia: Westminster, 1971.

Richardson, Kurt Anders. "*Christus Praesens*: Barth's Radically Realist Christology and Its Necessity for Theological Method." In *Karl Barth and Evangelical Theology*, edited by Sung Wook Chung, 136–48. Grand Rapids: Baker Academic, 2006.

Rosato, Philip J. *The Spirit as Lord: The Pneumatology of Karl Barth*. Edinburgh: T. & T. Clark, 1981.

Smit, Dirk. "'. . . The Doing of the Little Righteousness': On Justice in Barth's View of the Christian Life." In *Loving God with Our Minds: The Pastor as Theologian*, edited by Michael Welker and Cynthia A. Jarvis, 120–45. Grand Rapids: Eerdmans, 2004.

———. "Paradigms of Radical Grace." In *On Reading Karl Barth in South Africa*, edited by Charles Villa-Vicencio, 17–43. Grand Rapids: Eerdmans, 1988.

Thurneysen, Eduard. *Das Wort Gottes und die Kirche*. Munich: Kaiser, 1927.

Torrance, Thomas F. "Karl Barth and the Latin Heresy." *Scottish Journal of Theology* 39 (1986) 461–82.

———. *Karl Barth: An Introduction to His Early Theology*. London: SCM, 1962.

———. *Karl Barth, Biblical and Evangelical Theologian*. Edinburgh: T. & T. Clark, 1990.

Villa-Vicencio, Charles, ed. *On Reading Karl Barth in South Africa*. Grand Rapids: Eerdmans, 1988.

Webster, John. "Balthasar and Karl Barth." In *The Cambridge Companion to Hans Urs von Balthasar*, edited by Edward T. Oakes and David Moss, 241–55. Cambridge: Cambridge University Press, 2004.

———. *Barth*. London: Continuum, 2000.

———. *Barth's Earlier Theology*. London: T. & T. Clark, 2005.

———. *Barth's Ethics of Reconciliation*. Cambridge: Cambridge University Press, 1995.

———. *Barth's Moral Theology: Human Action in Barth's Thought*. Edinburgh: T. & T. Clark, 1998.

———. "The Church and the Perfections of God." In *The Community of the Word: Toward an Evangelical Ecclesiology*, edited by Mark Husbands and Daniel J. Treier, 75–95. Leicester: Apollos, 2005.

———. *Confessing God*. London: T. & T. Clark, 2005.

———. "'Eloquent and Radiant': The Prophetic Office of Christ and the Mission of the Church." In *Barth's Moral Theology: Human Action in Barth's Thought*, 125–50. Edinburgh: T. & T. Clark, 1998.

———. "The Visible Attests the Invisible." In *The Community of the Word: Toward an Evangelical Ecclesiology*, edited by Mark Husbands and Daniel J. Treier, 96–113. Leicester: Apollos, 2005.

———. *Word and Church: Essays in Christian Dogmatics*. Edinburgh: T. & T. Clark, 2001.

Weinrich, Michael. "God's Free Grace and the Freedom of the Church: Theological Aspects of the Barmen Declaration." *International Journal of Systematic Theology* 12 (2010) 404–19.

Welker, Michael. "Karl Barth: From Fighter against the 'Roman Heresy' to Leading Thinker for the Ecumenical Movement." *Scottish Journal of Theology* 57 (2004) 434–50.

Welker, Michael, and Cynthia Jarvis, eds. *Loving God with Our Minds: The Pastor as Theologian*. Grand Rapids: Eerdmans, 2004.

Wolterstorff, Nicholas. *Divine Discourse*. Cambridge: Cambridge University Press, 1995.

Wood, Ralph C. *The Comedy of Redemption: Christian Faith and Comic Vision in Four American Novelists*. Notre Dame: University of Notre Dame Press, 1988.

Work, Telford. *Living and Active: Scripture in the Economy of Salvation*. Grand Rapids: Eerdmans, 2002.

Yocum, John. *Ecclesial Mediation in Karl Barth*. Hampshire, UK: Ashgate, 2004.

Index

Printed in Great Britain
by Amazon